JOHANN SEBASTIAN BACH

COMPLETE ORGAN WORKS

A Critico-Practical Edition in Eight Volumes

Provided with a Preface containing General Observations on the Manner of performing the Preludes and Fugues

and

Suggestions for the Interpretation of the Compositions contained in Each Volume

by

CHARLES–MARIE WIDOR

Professor in the Conservatoire at Paris and Organist at the Church of St. Sulpice

and

Dr. ALBERT SCHWEITZER

Privataozent at Strassburg University and Organist for the Bachgesellschaft of Paris

VOLUME IV

Preludes and Fugues of the Mature Master-Period

(*Part 2*)

ED 870

G. SCHIRMER, Inc.

DISTRIBUTED BY

HAL•LEONARD®
CORPORATION

7777 W. BLUEMOUND RD. P.O. BOX 13819 MILWAUKEE, WI 53213

Contents of Volume IV

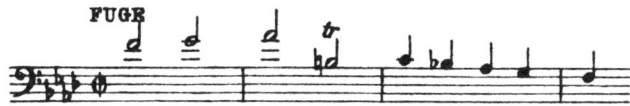
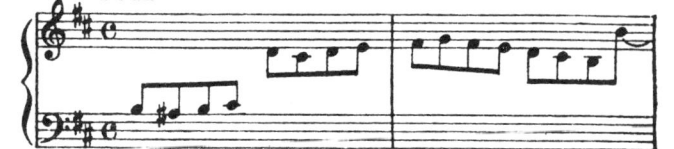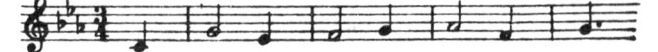

Literary and Critical Notes to the Fourth Volume

The Preludes and Fugues contained in the Fourth Volume, like those in the Third, were written in part during the later years of the Weimar epoch, that is, from about 1714 to 1717, and in part in Leipzig (1723–1750). Some of the works may be a product of the Cöthen period (1717–1723), or at least then took on their definite shape.

To the Weimar period may be referred the grandly simple Preludes in F minor (No. 2), G major (No. 3), A major (No. 5), and probably also the Toccata and Fugue in F major (No. 1).

The definitive revision of the virtuose Preludes and Fugues in G minor (No. 4) and A minor (No. 6) was probably made during the sojourn in Cöthen. It is impossible to trace these two works back to their beginnings. J. P. Kellner, one of Bach's pupils, preserved for us a copy of the Prelude in A minor in which the opening measures are presented in a primitively incomplete — and therefore earlier — form. In this copy they appear thus:

It will be seen that the full grandeur and majesty of the chromatic line was brought out only by the improvement on which the later version was based.

The original form of the fugue-theme is found in a three-part clavier-fugue, in the following shape:

Here all the elements of the finished theme are already at hand; only the grand, simple melodic line invoked by the composer's fancy is still too much clouded by accessories, and too short-breathed, to be fully effective. Only after long elaboration did it attain that tranquil plasticity with which it bears along the sixteenth-notes of the theme like ripples on a flood.

Furthermore, in this first form the plan of the fugue is already prefigured in its main developments.

It appears that Bach performed the fugue in G minor in the year 1720 at Hamburg, whither he had gone to pay his respects to the aged Reinken, and to introduce himself to the church authorities and musical connoisseurs in view of possible vacancies in organistships. Mattheson, the Hamburg composer and critic, quotes the theme in the second edition of his great Thorough-bass Method, in the following form:

The peculiar and not very favorable shape in which the Hamburg writer presents this Bach theme was regarded for a long time as a preliminary stage to the definitive form. But the evidence would seem to show that this version must be set down to Mattheson's own account. He mentions the fact, that in 1725 he gave it to the rival candidates at an organ-competition for extempore working out. The original Bach theme exceeds the limits of an octave, which transgresses the rules of fugal art. When the great critic and theorist gave it out for the competition, he was obliged, in order to save his own reputation, to prune it to fit the rule. Did it enter his head that, in so doing, he was robbing it of its beauty?

The Passacaglia (No. 8) also probably belongs, in its present shape, to the Cöthen period. The Fugue bears the traces of an earlier creative epoch more distinctly than the Passacaglia.

The Prelude and Fugue in B minor (No. 7) exhibit the characteristic features of the organ compositions from the later Leipzig period. They are companion-pieces to the great Prelude and Fugue in E minor (Vol. III, No. 9).

There have been preserved in autograph the Prelude and Fugue in A major (No. 5), and those in G major (No. 3). Of the latter we likewise possess a copy with corrections in Bach's own hand, which presents the pieces in an earlier form. Our notation of the Prelude and Fugue in A major follows, not the autograph, but copies handed down with the latter, and made from a later, perfected autograph which has been lost.

The other pieces we possess only in the shape of copies. The autographs of two of these did not disappear until the second half of the nineteenth century. Griepenkerl, who had charge of the old Peters edition, could still refer to the autograph of the Passacaglia (No. 8) and those of the Prelude and Fugue in B minor (No. 7). The last-named probably went to England. Rust, who edited the organ-works for the great Bachgesellschaft, remembered that he had seen it, and mentions that the pedal-part was written in with red ink.

22712

Suggestions for Performing the Preludes and Fugues

Preliminary Observations

The remarks on the interpretation of the several preludes and fugues will be strictly limited to a statement of formulas.

The directions are calculated, in most cases, for a two-manual organ. For the preludes and fugues Bach generally employed only his great-manual and his *Rückpositiv* (choir), his third manual not being sufficiently full-toned to be used on a level with the other two. On the earlier organs an alternation between choir and swell could not well be considered, because the great-manual lay between them. It is certain that all the Master's works can be performed on a well-arranged and finely-voiced two-manual instrument in a correct and wholly appropriate manner.

For a number of preludes and fugues, however, our "suggestions" are intended to be carried out on a three-manual organ. But the directions may be transferred without difficulty to one having only two rows of keys.

In a two-manual organ, Man. II should be in the swell-box; in a three-manual organ, Man. III.

All manuals are supposed to be provided with good foundation stops, compound stops ("mixtures"), and reeds. The swell-organ should be abundantly furnished with stops of all classes. The effect obtained by opening and closing the shutters should be such as to make itself felt when the swell-manual is coupled to the great and the hands are playing on the latter.

In its relation to the instrument as a whole, the swell-organ should impart flexibility and a capacity for modulating the tone-effects.

The Fifth, Twelfth, etc., are reckoned among the foundation stops; Thirds and Sevenths, and their octaves, are to be used with the compound stops.

For the arrangement of the combination or composition pedals, pistons, etc., and of the couplers, the suggestions of the international Regulations for Organ-building have been adopted as drafted by the committee headed by Dr. Albert Schweitzer and Abbé Dr. Xaver Mathias. The couplers and auxiliaries above-mentioned should be workable either by hand or by foot, as occasion serves.

The player is not expected to use the ordinary *crescendo*-pedals, which bring on the stops in a succession fixed beforehand.

The suggestions can be carried out, in general, only with the aid of an assistant for drawing or retiring the stops at the proper place. This is the method adopted by Bach himself when he wished to shade his registration with special care.

Should the player prefer to make the changes in registration himself, with the help of modern appliances, he may simplify our suggestions accordingly by drawing or retiring his stops in groups where the editors propose to bring them on or retire them successively.

The decisive factor is not the arrangements for facilitating registration — for in Bach-playing these may frequently be replaced to advantage by an assistant — but the tone produced. Your instrument must have at command fine, clear-voiced stops, neither too dull nor too blaring. The foundation stops, mixtures, and reeds, when combined, must produce a *forte* through which the polyphony can be clearly traced, and which does not weary the ear.

For such an ideal instrument, which any good organ-builder can construct if allowed the means and the time, the Editors' suggestions are calculated. They afford merely general indications as to place and direction in which an alteration of timbre or a change of manual is to be effected. It remains for the organist to fit these formulas to the instrument on which he has to play.

For instance, when choir and swell are not provided with good mixtures, the effect which the Editors propose to obtain on the ideal organ by drawing or retiring these registers will have to be realized by the use of foundation stops, more especially those of four-foot or two-foot tone, by coupling and uncoupling the manuals, or in some other suitable manner.

When some of the foundation stops are too dull or too harsh in tone, they should not be employed in every case where the Editors suppose all the foundation stops (eight, four, and two-foot) to be drawn. On the other hand, he may draw one or another of these stops as a substitute (but only in case of need) for a missing mixture stop.

Unfortunately, a good interpretation of Bach's organ works depends not alone on the artistic quality of the player, but also on that of the instrument. Organists of all nationalities should, therefore, see to it that in cathedrals, village churches, and concert-halls only simple, substantial, finely voiced and full-toned instruments are set up, to the end that coming generations may find it easier to play Bach well than our own, in which far too many organists are condemned, by the defects of organs built according to wrong principles, to an incomplete interpretation of the Master's works.

The better the instrument, the fewer will be the needful readjustments of the Editors' indications.

22712

Respecting the reinforcement and reduction of the pedal by drawing and retiring stops and couplers, the Notes contain hints only in exceptional cases; it being assumed that the pedal will follow the manuals with a suitable volume of tone [suitable bass!].

Suggestions for the intercoupling and uncoupling of the manuals are also seldom made. In this matter the player will be governed by the special arrangements of his instrument and the relations subsisting between the several manuals with regard to volume and quality of tone.

Of course, directions for using the swell are also given only in passages of special prominence.

The Editors have been particularly careful to indicate, as precisely as possible, the way in which a change of manual is to be effected, wherever it occurs, as a great deal depends upon this.

Wherever a phrasing is proposed, the "ideal" phrasing is intended, which shows the player how the phrase is to be understood and conceived. It will depend on his own artistic sense, the quality of the voicing of his organ and its keyboard facilities, how closely he can approximate the ideal phrasing in the audible interpretation.

The "breathing-mark" (') indicates a noticeable "lift" (break). Inserted between notes which are repeated in the same part, it signifies that they are to be sustained for only half their time-value.

Short slurs included under one long one ⌢⌢⌢ show the units which combine to form a period or figure. They should be set off by brief, hardly perceptible breaks.

Tenuto-dashes under a slur ⌒- - -⌒ call for a sort of free *legato* in which the notes are not smoothly connected, but slightly separated. In reality, such tones will frequently have to be played in an ordinary *legato*, as the organ does not control the more delicate nuances between *tenuto* and *legato*.

Notes marked with the simple *tenuto*-dashes, without a slur, are to be separated. They should be sustained for the greater part of their time-value, the key being allowed to rise just before the next key is depressed, so that an extremely brief break results.

During the progress of their work it has become increasingly evident to the Editors that the Notes have on the whole a tendency toward sketchiness. In many cases they had to content themselves with mere hints, instead of going into details; other points, which should have been reasoned out, had to be stated as simple assertions; and some more or less plausible alternative readings could not be mentioned at all.

Any one who realizes the difficulties encountered in concisely explaining the musical processes involved in the interpretation of preludes and fugues, will be indulgent toward the present attempt — the first ever made in this direction; in forming his opinions he will strive to penetrate the artistic thought of the Editors, and to associate himself with them in spirit as they, during their arduous common labors, were associated and felt themselves at one with each other and with other known and unknown colleagues, near or far. Such association is always found where men meet in a common striving after perfection, and hear a voice saying: "Put off thy shoes from off thy feet, for the place whereon thou standest is holy ground;" and feel that in being permitted to touch the sacred instrument and set forth the works of Johann Sebastian Bach, a blessing has entered into their lives.

Suggestions for Performing the Preludes and Fugues of the Mature Master-Period

I. Prelude (Toccata) and Fugue in F Major. (Pages 2-19.)

PRELUDE (TOCCATA)

The performance of the Toccata requires classic simplicity in both technical execution and registration. It tolerates no "modernizing" whatsoever.

In particular, all effects to be brought out by the alternation of the manuals should be eschewed. The style of Bach's writing, and the uninterrupted employment of the pedal, show clearly that he wished only the great-manual to be used. Why act contrary to his intention? It shall be admitted that the proportions of the keyboards in modern organs allow us to play the two great canonic divisions (measures 1–55 and 83–137) with the right hand on the second manual, while the left remains on the great; and also, in the further course of the piece, to introduce variety which was impossible for Bach. What is gained thereby? The canon loses in impressiveness, and any variety which exceeds what the Master proposed is superfluous, if not injurious.

In the main, foundation stops, mixtures and reeds are to be drawn. This does not mean that we are to play throughout with full organ. That was possible on the old organs; the tone of modern instruments does not permit it. Therefore, a selection should be made and a tone-color combined in which all species of registers are represented, but which falls short of the full organ in strength, and does not weary the hearer when continued through a long series of measures. Such a combination is meant when we speak, in what follows, of a "brilliant *forte*."

With this registration, the first canon commences. In the pedal only foundation stops are drawn. On the first beat in measure 47 it is coupled to the third manual; at the corresponding points in measures 51 and 53 the couplers to the second and first manuals will be thrown on; at the beginning of measure 55 the reeds will be added.

The same *crescendo* of the sustained bass will be carried out in measures 129–137; the pedal reeds, and manual-to-pedal couplers, having been thrown off (for the second canon) at the rest in measure 82.

For the chords in measures 81 and 82 bring on the full organ with the 16-foot manual registers. The second canon is to be played with the same registration as the first.

A repeated comparison between the performance of the canons on one manual and on two manuals will finally convince player and audience that their effect is most impressive when both parts progress together in the same tone-power and tone-color, *i.e.*, on the same manual. Besides, the transient addition of another stop in measures 35–45 and 121–127 supports the assumption that Bach used one manual.

The chords in measures 169–176 will be separated one from the other, as they do not result from the progression of *obbligato* parts. For these chords, employ full organ with the 16-foot manual stops.

Although the temptation to change manuals is not small, it is better not to alternate between the first and second manuals every other measure. In the nature of the music there is nothing responsive or echo-like. The entire interest concentrates on the modulation proceeding above the interrupted organ-point in the bass. Here the player's art must graduate the harmonic values, and whet expectancy of the final dénouement, by a delicate shading of the tempo, a slight acceleration on one chord and an imperceptible dwelling on another.

In like manner, and with the same registration, the chord-successions in measures 197–204, 263–270, 311–318, 375–382 and 417–424 are to be executed. There are organists, however, who retain for the chords the registration in which the two canonic divisions were played.

During the rest in bass, in measure 175, throw off the pedal reeds; after lifting the chord in measure 176, also throw off the reeds and 16-foot stops on the manuals. Thus measures 177–196 will be played with foundation stops and mixtures.

Whether the full organ should be brought on abruptly in measure 197, or prepared by adding stops during the four or five preceding measures, shall be left to the player's judgment. Reasons might be adduced for either procedure.

It would appear self-evident that one should play from measures 217–238 in the brilliant *forte*, and then continue with foundation stops and mixtures through measures 238–263.

It is doubtful, on the other hand, whether one should play the transitional measures 204–216 with full organ, in the brilliant *forte*, or only with foundation stops and mixtures. We would suggest that only foundation stops and mixtures be drawn, with the addition of one or two reeds; the balance of the reeds to be added on the first beat in measure 217 or 219 to mark the beginning of the new principal section.

Bach probably proceeded much more simply. He played from beginning to end with full organ, without the 16-foot manual stops. His sole change in the registration was to draw these 16-foot stops for the chords, and then to push them in. But it is likewise supposable that he retained them throughout.

On account of the intensity of the modern reeds it appears advisable to registrate so that the hearers may have intervals of relief from them. Where should they be used, and where not? Some solve the problem in one way, others in another. But probably all will agree that measures 176–196 and the corresponding periods are the passages where reeds can best be omitted. Whether they are to be renounced *in toto*, or only in part, will depend on the organ and the auditorium. When they are entirely omitted, you will return (after executing measures 263–270 with full organ) on the second eighth in measure 270 to the " brilliant *forte*," then play measures 290–311 with foundation stops and mixtures, and take full organ for the performance of measures 311–318.

Registrate the transitional measures 318–330 in the same manner as the corresponding measures 204–217.

From measures 332–352 you will play in the brilliant *forte*. After lifting the manual-parts in measure 352, throw off the reeds.

In measures 368–371 you will draw (taking advantage of the rests) registers in succession, and eventually add further reinforcements on the first beats in measures 372–375. You will arrive at full organ with the second eighth in measure 375.

From the lifting of the chord in measure 382 onward, you will again employ the brilliant *forte*. Retain it up to measure 412, without giving thought to the bringing out of *crescendi* and *decrescendi*. From measure 412 on, stops will be drawn successively on the first beats, arriving at full organ in measure 417.

According to his individual convictions the player will either throw off or retain the 16-foot manual stops for measures 424–436. They are unquestionably needed in the last two measures.

In cases where the manual reeds are not employed, those on the pedal will also not be drawn. Whether the 16-foot Posaune on the pedal is to be used in the brilliant *forte*, will depend on its character; at all events, the 8- and 4-foot pedal reeds are to be drawn for these sections. It is likely that Bach kept his 16-foot pedal reeds out throughout the entire piece.

For the organ-point in the pedal entering with measure 394, throw off your pedal reeds and the coupler to the great-manual, but retain the coupler to the second manual, so that its reeds and mixtures may continue the bass in the color in which the other parts proceed. On the first beats in measures 414–417, again draw the great-to-pedal coupler and bring on the pedal reeds.

Vain virtuosi plume themselves on rattling off the Toccata at a ridiculous speed. They find their reward. A genuine organist will rather fear playing too fast than too slow, and will seek to win applause by endeavoring to meet the demands for the elasticity of tempo required here in its highest perfection.

The fundamental tempo is set by the movements to be played in the brilliant *forte;* the periods containing chord-successions move somewhat slower, and those in which only foundation stops and mixtures are employed move somewhat faster. Let it be the interpreter's chief care to lead over from one tempo into another, playing with freedom, and still without disturbing the hearer's conception of a uniform fundamental tempo. Again and again should he mentally review and mould this piece, until he penetrates to a clear, living conception of its structural sequence as influencing the *tempo*; and then he will be able to let the Toccata arise like a Gothic edifice beneath the blue sky of the *F*-major tonality.

He should not expect his audience to comprehend this piece, and think it beautiful, on a first hearing. But let him perform it again and again as a postlude; in time they will forget to go out, and will remain till the last chord has sounded.

It should be observed, that the two-measure group forms the rhythmic unit. Hence, the Toccata should actually be conceived as if it were written in six-eight time.

FUGUE

The first principal section (measures 1–70) will be played on the great-manual with foundation stops and mixtures. Should an augmentation be desired, only the mixtures of the third manual will be drawn to begin with, those of the second and first following in succession. These reinforcements should be added on the first quarter in measure 30, the fourth quarter in measure 44, the second in measure 50, and the first in measure 56.

Some players also employ reed-stops for this augmentation; others even draw them at the start.

The episode begins in measure 70. The change of manual can best be accomplished by going over to the second manual with the right hand on the fourth quarter, and at the same time doubling the first half-note taken in the alto on the second manual, then releasing it on the first.

This episode extends to measure 128. Because of its length it is advisable to use the reduced great-organ as a subsidiary organ, so that one may alternate between three varying degrees of tone-power. The mixtures on the second and third manuals are to remain in action.

Bach probably performed the entire episode on the second manual. The construction shows that he did not intend to have the theme brought out specially. However, we shall not sin against his spirit by introducing a certain variety into the long episode, or by occasionally coupling the silent pedal to one of the manuals so that the theme may be allowed to display itself on a separate manual. But do not make matters too complicated for yourself or your audience.

We would suggest that both hands remain on the second manual up to measure 88. On the second quarter in this measure the right hand goes over to the third manual. The left hand follows on the last quarter in measure 89.

During the progress of measures 93–100 the swell-box closes.

From measure 101 onward the tenor-part is played on the second manual, the silent pedal being coupled to this manual and used for playing the tenor where the distribution of the parts calls for it. On the second eighth before the last in measure 106 the right hand likewise returns to the second manual.

Meantime the reduced great-manual has been uncoupled from the other manuals. From the last quarter in measure 110 onward the left hand takes over the alto-part on the great, while the tenor-part is assigned to the silent pedal coupled to the second manual.

From the second eighth before the last in measure 115 both hands play on the first manual, remaining there until the close of the Fugue. On the last quarter in measure 119 its coupler to the third manual is again drawn. The swell-box opens gradually.

On the third quarter in measure 128 the coupler of the great-manual to the choir is also drawn. For the entrance of the bass, the pedal is brought up to its original strength.

On the third quarter in measure 134 all the registers on the great-organ will be added which are required to make the combination the same as at the commencement of the Fugue.

The above *modus operandi* thus carries out the episode in a grand *diminuendo* and *crescendo*, and effects a fine transition into the closing principal section. Even on organs with only two manuals this plan may be realized in its chief features; the mixtures of the second manual will be thrown off, and this manual then utilized as a third manual.

There is a strong temptation to bring out the theme in alto, from measure 128 onward, on the reinforced great-organ (with the help of the pedal, which would take over the tenor-part), the right hand remaining on the second manual. But then both hands would necessarily have played on the second (or third) manual from measure 119 onward.

The return of the soprano and tenor to the great-manual would be effectuated by letting the latter transfer on the first quarter in measure 134, and the former on the third quarter in the same measure.

For bringing on a closing augmentation, stops will be added on the first quarter in measures 153 and 158. Some players already introduce reinforce-

ments with the beginning of measure 143, the soprano and bass being lifted a trifle prematurely.

In measure 163 the bass is increased to *fortissimo*.

II. Prelude and Fugue in F Minor. (Pages 20-29.)

PRELUDE

This piece may be played from beginning to end in a brilliant *forte* resulting from a combination of foundation stops, mixtures and reeds; dynamic variety would spring solely from the logic of the wonderful music.

But, on the other hand, the lines of the *crescendi* and *decrescendi* are so plainly indicated that it is to be assumed that Bach himself realized them to a certain degree by changing registration.

The *forte* extends to measure 32. Here enters a *mezzo-forte* which continues till measure 51. Through measures 51–64 an augmentation goes forward in which the *forte* of the beginning is arrived at.

Commence on the great-manual with the brilliant *forte* in which foundation stops, mixtures and reeds are represented. Of course, both hands play on the great-manual. Organists who have lost their distaste for triviality will venture to start with the right hand on the second manual and the left hand on the first, not playing with both together on the great until later.

There are players who affect an augmentation to full organ during the course of measures 15–32.

At all events, before striking the fifth sixteenth in measure 32, a portion of the active stops will be thrown off. We would suggest retaining the mixtures of the second and third manuals, then retiring them successively after the first quarter in measures 36, 37, 38 and 39, employing foundation stops alone from measures 40–50.

It is probable (though not certain) that the second manual should be used for measures 52, 54 and 56. The left hand would change over on the first or second eighth, and the right hand on the second sixteenth.

This change of manual permits of bringing on a fine *crescendo*. The great-organ stops will be added in the measures when the hands are on the second manual. In case you remain continuously on the great, the reinforcements can enter at the breath-pause between the first and second sixteenth-notes in measures 51, 53, 55 and 57.

When your swell-box is in good shape, you may, to begin with, do without reinforcing the great-organ, and add the mixtures and reeds of the second manual, after the shutters are closed, between the first and second sixteenths in measure 51. The swell-box will now open up to measure 60. Only from here onward are stops to be added on the first manual.

Whichever method be chosen, take care that the augmentation does not reach its climax too early, and that reinforcements remain in reserve, to be introduced on the first beats in measures 60, 61, 62 and 63, and also at the beginning of measure 64.

Properly conducted, this *crescendo* continued through thirteen measures has a most impressive effect. For measure 70 bring on the full organ with the 16-foot manual registers. Part of the reinforcements may, if you prefer, be introduced as early as the third quarter in measure 69.

From measure 71 onward let the 16-foot manual stops be retired; draw them again on the third quarter in measure 74.

It is not wholly improbable that Bach played with both hands on the *Rück-positiv* from the second sixteenth-note in measure 51 on, not returning to the great until the fifth sixteenth in measure 64.

FUGUE

In a spacious auditorium the first principal section of this marvellous Fugue — measures 1–42 — may be performed in an unchanging, brilliant *forte* of foundation stops, mixtures and reeds. Should the nave be too contracted to permit of such prolonged powerful playing, you should, on beginning, draw the mixtures and reeds only on the second manual, and successively add those of the great-organ on the first quarter in measure 17, between the first and second quarters in measure 27, and on the first quarter in measure 37.

Some players transfer the two highest parts to the second manual on the second quarter in measure 27, in order to emphasize the theme with the left hand on the great from measure 31 onward. Considered by itself, the effect is not bad. But then one must keep the right hand on the second manual till measure 37, and accept as part of the bargain that in measures 34, 35 and 36 a not especially important inner part asserts itself as a solo on the great. At all events, Bach had no intention of using the second manual in these measures.

Measures 42–64 are to be executed on the second manual with foundation stops and mixtures. The best way to proceed is as follows:—Retire the reeds of the second manual already on the second quarter in measure 41. Let the pedal sustain the *f* in the left hand at the beginning of measure 42, not repeating the note; the left hand takes instead (while the right sustains the three tones of the chord on the great-manual) the alto *f* on the second manual, so that it will sound on this manual when the right-hand chord is lifted. From the second quarter onward, both hands will be on the second manual.

The swell-box closes from measures 50–55. In case you wish to emphasize the theme in the inner part from measure 56 onward, play it with the right hand on Man. I (which has been reduced meanwhile), and play the lower part on the silent pedal coupled to Man. II. Or, you may play the two lower parts with the left hand on the great-manual.

From the third quarter in measure 59 onward, both hands are again on the second manual. Pedal and great are again increased to their original tone-power; the swell-box opens during the progress of measures 60–64.

If you have a third manual, play upon it from the second quarter in measure 52 to the corresponding point in measure 54; then go back to the second manual, and return to the third on the second quarter in measure 56 with the right hand by doubling the dotted *f*. From this measure forward the theme is played on the second manual with the left hand.

From the third quarter in measure 59 onward the left hand transfers the two lower parts to and joins the right hand on the third manual.

The return to the great-manual takes place at the beginning of measure 64. The soprano goes over on the first quarter; the sustained note in the part next below is struck afresh upon the great-manual on the first quarter; the left hand still sustains its half-notes on the third manual, not going over to the first till the beginning of measure 65. Some players leave the two half-notes in the left hand, at the beginning of measure 64, to sound in the same pedal-tone, without striking them; employing the thus liberated left hand to execute the second highest part on the second manual until the beginning of measure 65.

On the first beat in measure 73 the second-manual reeds may be drawn again. Increase still further for the last quarter in measure 87.

A *diminuendo subito* at measure 90, or a transference to the second manual, may offer a certain temptation to the modern player, but most assuredly formed no part of Bach's design. Remain, therefore, on the first manual, and, if you will, bring on further reinforcements.

On the other hand, a clever modernization of the following episode would scarcely be unsuitable. Properly, in measure 96, the theme in the left hand should enter on the second manual; from the fourth quarter of this measure onward it should then be played with both hands on this keyboard; and not until measure 120 ought the hands to return to the great-manual, the left on the second eighth, the right on the second quarter.—According to modern procedure the left hand remains on the great-manual in measure 96, only the right hand transferring to the second manual on the last quarter. In the registration nothing is to be changed. The swell-box closes from measures 97–101. On the third quarter in measure 99 the left hand also goes over to the second manual.

For the beginning of measure 102 the second-manual reeds are thrown off. An organist who fears that his auditors may not be able to follow the theme in measures 102–104, and is willing to spare no pains to help them out, will meanwhile have reduced the great-organ, and silenced the pedal so as to couple it to the second manual, and from measure 102 onward will play the theme on the great with his left hand while executing the lowest part on the pedal.

From the second eighth in measure 105 onward both hands, in any case, will be on the second manual again. The swell-box opens during the course of measures 106–110.

In measure 110 the left hand may take over the theme on the reduced great-organ, while the silent pedal, coupled to the second manual, carries on the lower part. A simpler way is to let the left hand play the two lower parts on the reduced great-organ. The right hand remains for the present on the second manual.

From the third quarter in measure 113 onward the left hand plays the two lower parts on the great. On the second eighth before the last in this measure the right hand likewise returns to the (still reduced) great-manual.

Before the second eighth before the last in measures 114, 115 and 116, and before the second eighth in measures 117, 118 and 119, you will add successive reinforcements in order to arrive, on the second quarter in measure 120, at the *forte*-combination of foundation stops, mixtures and reeds. By continuing to increase successively on the first beat in measure 123 and at the rests in measures 126–129, you will arrive at full organ. Or the augmentation may not reach its climax till the beginning of measure 134.

Certain players prefer to increase to full organ as early as measure 120. In measures 113–116 one may allow the soprano-part to alternate between the first and second manuals; the change will be accomplished each time on the second eighth before the last.

III. Prelude and Fugue in G Major. (Pages 30–39.)

PRELUDE

In construction the Prelude resembles the foregoing in *F* minor. In this case also the player — if he does not prefer to perform the entire work in an even

forte — will make up his mind to distinguish a middle section (measures 29–46) by means of a reduced registration, then increasing by degrees either to the initial *forte* or to full organ. No change of manual is provided for.

Begin with foundation stops, mixtures and reeds; but do not allow yourself to be misled into playing the *Vivace* so rapidly as the modern interpretation of the term would imply. In no event could Bach have intended to go beyond an *Allegro* in which his pedal reeds could just keep up with the rest.

We may mention, as a curious fact, that organists have actually been known to start the brilliant figurations of the beginning on the second manual, for the sake of effecting a *crescendo* which they *conceived* to be fitting for the first division of the piece.

Up to measure 29 no change will be attempted in the registration. Whether one should employ the 16-foot pedal reeds or not, depends on their character; if they are dull and heavy in resonance, it is best to omit them.

Before the third sixteenth at the beginning of measure 29 one may throw off reeds and mixtures all at once, and play the succeeding measures with foundation stops alone; though the effect is probably better when these stops are retired more gradually, the reeds being retired in measure 29, and the mixtures successively thrown off before the second eighth in measures 32, 34 and 38. The swell-box closes during the course of measures 43–45.

On the second eighth in measure 46 the second-manual mixtures are added. The swell-box remains closed, so that the second-manual reeds may be imperceptibly introduced on the third eighth-note before the last in measure 53.

Now the shutters begin to open, so that the next five measures continue in a fine *crescendo*.

On the second sixteenth-note in measure 59 add one of the great-organ mixture-stops. The subsequent reinforcements are best introduced on the rests in measures 63 and 64, on the second sixteenth-note before the last in measure 69, and on the second sixteenths in measures 74 and 77. However, the full organ may be brought on still earlier.

The effect of the composition depends chiefly upon plasticity in the execution. Be particularly careful to separate distinctly all notes repeated in the same part, and to play all the rest strictly *legato*. By this means the chord-successions will be most advantageously set out.

The phrasing must be consistently carried out according to the given motives in the first measures.

Phrase as follows in measures 10 and 11:

Play the pedal-part in measures 21–24 like this:

In measures 63 and 64 the left hand should phrase thus:

When care is taken to make the *legato* phrasing of the eighth-notes and sixteenths in each part correspond precisely with that demanded by the funda-mental motive interwoven throughout, it lends to the Prelude a wonderfully transparent and animated effect. But when the sixteenth-notes are simply reeled off without breathing into them the breath of life, the piece seems like the merest shadow of itself.

FUGUE

On a fine organ, and in a good-sized auditorium, measures 1–38 will be played in a clear, sonorous *forte* resulting from a combination of foundation stops, mixtures and reeds. Where the above conditions are not present, you must make up your mind to attain the *forte* by augmentation. In this case, mixtures and reeds are drawn only on the second manual. The swell-box is closed at the out-set; it opens during the course of measures 14–16. On the second eighth before the last in measures 17 and 22, the second quarter in measure 27, the second eighth before the last in measure 30, and the second eighth in measure 35, the player has a chance to add the mixtures and reeds on the great-organ until the desired *forte* or *fortissimo* is reached.

The episode may be performed in the classic, primitive manner, or with modern refinements. Choosing the former method, transfer the left hand to the second manual with the second sixteenth-note of the third quarter in measure 38; the right hand following with the soprano-part on the last quarter of the measure by doubling the half-note on the second manual and releasing it on the great-manual. If your choir-organ is good the effect will be excellent, despite the great contrast.

The return to the great-manual is effected just as simply. After the hands have kept continuously on the second manual from measure 38 onward, not even being misled into making a change by the entrance of the pedal in measure 52,

they return to the great-manual in measure 53, the left hand on the second six-teenth in the third beat, the right on the second sixteenth in the first beat. To proceed quite correctly, take the *g* in the last eighth of the alto-part in measure 52 with the left thumb on the great-manual, the fourth or fifth finger of the left hand meanwhile sustaining the quarter-note (*a*) in the lower part on the second manual. The narrow space between keyboards on the organs of Bach's time rendered this manœuvre quite easy. On the organs of to-day it may appear rather venturesome. The procedure will be simplified by relinquishing the tenor-part on the last eighth, as its note is contained in that of the pedal. The left hand is thus set free to take the last eighth in the alto-part on the great-manual.

The modernized interpretation of the episode seeks to moderate the con-trasts. From measures 38–43 both hands remain on the great-manual. By successively retiring stops, a *diminuendo* is effected. For doing this you will choose the first quarters in measures 39, 40 and 41, and the rests in soprano before the second sixteenth-note before the last in measure 41 and before the fifth six-teenth in measure 42. The effect of this procedure is not bad, because the throwing off of single registers on the first quarter in measures 39, 40 and 41 acts like a *decrescendo* on the suspension.

At the beginning of measure 43 there will be only 8- and 4-foot foundation stops left on the great-organ, and only foundation stops and mixtures on the second manual. On the second sixteenth-note before the last in measure 43 the right hand goes over to the second manual, the left hand following on the last eighth of the same measure or on the second sixteenth before the last in measure 44.

During measures 45, 46 and 47 the swell-box closes. At the same time the 4-foot stops of the great-organ are thrown off. With the second eighth in meas-ure 48, transfer the left hand to the reduced great-manual. The swell-box opens during the progress of measures 48–52.

In the course of measure 52 the 4-foot foundation stops of the great-organ will be drawn again. From the last eighth in this measure onward, the left hand will play two parts. On the last quarter in measure 53 the soprano-part will also return to the great. No harm is done by having the great-organ comparatively weak during measures 53–55; the theme in the pedal comes out all the more clearly.

On the second sixteenth-note in measure 56 the 2-foot foundation stop of the great-organ will be drawn. On the second eighth before the last in measure 59 the second-manual reeds are also to be added. Further reinforcements are introduced on the second eighths in measures 63 and 65, the first quarter in measure 68, and *a piacere* on the second sixteenth in measure 69 and during the rests in measures 70 and 71. You must arrive at full organ with the hold ($\frown$) in measure 71. Continue in this tone-power to the end.

As in the Prelude, the life and transparency in the movement of the Fugue depend upon consistently maintaining the phrasing in each of the several parts. Take care not to group the sixteenth-notes in measure 48 and the following simply according to the formula

In reality the phrasing should run thus:

Avoid taking the tempo too fast.

The theme is identical with that of the first chorus in the cantata "Ich hatte viel Bekümmernis" (No. 21), except that in the choral work it appears in minor. The cantata dates from the year 1714. It is likely that the Fugue was written about the same time. It was doubtless composed together with the Prelude. Observe how its theme is announced, in the Prelude, in the groups of eighth-notes repeated by the pedal during the course of measures 63–69:

Over this Prelude and Fugue something like a sunny sky seems to be spread. They are eloquent with a great, serene confidence that banishes care from troubled hearts.

IV. Prelude (Fantasia) and Fugue in G Minor. (Pages 40-53.)

PRELUDE (FANTASIA)

Measures 1–9 will be played with full organ, omitting the 16-foot manual-stops. At the end of measure 3 throw off the pedal reeds and the great-to-pedal coupler.

Some players like to go over to the second manual after the first quarter in measure 9. But the marvellous four-part movement requires a certain broad and mellow tone which only the foundation stops of the great-organ can produce. We would, therefore, suggest throwing off the reeds and mixtures of the great and second manuals after the second eighth in measure 9, and playing what follows on the great-manual. But the change in registration must on no account cause any disturbing delay in the entrance of pedal or manual.

At the end of measure 13 the swell-box will close coincidently with the natural *ritardando;* on the rest in measure 14, before beginning the ascending run, introduce the mixtures and reeds of the second manual. From the end of measure 14 to the beginning of measure 17 the swell-box opens; the motion of the swell-pedal should be so timed that a considerable volume of the *crescendo* can still be given out on the first two notes in measure 17, which are separated one from the other. After the second eighth in measure 15, on the second thirty-second-note of the second quarter in measure 16, on the second eighth in measure 17, and on the second sixteenth of the second quarter in measure 18, the great-organ mixtures should be successively introduced; its reeds will be added on the rest in measure 20 and on the first quarter in measure 21.

During the rest in the bass-part in measure 20, draw the great-to-pedal coupler; draw the pedal reeds at the beginning of measure 22.

After the second eighth in measure 25, retire the mixtures and reeds of the manuals (as at the corresponding point in measure 9).

In order that the change in the pedal-registration may not have to be effected here, too, the great-to-pedal coupler and the pedal reeds should already have been thrown off during the rest in bass in the preceding measure; and likewise take the pedal-note on the last eighth in that measure with the left hand, on the great-manual, so as to cover the reduction in the pedal. In any event, the left hand will help in sustaining the pedal-note at the beginning of measure 25. By this means the premature reduction of the pedal, which essentially facilitates the change of registration in measure 25, will remain unnoticed even by experts in the audience.

From the second quarter in measure 25 to the first in measure 31, you will employ foundation stops. At the transition from measure 30–31 the swell-box closes concurrently with the natural *rallentando.* At the breath-pause between the first and second quarters in measure 31, add the mixtures and reeds of the second manual, drawing the great-to-pedal coupler at the same time. The procedure is facilitated by lifting the pedal-part at the very beginning of the measure, and sustaining the bass note with the left hand. This will not be noticed at all by the hearer.

During the course of measures 31–34 the swell-box opens. In order that the right foot may be free to work the swell-pedal, the last three and the first two eighths in the bass in these measures should regularly be taken by the left foot. Just here the control of the swell is rather complicated, and requires practice. The outcome will reward your pains.

On the first quarter and the fourth eighth in measure 35, the first quarter in measure 36, and the second quarters in measures 37 and 38, introduce reinforcements leading up to full organ. The pedal reeds enter on the first eighth in measure 37. Between the first and second sixteenths in measure 39, retire the 16-foot manual stops. The effect is also very good here if you throw off the great-to-pedal coupler. The pedal then retains its full tone without sounding heavy or overpowering the inner parts. At the beginning of the last measure but one, draw the great-to-pedal coupler again.

For the chords occurring in measure 44 to the close, the 16-foot manual stops may be added; for the runs they should be retired. The effect is excellent.

However, there are players who keep these registers out continuously.

At all events, do not undertake any radical changes in the registration during measures 39 to 49. The piece should close majestically, in a grand, uniform *forte*.

It should be observed that some organists, in order to obtain a still stronger *crescendo*, go over to the second manual with the second quarter in measure 31, and execute the pedal-part for a time with the left hand, which plays in octaves. Not until the swell-box is fully opened do they transfer both hands back to the great-manual and take up the bass again with the pedal. But they fail to consider that the *crescendo* desired by Bach ought to commence with a rich *mezzo-forte* on the great-organ, this being plainly indicated by his employment of the pedal.

The simplicity and naturalness of the plan detailed above for interpreting this splendid Fantasia, should be its highest recommendation. In case your swell-organ is not of the best, the *crescendi* otherwise to be effected by its aid will have to be realized by the successive addition of registers on the second manual.

It is self-evident that Bach himself operated in this piece by successively adding registers. But he probably did not prolong the lines of the *crescendi* and *decrescendi* to the extent that modern players will.

The balancing of the tempi is a matter of high importance in the execution of this piece. It is clear that it should be played with a certain freedom; but any exaggeration whatever must be avoided. The touchstone of the artist will be found in playing with freedom, but never letting the hearer lose track of the measure, rhythm, and fundamental tempo.

Anything approaching haste is to be condemned. The sixteenth-note figurations must roll out in tranquil majesty. Not the least note therein should escape the auditor. At the same time the structural development should be plainly set forth by the phrasing, so that it may not seem like a mere stream of rushing notes, but an evolution of living forms.

FUGUE

Many players may prefer the following phrasing of the theme:

This latter has the advantage, that the several motives are better contrasted than in the former. The arguments of musical logic are on its side.

For the former phrasing, on the other hand, the principles of æsthetics contend. The binding of the ascending octave is more pleasing to the ear than the lifting, and is more sonorous, and still does not destroy the conception of the structure of the theme. A decision can hardly be reached.

Inconceivable it is, that there have been "virtuosi" who so far misunderstood the proud, vigorous character of this theme as to let it enter, at the outset, in *piano* on the second manual.

Begin on the great-organ in a *forte* in which foundation stops and mixtures are combined. On the last eighth in measure 21 — and also on the first in measure 25, if desired — reinforcements are added. In this first principal section it is better to dispense with reeds altogether.

On the second eighth in measure 37 the right hand goes over to the second manual. It is likely that Bach would have already transferred the left hand on the last eighth in measure 36. But a modern player will scarcely withstand the temptation to improve the fine opportunity of presenting the theme to his auditors on a different manual. Let him not forget, however, to retire the great-organ mixtures at the moment when his right hand changes over, so that the theme may not stand out with too harsh effect, and that the section may preserve the character of an episode.

Some players think it best to retire the registers of the great-organ successively — say after the last eighth but one in measures 37 and 38, and before the second sixteenth before the last in measure 39.

Certain organists transfer the left hand to the second manual on the second sixteenth-note before the last in measure 39; others do so in the middle of measure 41, and others again on the second eighth in measure 42. Some remain on the great-manual until the tenor-part pauses in measure 43. The most natural way is, probably, to change on the second sixteenth before the last in measure 39. In any case, both hands will be on the second manual from the second eighth in measure 43 onward.

From the last eighth in measure 43 to the middle of measure 46 the swell-box closes, so that the theme appears to be vanishing in the distance. The effect is very good when you dwell slightly on the last eighth in measure 43; and for the following transition to measure 44 let the swell-box close to a sensible extent.

During the progress of measures 47–49 the shutters are reopened.

On the last eighth in measure 50 the left hand goes over to the great-manual, on which only the 8-foot foundation stops are drawn. You may change over with the right hand on the second sixteenth in the third quarter of measure 53, or on the last sixteenth in that measure, or on the second eighth in measure 55. This change by the right hand does not afford genuine satisfaction, whichever point be chosen. One cannot get rid of the impression that Bach probably did not intend a change of manual in this passage. It is possible that he kept both hands on the second manual — despite the pedal-entrance — up to measure 57, not making the change until the second eighth before the last in this measure. Naturally, he likewise forbore bringing out the theme on the first manual from measure 30 onward. Nevertheless, no objection can be made to the procedure outlined above. The return of the right hand to the great-manual, although logically unsatisfactory, is perfectly correct in sound if the great-organ be properly reduced. On the second manual the mixtures are to be retained.

With three manuals at your disposal, you may transfer both hands to the third on the second eighth in measure 43, after having employed the second manual in the manner indicated above. On the second eighth before the last in measure 46 the left hand returns to the second manual; the right may follow on the last sixteenth in measure 48. From here onward you will carry out the directions already given for a two-manual organ. It is improbable that Bach himself used his third manual during this episode.

Whichever method be chosen, one should perform the episode on a modern organ with a *decrescendo* extending to the middle of measure 46, and from that point in a continuous *crescendo*.

On the last sixteenth-note in measure 54 — provided that both hands are now on the great-manual — the 4-foot foundation stops of the great-organ may be added. Some organists will not add them until the second eighth before the last in measure 57, which is probably the better way.

Much depends on correctly carrying out the subsequent augmentation. It must proceed neither too swiftly nor too slowly. The following suggestions are offered.

On the last sixteenth-note but one in measure 62 (or on the fourth eighth in measure 63) add the 2-foot foundation stop of the great-organ together with one of its mixtures. A further reinforcement will be introduced on the second beat in measure 66. Under cover of the mixtures of the great-organ, you can imperceptibly close the swell-box during the course of this measure and the next, and then add the second-manual reeds on the second eighth in measure 68. For the present the swell-box remains closed, so that the tone of the reeds sounds merely like a discreet coloring of the foundation stops and mixtures.

On the fourth eighth in measure 72 add whatever mixtures are still in.

With measure 80 the swell-box begins to open, thus bringing out the tone of the reeds on the swell-manual. This *crescendo* attains its climax about in measure 84. On the second eighth before the last in measure 84, and the third beat in measure 86, add the great-organ reeds.

Instead of bringing on an uninterrupted *crescendo*, one may alternate between a more and a less powerful tone-effect. The sections to be played more loudly would be from the second quarter in measure 66 to the first in measure 68; from the fourth eighth in measure 72 to the second eighth before the last in measure 82; and from the third quarter in measures 86–93. The intermediate sections would be played somewhat softer, without reeds.

The pedal-reeds may be used from measure 82 onward. But it is better to dispense with the 16-foot Posaune until measure 110, so as not to render its effect stale.

How the close of the Fugue shall be performed, depends on the conception one has of measures 93–110. According to rule, they should be regarded as an episode. Bach, on the last eighth in measure 93, probably went over to his *Rückpositiv* with the soprano, letting the left hand follow on the second sixteenth-note before the last in measure 94. Up to the rest in measure 110 he then kept both hands on this manual, not returning to the great until the last eighth in that measure. The abrupt and overwhelming entrance of the theme in the pedal, with the succeeding *finale* of the other parts, were admirably brought out by this means.

The modern organist — who, moreover, has not the brilliant, sonorous tone of the old *Rückpositiv* at his command — is not wholly satisfied with the interruption of the closing intensification by an episode performed on the second manual.

Some players completely obliterate the character of the episode by involving it in the intensification. They arrange their registration in such a way, that in measure 93 they still have at their disposal reserves which they can introduce on the last beat in this measure and, if they desire, on the rest in soprano in measure 104, and on the second sixteenth-notes in measures 107, 108 and 109. They emphasize the theme in measures 100–103 by entrusting it to the pedal, which is coupled to the manuals, and whose 16-foot registers are thrown off at this conjuncture.

Others steer a middle course. After measure 93 they draw no more stops, and play in part on the second manual. In measure 93 they keep the right hand on the great-manual, transferring only the left (towards the end of measure 94) to the second. From the second sixteenth-note before the last in measure 96 onward they let the right hand also play on the second manual; and on the last eighth in measure 100 transfer the left hand to the great-manual.

Meanwhile, all the pedal stops, and the great-to-pedal coupler, have been thrown off. On the fourth eighth in measure 103 this silent pedal, coupled to the second manual, takes over the lowest part, in order that the left hand may execute the theme in alto on the great. From the second eighth in measure 106 onward both hands again play on the great-manual. The pedal is brought up to *fortissimo*.

This procedure, a compromise between ancient and modern views, has many good points. But from time to time the player should not neglect to perform the entire episode on the second manual to familiarize himself and his audience with the classical conception. It is still the sole correct one, however strange it may seem to us at first.

V. Prelude and Fugue in A Major. (Pages 54-61.)

PRELUDE

Together with the Fugue, this Prelude belongs to a special category among Bach's works for the organ. Neither is distinguished by majestic traits; they are rather lyric in character. In their style, too, they exhibit various peculiarities. The other works of this kind offer nothing analogous to the last twelve measures of the Fugue. In what other composition does Bach lead the parts on the organ away from each other in ascending and descending thirds, as in measures 171 and 172 of this Fugue? Where else does he finish an organ-fugue without a real *conclusio*?

The individuality of these pieces must be reflected in their performance.

Beware, in the Prelude, of all striving after effect and of any modernizing tendency to exploit this piece by means of a grand augmentation. The more simply it is played, the more natural will be its effect.

Draw foundation stops on the great-organ, and foundation stops and mixtures on the second manual. Begin on the great. On the first quarter in measure 8, couple the pedal to the second manual; at the same point in the next measure, couple it to the great-manual also. Execute the pedal solo in measure 10 without the addition of stops.

On the second quarter in measure 11, retire the great-to-pedal coupler; at the corresponding point in the next measure, retire the coupler to the second manual.

On the sixteenth-rest in soprano in the middle of measure 14 the volume of tone may be somewhat reduced by throwing off one or two stops or uncoupling the second manual.

On the second sixteenth in the third quarter of measure 16 the hands go over to the second manual, where they remain. On the second sixteenth in measure 19 the soprano returns to the great-manual; the alto follows on the second sixteenth in the second quarter, the tenor on the second sixteenth before the last.

During the rest in soprano in measure 22, increase the great-organ to its original strength; at the same time draw the manual-to-pedal couplers, unless this was already done in measure 19. The Prelude closes in the same tone-power in which it began.

In this piece much depends on graceful, smooth execution. It should glide past the hearer like a vision.

We must mention that many players do not care to reduce the great-organ in measure 14, and object to the change of manual in measure 16. They play the Prelude from beginning to end on the same manual and in the same volume of tone.

FUGUE

Its theme is closely related to that of the orchestral prelude to the Cantata "Tritt auf die Glaubensbahn" (No. 152), which runs thus:

The two themes are, however, developed quite differently.

The fugue-theme is much completer than that of the Cantata. It presents the mature form of the idea. Hence, the organ composition was probably written later than the Cantata; but the difference in date cannot be determined. The Cantata was composed in Weimar, presumably about 1715.

The theme symbolizes footfalls. But what Bach represents in this Fugue is not the strong and steadfast stride, unfaltering and unswerving, with which he elsewhere so drastically expresses the confidence and strength of Faith. The impression is rather as if his intent were to portray the steps of those blessed ones, who in life held to the straight path of belief, and are now wandering through the fields of Paradise. Through this music there shines the sunlight of joyfulness — almost of playfulness.

Observe also that the Fugue appears, in reality, like a kind of Chaconne. It consists, in the main, of a succession of sections in each of which the theme enters in either one part, or two parts. There is no question of an actual development, such as one otherwise finds in the organ-fugues.

This means, that this fugue admits of no general and continuing augmentation.

The player who tries every possible and impossible registration over and over will arrive at the conclusion, that in this case his sole salvation lies in the greatest simplicity.

It will be best to use only 8- and 4-foot foundation stops. Let the player prevail upon himself neither to add nor to retire any stops during the progress of the piece.

Variety will be taken care of by changing manuals, coupling and uncoupling them, and closing and opening the swell.

As Bach himself probably played likewise with foundation stops only, he was enabled to employ his third manual, which he usually dispensed with for the other fugues on account of its weak array of stops. It is plainly to be seen that he expects the episodes to be played in two degrees of tone-power.

The Fugue starts on the great-manual, to which the second and third are coupled; the swell-box is open. In case the auditorium is small, you may dispense with your Diapasons and Principals if they are rather loud. Between the first and second eighths in measure 45 throw off the couplers of the second and third manuals to the great; but the hands remain on the great.

On the second eighth in measure 49, go over to the second manual. Should you wish to bring out the theme in the tenor, let the left hand stay on the great-manual. But it is likely that Bach changed with both hands.

From the second eighth in measure 57 onward both hands play on the third manual. The swell-box closes gradually up to measure 65.

From the second eighth in measure 65 onward both hands are again on the second manual, which is coupled to the third throughout the entire piece. The swell-box opens gradually up to measure 76.

With the second eighth in measure 77 both hands return to the great-manual, which has been recoupled meanwhile to the other two. Between the first and second quarters in measure 89, throw off the couplers. Between the first and second eighths in measure 97, again draw the III to I coupler. At the corresponding point in measure 102, or as early as the first eighth in that measure, likewise draw the II to I coupler.

Players who already go over to the second manual on the second eighth in measure 110, are probably in error. The episode does not begin until measure 115. From the second eighth in this measure onward both hands play on the second manual; at the corresponding point in measure 123 they go over to the third. The swell-box closes slowly from measure 131 to measure 135.

From the second eighth in measure 136 onward both hands are once more on the great-manual, its couplers to the other two having been retired previously. On the second quarter in measure 145, again draw the III to I coupler.

During the course of measures 153–159, the swell-box opens. It will not be difficult to divide up the pedal-part between the feet so that the right foot may find various momentary opportunities to operate the balanced swell-pedal.

On the second eighth in measure 161 also draw the II to I coupler; play from here to the close with unchanging tone-power.

A player who follows this or some similar plan will thus renounce, as a matter of principle, all stratagems aiming at the reservation of a special manual for the theme. Admittedly, the temptation to this latter procedure is not small in the present case. Supposing that, in the episodes, one gives the lowest part to the silent pedal coupled to Manual II or III, and considers it allowable, in the principal sections, to play with one hand on one manual and the other hand on another, there will be little trouble in bringing out the theme as a solo almost anywhere.

But precisely because this effect is so cheap, let us do without it, and rather win applause by an exposition of the theme to our hearers by virtue of an artistic development of its characteristic phrasing. Besides, do not forget that by continually emphasizing the theme the contrast between principal section and episode is wholly obliterated.

The chief difficulty in performing this Fugue consists in so executing it that it shall have no unrestful effect. In the theme the accents fall on the second beat in measures 2, 4, 6 and 8, the first quarter in each of these measures bearing the preparatory accent. Consequently, the entire Fugue moves in a rhythm opposed to the natural measure-accents! Compare it with the Passacaglia, whose theme flows on smoothly in the rhythm of its three-four time!

There is also danger of breaking the continuity of the numerous short periods of which the piece is built up. At the close of each, one involuntarily makes a slight — though never so slight — *rallentando*, returning directly into the normal tempo. This also lends an unrestful effect to the whole.

It is the player's task to overcome these difficulties and interpret this composition with quiet elegance, though for the organ it is almost too graceful and sharply rhythmical. Let him show himself a master of the key, a master of the movement. Otherwise he will discover that his auditors are weary and irritated after twenty measures, and quite unable to enjoy this peculiar and — even though it wellnigh overpasses the bounds of the organ-style established by Bach — so admirable composition.

It should be said, that the work may be played in much simpler fashion than is shown in the foregoing. The coupling and uncoupling of Manuals II and III to and from Manual I may be dispensed with. Bach contented himself with the three grades of power afforded by the three manuals.

VI. Prelude and Fugue in A Minor. (Pages 62-75.)

PRELUDE

The transcriptions for piano which this Prelude has undergone, have made it a household word in the world of music. Nevertheless, its fate is far from enviable. Whatever favor it may have enjoyed was really due to the fact that the virtuosi of the piano and organ have vied with each other in burdening it with *crescendi* and *decrescendi* abhorrent to its character.

In point of fact, it should be played from beginning to end on one manual in an equal *forte*.

The first who ventured to advocate this conception — a conception founded on the style and construction of the piece, and taken as a matter of course in the eighteenth century, and as late as the first half of the nineteenth — were jeered at as pedants and fools. Fortunately, in this matter, as in others, unwisdom was permitted to darken the truth only for a season, and not for long.

On organs of the eighteenth century the full organ was drawn for this piece — probably without the 16-foot manual stops — and it was played through to the end with the same combination. On the pedal, the reeds — including the 16-foot Posaune — could remain out continuously, in spite of the sustained notes. The tone was clear and penetrating, but did not drown the other parts in any manner.

When performed on our modern organs, their greater fullness of tone, and especially the intenser sound of the reeds, must be taken into account. For the long organ-points the pedal must be reduced. In the *forte* certain shadings must be introduced, that it may not grow intolerable to the listener. No change is to be made in the foundation stops and mixtures drawn; but the reed-groups may be reduced or increased. Any foundation stops or mixtures which are either too dull or too harsh, should be eliminated from the start. What one should aim at is less a high degree of power, than richness of tone and clearness of combination. But hold fast to the principle that reeds in some shape, however weak, ought to be continuously represented in your combinations. Let the color of the *forte* remain the same throughout; vary it only in the intensity.

The following plan is calculated for a three-manual organ.

Begin on the great-organ, and remain on it throughout. Prepare the foundation stops and mixtures of the great, swell and choir, and the swell-reeds; the swell-box is open.

On the pedal, which is coupled to Man. III, only foundation stops are drawn.

For the beginning of the triplets in sixteenth-notes in the middle of measure 9, the swell-box is closed. It opens again during the progress of measures 10–21.

On the second 32d-note in measure 22, add the reeds of Man. II; on the first quarter in measure 23, couple the pedal to Man. II; and on the third quarter of the same measure couple it to Man. I. During the breath-pause between the first and second sixteenths in bass in measure 24, throw on the pedal-reeds.

On the second quarter in measure 30 throw off the pedal-coupler to Man. I; on the fourth quarter in measure 31, retire the 16-foot Posaune. Between the second and third sixteenth-notes before the last in measure 35, increase the bass again up to full strength.

With the second 32d-note in measure 33 add the 8-foot reeds of the great-organ, at the same instant lifting the first eighth in soprano; add the 4-foot reeds at the beginning of measure 36. The *forte* thus attained will be maintained through the entire closing section. He who hath ears to hear will notice that the natural intensification immanent to the music is most gloriously manifested when no extrinsic aids are employed to bring it out.

Many organists use the 16-foot manual stops all through the piece; others add them at the beginning of measure 36.

Perform the Prelude strictly in time and in a tranquil tempo, that it may unfold before the listener in grandeur and majesty.

FUGUE

The admirably simple plan of the Fugue is unmistakable. It discovers one rather long episode, which commences in the middle of measure 51 and ends somewhere before the entrance of the pedal in measure 95.

Begin on the great-organ with foundation stops and mixtures. Should there be reason to fear that a continuous *forte* would become fatiguing, draw at first the mixtures of the other manuals only, and add those of the great on the first eighth in measure 44. It is best to dispense with reeds altogether in the first principal section of the Fugue. But it is quite possible that Bach used his reeds from the start. He certainly had them drawn on the pedal.

With the fourth eighth in measure 51 the right hand goes over to the second manual; the left follows on the second sixteenth in measure 52. By this means the descending figure, which runs through all the parts from the middle of measure 50 onward, comes out finely.

Some players like to keep the left hand on the great-manual beyond this point, because it executes the second part of the theme in measures 52–56. In this case it is a good plan to retire the mixtures at the beginning of measure 52. Then the transfer to Man. II is best effected on the second sixteenth in measure 56.

The effect of the episode is very fine if you begin it with a *diminuendo* and finish with a *crescendo*. The swell-box should begin to close on the sustained soprano note in measure 60. At the beginning of measure 62 one-half of the *decrescendo* will be completed; on the first sixteenth in measure 63 — or already on the second sixteenth in the second half of measure 62 — throw off the swell-mixtures all at once, and let the swell-box close completely by the beginning of measure 66. Some players will prefer to finish closing it as early as the beginning of measure 63, in view of the retirement of the swell-mixtures.

It opens again between measures 67 and 70. On the first sixteenth in measure 71 the second-manual mixtures are drawn again.

With the fourth eighth, or the second sixteenth in the fourth eighth, in measure 78 the left hand goes over with the alto to the great, whose mixtures have not yet been drawn. They will be introduced later, on the fourth eighth in measure 87 and the first eighths in measures 95 and 97.

On the first eighth in measure 91 the right hand returns to the great. Some players already accomplish the change on the fourth eighth in measure 87, and then begin to increase as soon as the first eighth in measure 91. Have one of the pedal-reeds drawn, if possible, for the entrance of the pedal-part — but not the 16-foot Posaune.

On a three-manual organ the *decrescendo* and *crescendo* in the episode can be still more cleverly effected. Both hands having played on Man. II up to measure 60, double the sustained soprano note on Man. III at the first eighth in measure 61, at the same time releasing it on Man. II; on the fourth eighth in the same measure the left hand also goes over to Man. III, whose mixtures remain drawn.

Toward the end of measure 62 begin to close the swell-box, taking care that during this measure only about one-third of the full sweep of the balance swell-pedal has been used up. Before the first eighth in measure 63 the shutters will be suddenly closed by one-third more. The excellent effect of this abrupt *decrescendo* is properly brought out by slightly dwelling on the first sixteenth-note in measure 63. Up to the end of measure 65 the closing of the swell-box should be finished.

Meanwhile the mixtures of the choir-organ have been retired. From the beginning of measure 71 onward, the right hand plays on the choir, and is joined by the left on the fourth eighth in measure 75. The sustained lower note is doubled on the choir-manual, then letting go of it on the swell. The swell-box has reopened from measure 67 onward.

On the fourth eighth in measure 78, while the left hand goes over to the great-manual, the mixtures of the choir-organ are reintroduced. But they may be added just as well on the first eighth in measure 80.

Whoever likes to emphasize the theme everywhere, will entrust the tenor-part, from the fourth eighth in measure 61 onward, to the silent pedal coupled to the third manual (having previously transferred the right hand to the third manual at the beginning of the measure), and will bring out the theme in alto on the second manual. This procedure is not to be recommended, as you will find it very hard to bring the alto back neatly to the third manual from the second.

Some organists plume themselves on showing off the figurations in eighth-notes in the tenor, from the beginning of measure 66, on a special manual.

It shall not be denied that striking effects may be obtained by these and similar devices. But the grand line of the *decrescendo* and *crescendo*, which forms the peculiar charm of the episode, is then wholly lost. We provide for the listener's recreation, instead of stirring his conceptive faculty, wherein the feeling for grandeur and sublimity takes its rise.

From measure 91 to the close both hands remain on the great-manual.

From measure 97 onward all the foundation stops and mixtures of the organ should be in action. By adding the great-organ mixtures at the beginning of measures 95 and 97, an admirable *crescendo* is brought on. It sounds to the hearer like an uninterrupted swell of the sustained soprano tone.

On the first eighth in measure 113, bring on the swell-reeds. Whatever reinforcements may still be at your disposal on the choir, may be added on the first and fourth eighths in measures 126 and 127. At the beginning of measure 131 introduce the reeds of the great-organ. Herewith the augmentation has reached its climax.

It is petty and unrefined to save up stops here in order to increase during the course of measures 135–141. Neither should the 16-foot Posaune on the pedal wait to be drawn until the beginning of measure 139; if it is half-way bearable, draw it at the same moment that the reeds on Manuals II and III come into action — or, at least, draw it together with the great-organ reeds.

A piece of puerility that enjoys almost canonical authority, consists in going over with the right hand to Man. II at the beginning of measure 126, so as to let the sixteenth-note line stand out well on the great. By this means, of course, the listener wholly misses the boldly upstriving soprano-line.

There are even Apostles of Pettiness who do not hesitate, in measure 146, to start in on Man. III, and thereafter find their way over into the **fortissimo** of Man. I during the further progress of the 32d-note figure.

VII. Prelude and Fugue in B Minor. (Pages 76-90.)

PRELUDE

The construction of this piece is unmistakable. Its registration and performance on the old organ proceeded very simply. On the great-organ foundation stops, mixtures and reeds were drawn; on the *Rückpositiv*, foundation stops and mixtures. On the pedal the reeds were in action from the start.

The player stayed till the beginning of measure 17 on the great-manual. With the first 32d-note in this measure he went over to the *Rückpositiv*, remaining there with both hands till measure 23; from here onward he alternated, measure by measure, between the great-organ (whose reeds had meanwhile probably been retired) and the *Rückpositiv*.

With the first or second 32d-note in measure 27 the reeds of the great-organ were drawn again; from this point to the beginning of measure 43 both hands remained on this keyboard. They then went over to the *Rückpositiv*; in measure 50 they went back to the great-manual, the right hand on the second 32d-note, the left hand on the second thirty-second of the fourth eighth.

From the second sixteenth in measure 56 onward they were again on the *Rückpositiv*. The pedal-reeds were thrown off.

With the second 32d-note in measure 61 they were transferred to the great-manual, the pedal meanwhile being brought up to its original strength.

From the second sixteenth in measure 69 onward they played on the *Rückpositiv*. The pedal-reeds were again retired.

After the rest in measure 78 the soprano returned to the great; the alto followed on the second 32d-note in measure 79, the tenor on the second thirty-second in the second eighth in that measure.

The reeds of the pedal were again thrown on.

Do not neglect to play the Prelude thus simply, in case you have access to an old organ with *Rückpositiv;* you will be astounded at the elementary effect.

There is hardly another prelude, however, which so lends itself to the modernizing tendency. It fairly invites the player to work out transitions between episodes and principal sections, and to bring out the theme, in the episodes, on special keyboards.

Do not reward this obligingness with the ingratitude of a plebian modernization which feels no reverence for the nobility of form displayed in this piece, and sets aside the distinction between episode and principal section by the proclamation of liberty, equality, and fraternity. The modernization should

extend only to the episodes; the prerogative of the principal section must be maintained.

Following is a plan of performance intended for a three-manual organ. In its main features it is also adaptable to a two-manual instrument, by reducing the great-organ during the episodes in such a way that it may be employed as a subsidiary organ.

Foundation stops, mixtures and reeds should be represented in the *forte* of the principal sections. In case there is reason to fear that a strong combination on a certain organ or in a certain auditorium may grow intolerable, make a selection of registers embracing these three species. A change of registration within any given principal section can find no musical justification. Dispense with the reeds on Manuals II and III (as in the grand Prelude in *E* minor) so as not to complicate the registration needlessly; at the instant when the transition is accomplished, only foundation stops and mixtures should be standing on the second and third manuals. Whether or no the Posaune on the pedal shall be used in the principal sections, depends upon its quality.

Commencing on the great-manual, the hands will pass over to Man. III on the second sixteenth in measure 17 and stay there till measure 20. The contrast is strong, but has a fine effect when the player is careful to dwell a trifle on the first notes after the transition; this applies equally to the corresponding point in measure 43.

The swell-box closes gradually up to the beginning of measure 20. The effect is as if the episodical theme were at first borne away to a distance, and then came nearer and nearer from measure 20 onward.

At the beginning of measure 20 the left hand goes over to Man. II; the right remains for a time on Man. III, but goes over to Man. II in measure 22.

During the progress of measures 20-22 the swell-box has opened again. The great-organ reeds are retired.

From the second thirty-second in measure 23 onward, the hands will be on the great-manual thus reduced; at the corresponding point in measure 24 they go over to Man. II, and return — again in the same place — in measure 25 to the great-manual, transferring once more to Man. II in measure 26.

Draw the great-organ reeds again during the course of this last measure. In measure 27 the hands go back to the great-manual, which has meanwhile been increased to its original strength; the right hand on the first or second thirty-second, the left on the second eighth. Here they remain till the beginning of measure 43.

On the third thirty-second in measure 43 the left hand goes over to Man. III; the right follows on the third eighth; the swell-box closes gradually until measure 45.

With the third thirty-second in measure 46 the right hand passes to the second manual, the left remaining on the third. The swell-box opens during the course of measures 46–47. In the meantime the reeds and mixtures of the great-organ have been retired.

On the third thirty-second in measure 48 the left hand, after touching the first eighth-note in the alto-part on Man. II, passes over to the reduced great-manual. The right hand stays on Man. II.

On the first and fourth eighths in measure 49 the great-organ mixtures are thrown on again; on the second 32d-note in measure 50, add its reeds also; at the same point the right hand (which has been playing continuously on Man. II) returns to Man. I. It is easier to change on the first 32d-note, but (strictly speaking) incorrect, as the principal section does not enter till the second 32d-note. In this measure the first eighth in the tenor-part is "lifted" before the second just before the reeds are thrown on.

From the second sixteenth in measure 56 onward you may go over to the second manual (the pedal being correspondingly reduced), and return to the first manual with the second 32d-note in measure 61. Instead of this, however, it is advisable to remain, during this episode, on the great-organ, which has been reduced to the level of a subsidiary organ. This latter procedure presents the advantage, that one can effect the transition into the principal section with a fine *crescendo* in measure 60 by the successive addition of registers.

At the breath-pause in soprano and alto between the first and second sixteenths in measure 56, while the tenor part is held over, the reeds and mixtures of Man. I will, therefore, be thrown off together. At the same time the swell-box closes *subito;* it opens again from the middle of measure 58 to the beginning of measure 60. Both hands play on the great-manual. The construction shows that Bach did not expect the player to use different manuals.

On the second thirty-seconds in the first and fourth eighths in measure 60 the great-organ mixtures are drawn. On the second 32d-note in measure 61 its reeds are also added, the eighth-notes in alto and tenor having been lifted beforehand. In the course of measure 60 the pedal is increased to its original strength.

Until the beginning of measure 69, continue in the *forte* of the great-organ. Between the first and second sixteenth in this measure (as in the corresponding place in measure 56) throw off the reeds and mixtures of Man. I, at the same time closing the swell-box. Reduce the pedal, too, during the progress of the measure.

Both hands stay on the great-manual up to measure 73; the swell-box opens through measures 71 and 72.

In measure 73 both hands go over to Man. III; the left hand on the third thirty-second, the right hand on the second eighth. The swell-box closes in the course of measures 73 and 74.

On the third thirty-second in measure 75 the left hand, after taking the first eighth in the alto on the third manual, goes over to the second manual; the right hand does not follow until the third thirty-second in measure 76.

With the first 32d-note in measure 77 the left hand transfers to the (still reduced) great-organ. On the fourth eighth in the same measure and the first eighth in measure 78, draw the great-organ mixtures. The right hand plays on Man. II. After taking the fourth eighth in measure 78 on this manual, it passes over with the next-following 32d-note in the soprano to the great-manual. At the moment when this change is made, throw on the great-organ reeds. For the beginning of the next measure the pedal will be reinforced to its original strength.

Hasty execution reduces this Prelude to a caricature of its true self. It demands repose and rhythm. Play the 32d-notes but little faster than the sixteenth-notes of the great Prelude in *E* minor.

The small notes in measures 1, 2, 8, 9, etc., are to be played as if they were sixteenths. According to the ancient custom, this style of notation is meant to show that the first note — that is, the small one — takes a special accent.

The dots over the eighth-notes in measures 18, 19, etc., do not imply that these notes, and other similar ones, should be executed in a modern *staccato*. Bach's dot nearly corresponds to our *tenuto*-dash. These eighth-notes, therefore, are to be held for almost their entire time-value, separated from each other only by very brief pauses.

Different organists phrase the motive of the episode differently. Some play thus:

while others prefer the following phrasing:

The second mode is doubtless the correcter one; but the first is more characteristic and more readily caught by the ear.

See to it that the phrasing is most exactly carried out in all the parts. Do not play the long runs in 32d-notes like scales, but bring out distinctly the natural grouping of the notes upon which the figurations are founded. For instance, in measure 23, play this way:

FUGUE

For the sake of variety in the lengthy episode, our plan of execution is calculated for a three-manual organ. Begin on the great-manual with the foundation stops of all the manuals coupled together. On the swell, the mixtures are also drawn.

The swell-box, closed at the start, opens during the course of measures 10 and 11. On the third beat in measure 15, add the mixtures of the choir-organ.

In consideration of the entrance of the theme at the beginning of measure 20, some players bring on further reinforcements at the breath-pause between the first and second sixteenths. Others draw the new stops on the third beat in measure 21. Still others add them on the fourth beat of the same measure. In this last case it sounds as if new voices fell in on the second half of the soprano half-note in order to accentuate the last beat in the midst of said half-note, this last beat being regarded as forming an entity with the following sixteenths, in conformity with the grouping of the subsequent figures. So they play as if the text read as follows:

Neither of these three possible ways of adding stops produces an entirely unobjectionable result. Consequently, many players do not care to add any stops at all after measure 15.

On the first eighth in measure 28 the left hand goes directly over to the choir-manual; the right follows with the beginning of the sixteenth-note figuration in soprano. It is advisable to let both hands remain on the same manual till the beginning of measure 35. However, some organists will prefer to employ choir and swell together, so as to have a special manual at their disposal for the theme. In order to play it from measure 30 onward in the alto on the choir-manual, the tenor part is given for two measures to the silent pedal coupled to the swell-manual. But the simple course of playing with both hands on the choir-manual from measure 28 onward, is preferable to all these artificial manipulations.

With the first eighth in measure 35 the right hand transfers to the swell, the left hand not following until the second sixteenth in the third beat. The swell-box closes during the progress of measures 37–40.

At the same time, the choir-mixtures are thrown off.

On the third beat in measure 40 the left hand takes the theme over to the choir-manual; the right hand follows with alto and soprano on the third beat of measure 42. The swell-box opens from the middle of measure 40 up to the middle of measure 42, and closes in the course of measures 45–47.

On the first eighth in measure 49 add the mixtures of the choir. The swell-box opens through measures 49–52.

In the middle of measure 53 both hands — the left on the third beat, the right with the second sixteenth in the third beat — go over to the great-manual, whose 4- and 2-foot foundation stops and mixtures have previously been retired; the couplers of swell and choir to great remain in action.

At the beginning of measure 59, where the second principal section commences, draw the 4-foot foundation stops of the great-organ again.

Some organists arrange matters, for the sake of the theme, so as to have both hands still on the second manual in measure 58, and keep the right hand there in measure 59 while the left hand brings out the theme on the great-manual.

This advantage is dearly bought. In the first place, the listener is not convinced that the principal section starts here; in the second place, he does not notice that at this point a motive enters in soprano and alto which will dominate the entire closing section of the Fugue; in the third place, at the beginning of measure 61 his right hand has to get back to the great-manual in an awkward manner. Some players remain on the second manual till the beginning of measure 59, and then transfer both hands together to the great-manual.

In any event, it is better to play measures 59 and 60 with both hands on the great-manual. If your pedal goes up to g, throw off its 16-foot stops and carry out the theme with the 8- and 4-foot stops on the pedal in unison with the left hand. This procedure is advisable even where your pedal does not reach so high; for the compulsory omission by the pedal of the top note — or possibly of the two highest notes — of the theme will scarcely be noticed.

At the beginning of measure 61, draw the 2-foot foundation stops on the great-organ. In case the 16-foot pedal registers were previously retired, bring them on again here.

On the first eighth in measure 68, add the great-organ mixtures. Towards the end of measure 72 close the swell-box, so that the swell-reeds may be imperceptibly introduced at the beginning of measure 73.

Gradually open the swell-box through measures 73–75. Add whatever reserves may still be at your disposal successively, during measures 76, 77 and 78. At the beginning of measure 79 the climax of the intensification should be reached. For the triumphant entrance of the theme in the pedal, draw the 16-foot Posaune.

For the addition of registers in measures 76 and 77 some players will choose the first and third quarters, others the second and fourth. Reasons may be advanced both for and against either procedure. It is equally difficult to decide the question whether the final reinforcement should enter on the last eighth in measure 78 or the first sixteenth in measure 79.

There are organists who prefer not to arrive at full organ until the second eighth in measure 85.

VIII. Passacaglia et Thema fugatum in C Minor. (Pages 91-107.)

PASSACAGLIA

Passacaglia (Passacaille) was originally the name of an old Spanish dance in three-four time. In musical literature the term was understood to mean a piece built up over a continually repeated bass theme. In the Ciaccona (Chaconne) it was allowable to employ the theme in any part. Bach's composition is not a pure Passacaglia, because the theme appears several times in the higher parts. It partakes of the character of both Passacaglia and Chaconne.

It is evident, from the manner in which the fugued section grows out of measure 169, that this piece was not conceived solely for the organ, but concurrently for the cembalo with pedal. On the organ this transition is fairly impracticable, unless the player makes up his mind to finish the series of Variations with the same volume of tone in which the Fugue is to begin.

However, this does not mean that this work of Bach's cannot be played with fine effect on the organ. We admit that a general agreement as to conception and registration is hardly attainable.

Some players are of the opinion that only the foundation stops of the organ should be used, for the most part, in Passacaglia and Fugue. They base this opinion on the ground that the piece is properly a clavier composition adapted for organ; that it is not admissible to develop the full tone of the church-instrument, because the work would then be divested of its light and graceful character.

There is considerable force in this argument. Nevertheless, it is ill-founded. Once this work is reproduced on the organ, it would be wrong to renounce the fullness of tone and variety of combination afforded by this instrument. These do, indeed, invest the composition with an atmosphere of grandeur which one does not discover when playing it on the pianoforte. But this does not mean that it is not a characteristic of the piece. It means simply that the effect is somewhat different on the two instruments. But, in point of fact, this piece belongs to the organ. Though it may externally bear certain marks of the cembalo-style, its cast and construction show it to be a conception of the great organ-master. How meagre must it have sounded on the pedal-cembalo! Even

the modern grand pianoforte, with its full and richly variable tone, is by no means capable of effectively bringing out the grand *crescendi* and *decrescendi* implied by the organ-concept and continuing through Variations and Fugue. Neither the pedal-cembalo nor the pedal-piano has been able to win recognition as an individual instrument. Hence, the Passacaglia now belongs to the organ alone. To us it is a matter of purely historical interest that the composer allowed for the pedal-cembalo when writing it. We have to interpret it as an organ work pure and simple.

For the Passacaglia the player may adopt either of two methods. He may either strive — without wasting much thought on the broader possibilities of grouping — after interesting tonal combinations for effectively setting off the several Variations; or he may endeavor, even in these latter, to obtain his effects by means of lines rather than colors, and to present distinctly the construction of the whole composition. This way is probably the better of the two.

The first grand *crescendo* proceeds from the beginning of the piece up to measure 105. Here it is interrupted by an episode reaching to measure 129. At the end of this intermezzo the *crescendo* is resumed at the point where it was broken off, and increased up to full organ.

For the realization of this idea we shall present a plan worked out for a three-manual organ.

In what degree of tone-power shall the theme be introduced? Some let it enter *fortissimo;* others, *pianissimo;* still others incline toward a *forte* or *mezzoforte*.

We would suggest, that on pedal and great-manual the foundation stops should be drawn and the first nine measures played *pedaliter* and *manualiter* together in octaves. Then, after lifting the half-note in measure 9, reduce the pedal to a single 8-foot string-tone stop — carefully avoiding any awkward "artistic" delay — and bring in the quarter-note strictly in time.

No couplers are drawn, either of manual to pedal, or of manual to manual.

The 8-foot pedal-tone has an excellent effect. It will be best to add only 8-foot stops in the bass — possibly some 4-foot registers with them — up to measure 41, not drawing your 16-foot stops until then. But many players, although the advantages of the above procedure are plain as day, will employ 16-foot stops from the start, for the sake of the principle.

On Man. III an 8-foot flute-stop is drawn, on Man. II an 8-foot string-tone stop. The right hand plays, to begin with, on Man. II, the left hand on Man. III. The swell-box is half-open.

On the rest in measure 17 the swell-box closes; from the end of this measure onward the right hand plays on Man. III, the left on Man. II.

From the second eighth in measure 25 onward both hands will be on Man. III, on which several 8-foot stops have been drawn. The swell-box reopens during the course of measures 30-32.

From the second eighth in measure 33 onward both hands are on Man. II, on which some 4-foot stops have previously been added to the 8-foot foundation stops.

On the second eighth in measure 41, couple Man. III (on which meanwhile 4- and 2-foot foundation stops have been added) to Man. II, the hands remaining on the latter.

With the second sixteenth in measure 49, the hands go over to the great-manual, whose 8-foot foundation stops have already been drawn.

On the second sixteenth in measure 57, draw the swell-to-great coupler; at the corresponding point in measure 65, draw the choir-to-great coupler. On the choir-organ all the 8- and 4-foot foundation stops have previously been drawn.

With the second sixteenth in measure 73, add the 4- and 2-foot great-organ stops. At the corresponding point in measure 81, draw the swell-mixtures; on the third eighth in measure 89, the choir-mixtures. With the third quarter in measure 97, add the great-organ mixtures.

These suggestions follow the general idea, that the organist should endeavor, without dwelling too long on the subsidiary manuals and dallying with solo stops, to carry out the *crescendo* evenly and on broad lines. At the beginning of the episode in measure 105 there should be in action all the foundation stops (excepting the 16-foot stops on the manuals) and all the mixtures of the organ. The reeds are to be saved for the augmentation following the episode.

According to some players, the *crescendo* ought not to proceed continuously; instead, they reduce the registration for some section to a lower level than that of the preceding one, thus producing an interruption which allows the listener a respite and throws the subsequent reinforcements into fine relief through contrast. The period commencing with the last quarter in measure 89 is very often chosen for thus checking the *crescendo;* it is then played on Man. III with foundation stops and mixtures, the swell-box closing during the progress of measures 90–96. With the last quarter in measure 97 the right hand enters abruptly with the foundation stops and mixtures of the great-organ. The left hand follows on the second sixteenth before the last in that measure.

The above-described interruption of the *crescendo* is in certain respects more effective than the uninterrupted augmentation. But it presents the disadvantage of partially anticipating the effect of the entrance of the episode in measure 105. The sudden transition to *piano* on the third quarter in measure 105 makes a far stronger impression when preceded by *crescendi* alone, with no *decrescendi*.

From the third quarter in measure 105 onward both hands play on Man. II, its mixtures having been retired previously. It is coupled to Man. III, whose mixtures are still drawn. The swell-box closes in the course of measures 110–113.

With the second sixteenth before the last in measure 113 the right hand goes over to Man. III; the left follows on the second sixteenth in measure 114. During the progress of measures 114–120 the swell-box opens at first, and then (from measure 118 on) closes.

Before the second sixteenth in measure 121 retire — after lifting soprano and alto — the mixtures of Man. III. During measures 121–129 a *crescendo* and *decrescendo* is produced by the swell-box similar to that in the preceding section.

There are players who like to divide these arpeggios between two manuals, performing the first eight in each measure on Man. II and the last four on Man. III. Others go so far as to employ two manuals for the preceding section (measures 113–121); they transfer to the choir with the second sixteenth before the last in measure 113, the left hand then going over to the swell on the second sixteenth in measure 114, and the right hand following after playing the first two eighths in this measure on the choir. From the third quarter in measure 114 onward, both hands perform their sixteenth-notes on the choir. With the second sixteenth in measure 115, the left hand returns to the swell, followed by the right hand after it has played its two eighths on the choir — and so forth. The gist of this procedure is, therefore, that the arpeggios ascending through both hands are given to the swell-manual, while the rest are played on the choir. Some players — and they may be in the right — reverse the order of the manuals during the above changes.

Whoever practises either alternation should first throw off his swell-to-choir coupler.

From the last eighth in measure 129 onward, you will again play on the great-manual, whose registration has remained unchanged. Its couplers to the other manuals also remain out. The rests found in the succeeding measures afford an opportunity to draw successively those registers which were retired on choir and swell during the course of the episode. The swell-box opens in the course of measure 136; during the first two beats of measure 137, however, it is closed, in order that the swell-reeds may be imperceptibly introduced on the third beat of this measure.

Through measures 138–145 the swell-box opens. On the third beat in measure 145, bring on the choir-reeds; the great-organ reeds follow on the second eighth before the last in measure 153 and the last eighth in measure 161.

Keeping pace with the augmentation of the manuals, the pedal will be continuously reinforced. Many players employ the sixteen-foot manual stops from the third beat in measure 145 onward.

THEMA FUGATUM

The technical side of the problem involved in the transition from Passacaglia to Fugue, no longer exists for the modern organ. Its aids to registration permit the player to close measure 169 with full organ, and then to set any desired combination for the entrance of the second tone of the fugue-theme.

The problem is now, therefore, wholly æsthetic. None the less, a satisfactory solution is not possible. Whatever may be done, the first tone of the theme is lost. This is not the case on either cembalo or pianoforte. True, even on these it is swallowed up in the chord; but the ornament leading over from it to the second tone permits the listener to infer *a posteriori*, so to speak, that the first tone of the theme entered with the closing chord.

On the organ the execution of the ornament is prevented by the change in tone-power taking place at that instant. For the listener, the theme actually begins with the second tone.

A radical solution would be to close the Passacaglia in the same volume of tone with which the Fugue enters. Then the ornament can be executed. But not many players will be found who care to sacrifice the grand augmentation to this transition. When closing with full organ, two modes of further progression are open. One may continue to sustain the first tone of the theme by itself after lifting the closing chord in which it entered, taking care at the same time that, at the moment of lifting the chord, the "full organ" gives way to a combination previously prepared. Or, one makes up his mind to allow a short pause to ensue after the chord, and then to start anew with the first note of the theme. One solution is as good — and as bad — as the other. They both save the first note of the theme at the expense of the natural rhythmical connection of the two measures, and arbitrarily interject a few extra beats at precisely the moment when the listener, under the influence of the foregoing unavoidable *ritenuto*, had a sense of insecurity in his hold on the rhythm.

For the Fugue, foundation stops are drawn on all three manuals. On choir and swell the 2-foot registers, and on the great-organ the 2- and 4-foot registers, are not drawn. The manual-to-pedal couplers, and the great-couplers to choir and swell, are not drawn; but the swell is coupled to the choir. The swell-box is closed.

Begin with both hands on the great-manual, and stay on it till the beginning of measure 29. On the third beat in measure 17 the swell-to-great coupler is drawn; the swell-box opens during the course of measures 18–23.

On the second sixteenth in measure 23, couple choir to great. For the first principal section of the Fugue — that is, up to measure 29 — many players employ, on the pedal, only the 8-foot (with possibly the 4-foot) stops. Whether this is the correct way, we shall not decide. The effect is certainly excellent.

Instead of the above simple plan some players will prefer to play the theme, and the contrapuntal eighth-note figurations, on different manuals. True, from Bach's style of notation it is evident that he did not have in mind the continuous simultaneous employment of two manuals in the first principal section. But, on the other hand, the parts are so arranged that up to measure 23 the theme can always be executed on a separate keyboard, without imposing any too glaring inconsistencies as a consequence.

We proceed as follows: The right hand begins on Man. I, the left on Man. II. The silent pedal is coupled to Man. II.

From the third quarter in measure 5 onward the pedal executes the tenor part; the right hand plays on Man. I, the left on Man. II. From the end of measure 6 onward the left hand can play the alto and tenor parts together. From the second sixteenth in measure 10 onward, the right hand takes over the alto part; in the middle of measure 11 the left hand also transfers to Man. I.

Thus, when the pedal enters, both hands are on Man. I.

Meanwhile the 2-foot foundation stops and the mixtures have been added on the swell (which is coupled to the choir). With the second eighth in measure 13 the right hand goes over to the choir; the left hand performs the alto and tenor on the great. In measure 13 the second sixteenth before the last in the alto part lies beyond the reach of the left hand; we may assume it to be contained in the identical coincident note in soprano, without committing a fatal mistake. But if, for correctness' sake, one shrink from no complication, the right hand may here take the soprano note with the fifth finger on Man. II, and strike the sixteenth in the alto part with the thumb on Man. I.

Couplers I–II and I–III are not drawn.

On the second sixteenth in measure 17 the alto part also goes over to Man. II. The 4-foot foundation stops on Man. I come into play. The swell-box, closed till now, opens during the course of measure 17.

From the last quarter of this measure onward the left hand plays on Man. I; the right hand performs soprano and alto as best it may on Man. II. In measure 18 the two eighths before the last have to be taken by the left hand.

On the second sixteenth in measure 23, draw the choir-mixtures. The right hand remains with the soprano upon Man. II; the left, from the end of measure 23, carries out both alto and tenor on Man. I.

When the first principal section is performed on two manuals, it becomes necessary to employ the mixtures of the subsidiary manuals to counterbalance the weight of Man. I. But if, according to the simpler plan, Man. I alone is employed, the unmixed tone-color of the foundation stops can be retained.

Some players push their freedom of conception so far as to commence the Fugue on choir and swell. Justification for this procedure would be hard to find. In the first place, it is wrong in principle; in the second place, the effect of the entering episode in measure 29 is lost.

For the performance of the episode the player again has a choice between a simple and a complicated plan. It should be noted, that at the instant when the hands go over to the subsidiary manuals, any mixtures which may be standing on the latter are to be thrown off.

According to the simpler plan, both hands play on Man. II from the second sixteenth in measure 29 onward. On the second eighth in measure 36 the right hand is transferred to Man. III. The swell-box closes during the progress of measures 36-39.

At the beginning of measure 40 the left hand also goes over to Man. III. It doubles the first quarter in the tenor part which is already held on Man. II, and releases it on the second quarter. The swell-to-choir coupler is thrown off. On the second eighth in measure 44 the left hand carries the tenor part back to Man. II. During the progress of measures 44-49 the right hand either remains on Man. III, or alternates between Man. II and Man. III. In the latter case we would suggest that the sections between the second sixteenths in measures 45 and 46, and 47 and 48, should be performed on Man. II, and those between the second sixteenths in measures 44 and 45, 46 and 47, and 48 and 49 on Man. III.

Through measures 44-48 the swell-box opens gradually.

On the second sixteenth in measure 49 the right hand goes over to Man. II, whose coupler to Man. III was again drawn on the preceding sixteenth-rest. On the second quarter of the same measure the left hand goes over to Man. I.

Meanwhile the 16-foot pedal stops have been added. While the left hand is playing the tenor part in measures 49-52 on Man. I, the 4-foot foundation stops of the latter are successively drawn. On the third quarter in measure 52 the right hand also returns to Man. I.

The more complicated performance of the episode is distinguished from the other by undertaking to emphasize the theme on another keyboard. To this end the tenor part, from measure 29 to the middle of measure 35, is committed to a combination of 8-foot pedal stops. From the middle of measure 40 onward, the tenor part is again taken over by the silent pedal, which has meantime been coupled to Man. III, so as to leave the left hand free to bring out the theme on Man. II while the right hand is occupied on Man. III.

From measure 44 onward no distinction is made between the simpler and the more complicated plan of performance.

For carrying out the long augmentation in the second principal section, the following suggestions are submitted. After playing on the great-manual alone, without coupling swell or choir, from the third quarter in measure 52, draw the swell-to-great coupler on the first beat in measure 57, and the choir-to-great coupler on the second sixteenth in measure 64. The swell-box is closed.

The 2-foot foundation stops and the mixtures of Man. III are drawn on the first or second eighth in measure 71. The swell-box opens through measures 71-76.

On the third quarter in measure 77 the 2-foot foundation stops and the mixtures of Man. II are added.

On the second sixteenth in measure 85, add the 2-foot foundation stops of the great-organ and one of its mixtures. In the pedal a reed-stop is already drawn in preparation for the entrance of the theme in measure 87.

Covered by the mixture-stop drawn on Man. I, close the swell-box in the course of measure 87, and on the second sixteenth before the last in that measure throw on the reeds of Man. III. For the augmentation invited by what directly follows we have at our disposal the opening of the swell-box (whereby the swell-reeds make themselves felt), and the successive addition of the great-organ mixtures. These latter may best be introduced before the second sixteenths in measures 92, 93 and 94; the swell-box has been opening during the course of measures 88-92.

On the second sixteenth in measure 99, draw the choir-reeds. At the beginning of measure 102, and on the third quarter in measure 103, the great-organ reeds are drawn. The climax of the augmentation is, therefore, reached at the final entrance of the theme.

Some players like to keep reserves ready in order to bring on still more stops after measure 113; and there are others who do not arrive at "full organ" until after the rest in measure 117, or even — successively — not until between measures 118 and 123.

In this Fugue as in others, however, the judicious organist will not seek to realize the last intensification by means of registration, but confidently leave the effect to the structural winding-up of the composition.

In order that the alto part may be well brought out in measures 104, 105 and 106, some organists play it an octave higher than it is written; ascertaining thereafter that even connoisseurs who were not in the secret failed to notice the deception, but afterwards admitted that they had never heard the alto stand out so beautifully in this passage.

It should also be mentioned, that some players succumb to the temptation to emphasize the theme on the great-organ from measure 65 onward, and so have to banish the alto from the great-manual to another. He who would sin with propriety will already transfer his right hand to Man. II on the second sixteenth in measure 64, at the same time drawing (in order to mitigate the contrast) the mixtures of Man. III (which is coupled to Man. II). The alto must then, of course, remain on Man. II until the beginning of measure 71. Through this addition of the swell-mixtures the accomplishment of the augmentation, compared with the plan suggested previously, is somewhat hastened.

The counterpoint to the theme is variously phrased.   Some organists play thus:

Others prefer the following phrasing:

The second way is probably the correcter one; but the first is, on the whole, more effective.   The slur between the first two notes belongs to the traditional notation.   It supports the first phrasing, since it implies that only these two eighth-notes are to be played *legato*.

PRELUDES AND FUGUES OF THE MATURE MASTER-PERIOD

PART II

I
Praeludium und Fuge in F-Dur

22712 x

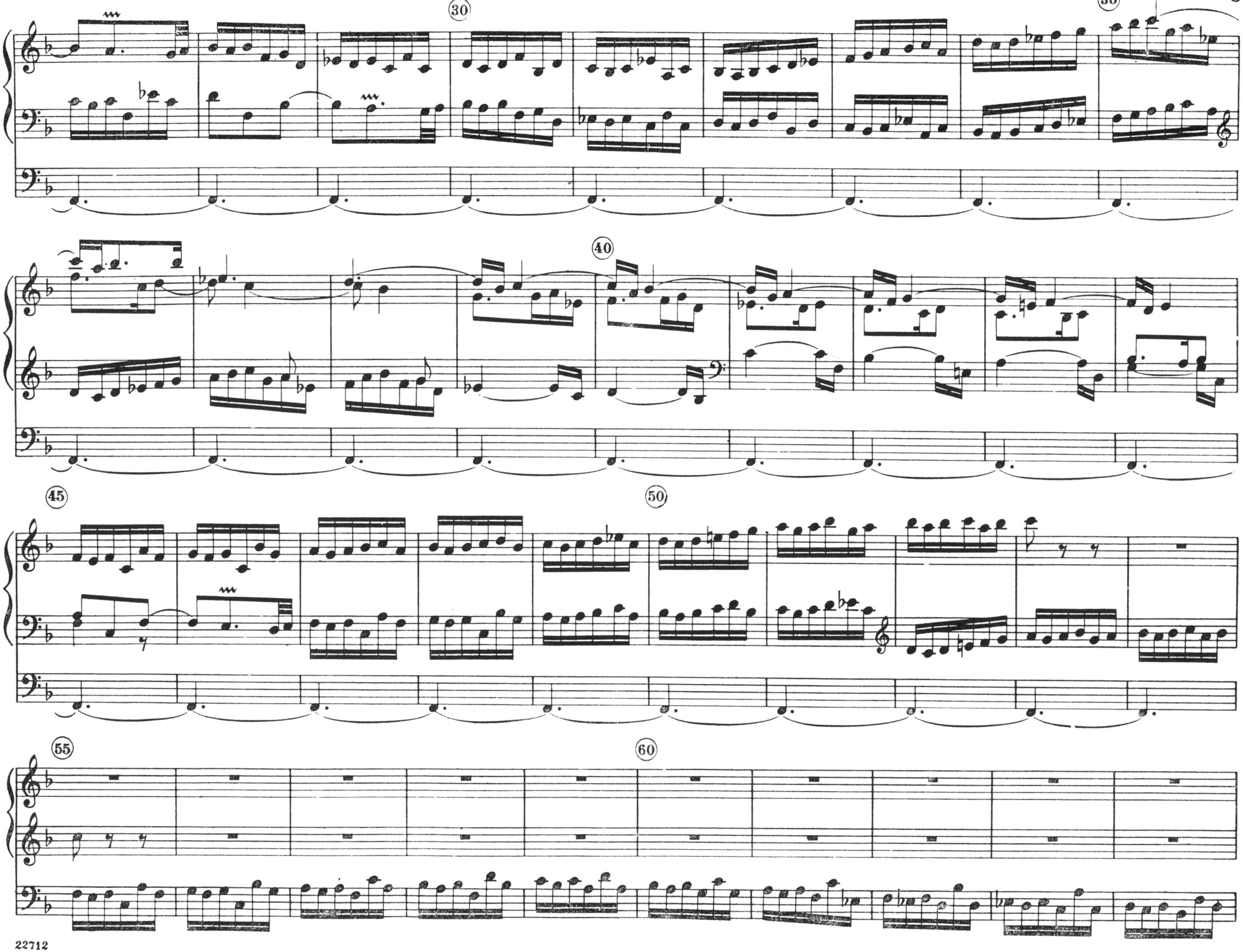
30
35
40
45
50
55
60

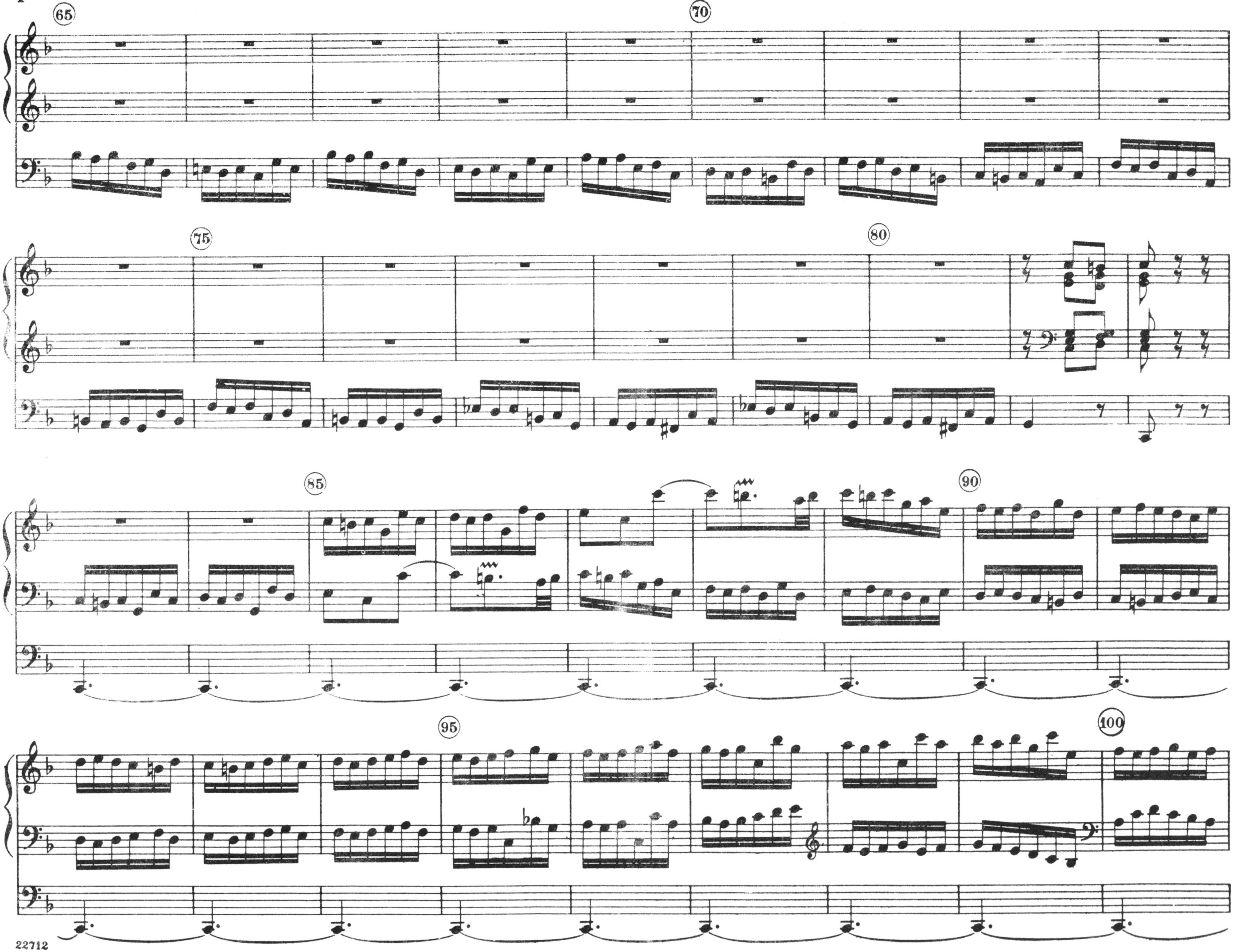
65
70
75
80
85
90
95
100

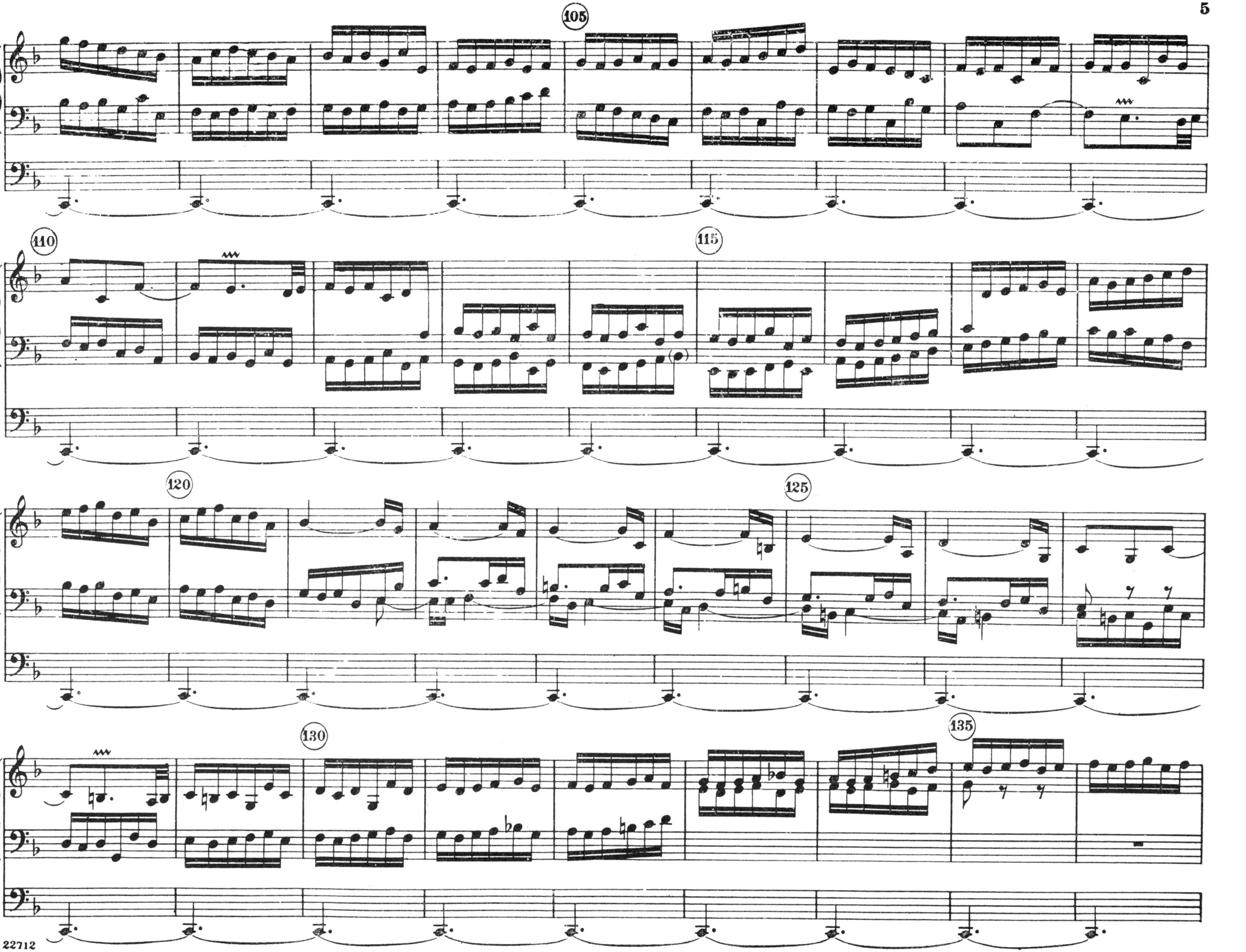
105
110
115
120
125
130
135

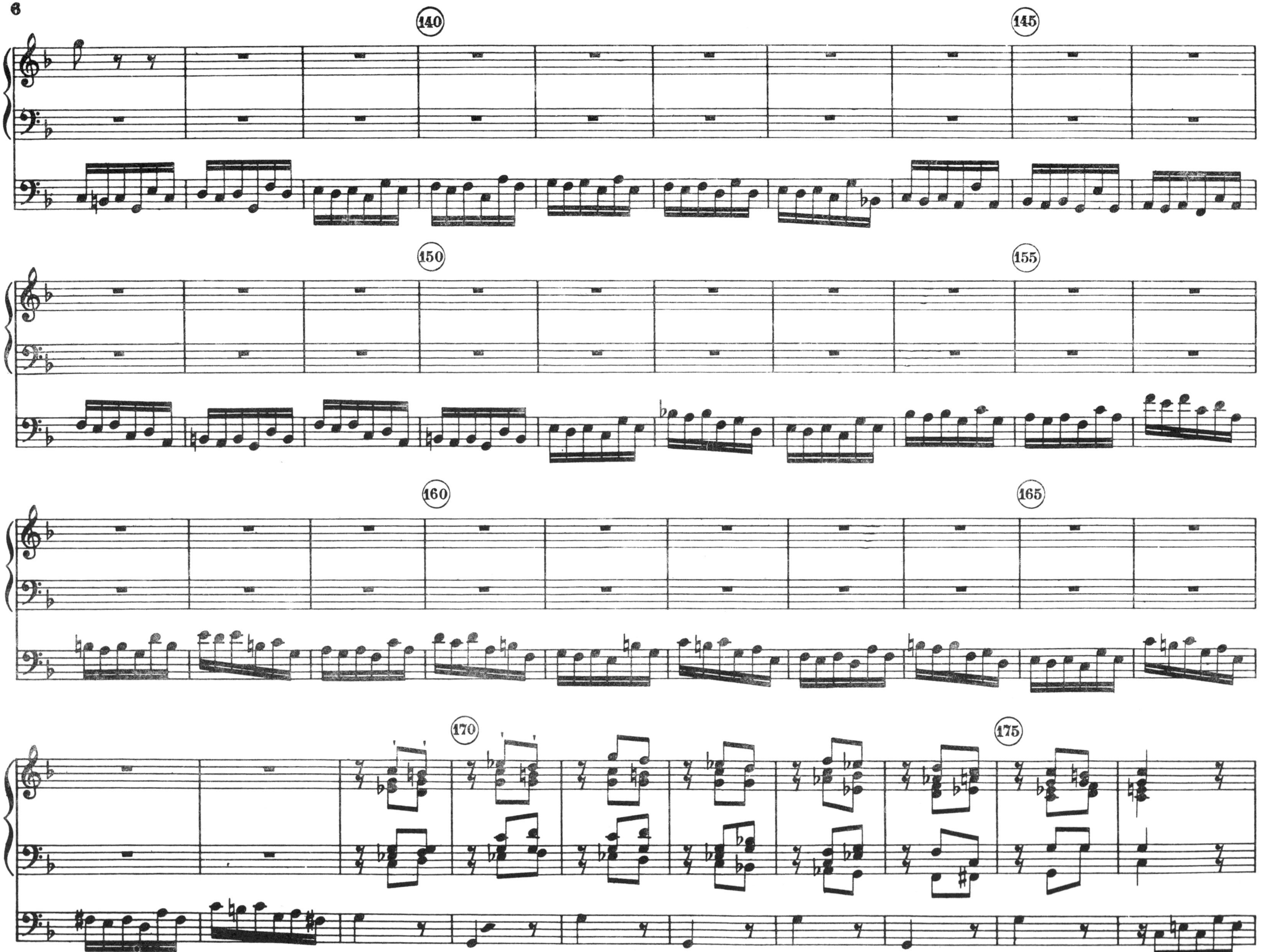
140
145
150
155
160
165
170
175

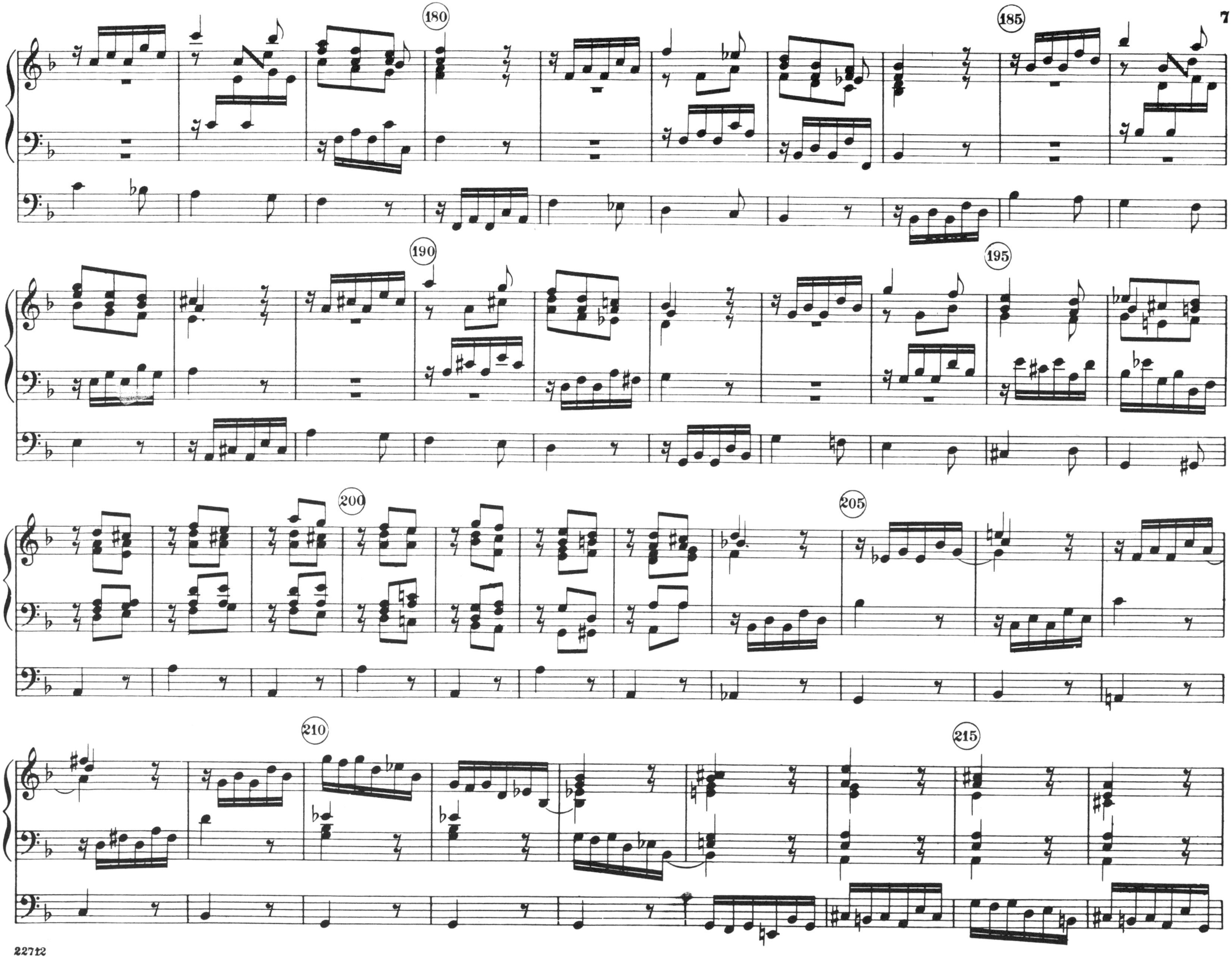
180
185
190
195
200
205
210
215

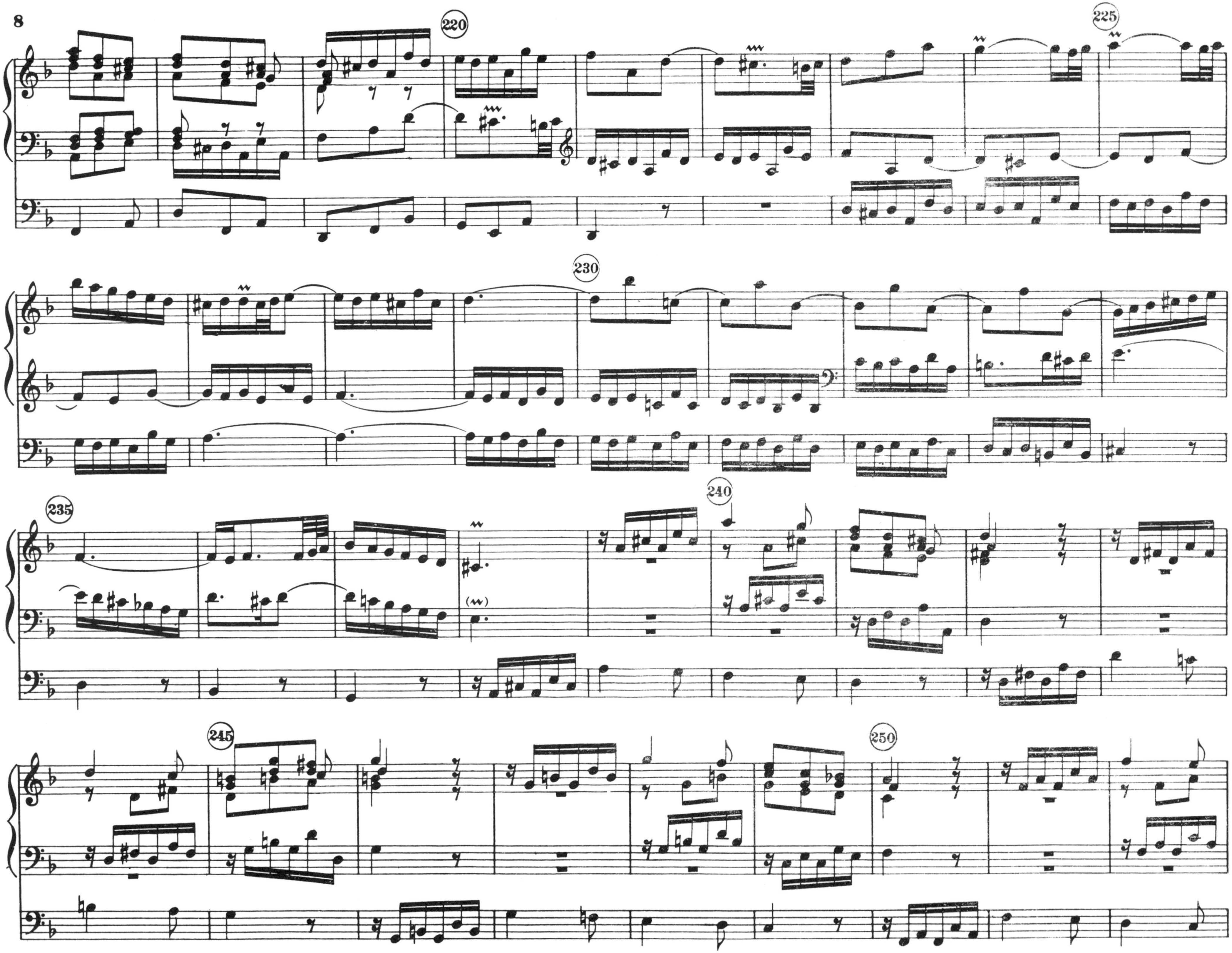
220
225
230
235
240
245
250

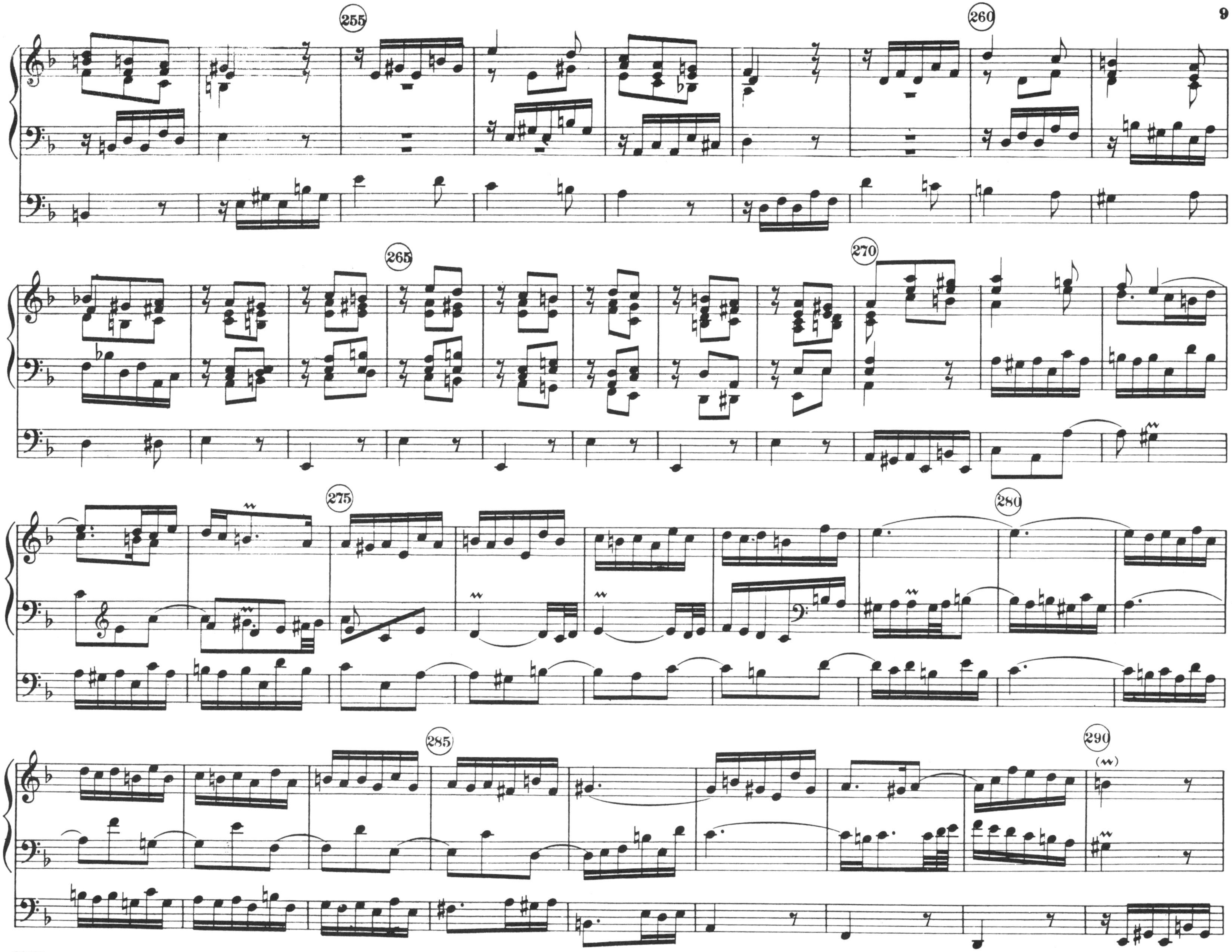

255
260
265
270
275
280
285
290

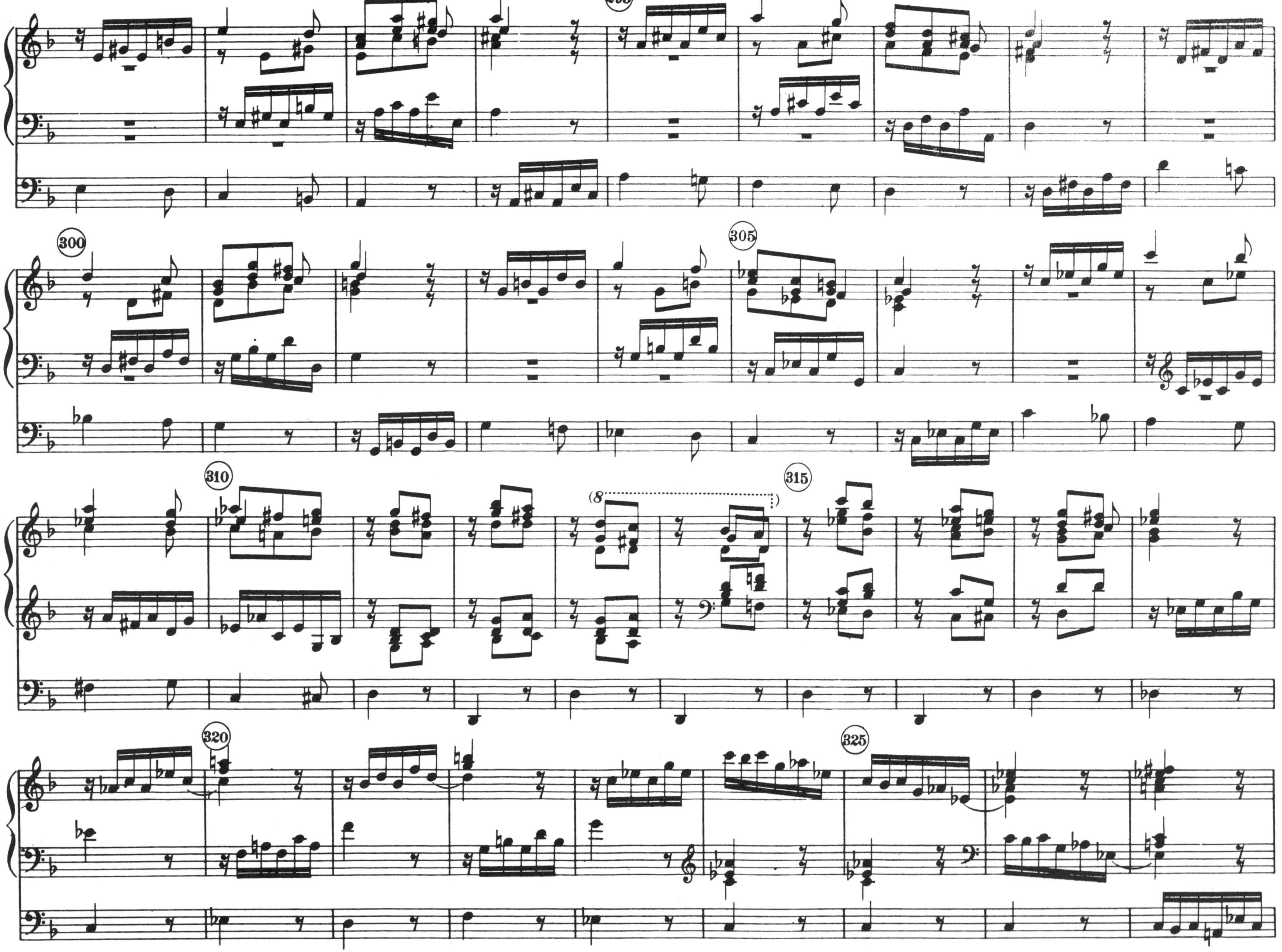
295
300
305
310
315
(8
320
325

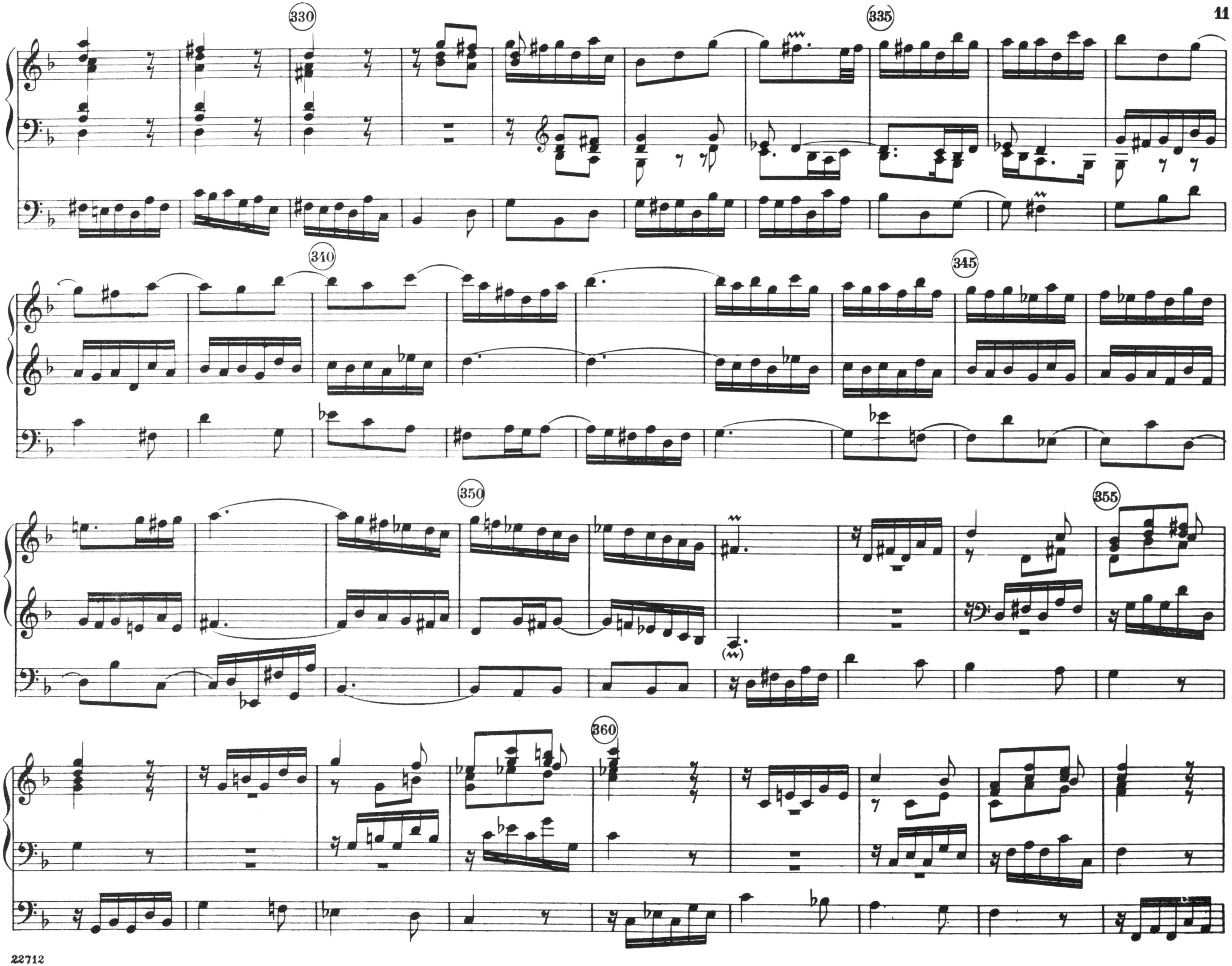
330
335
340
345
350
355
360

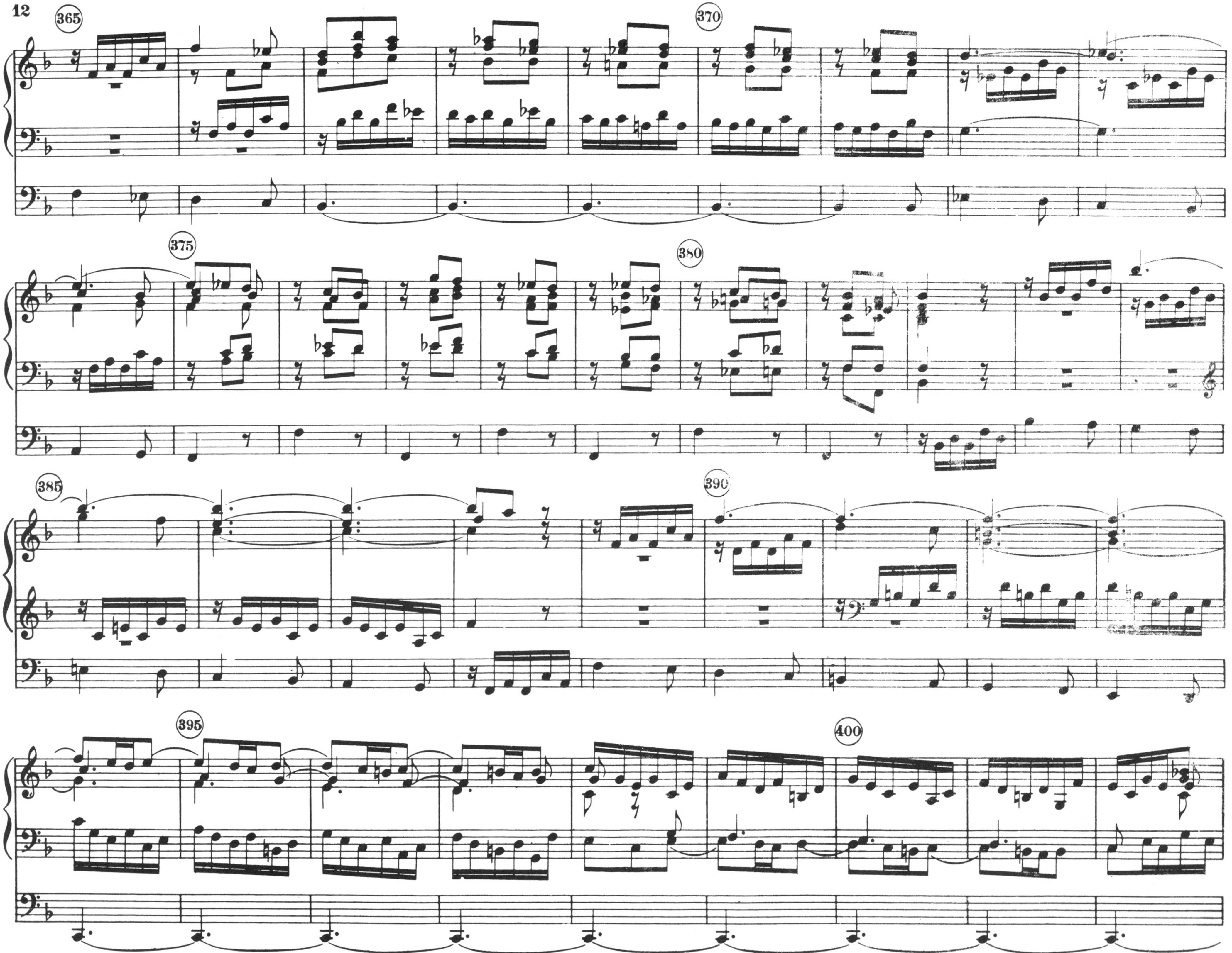
365
370
375
380
385
390
395
400

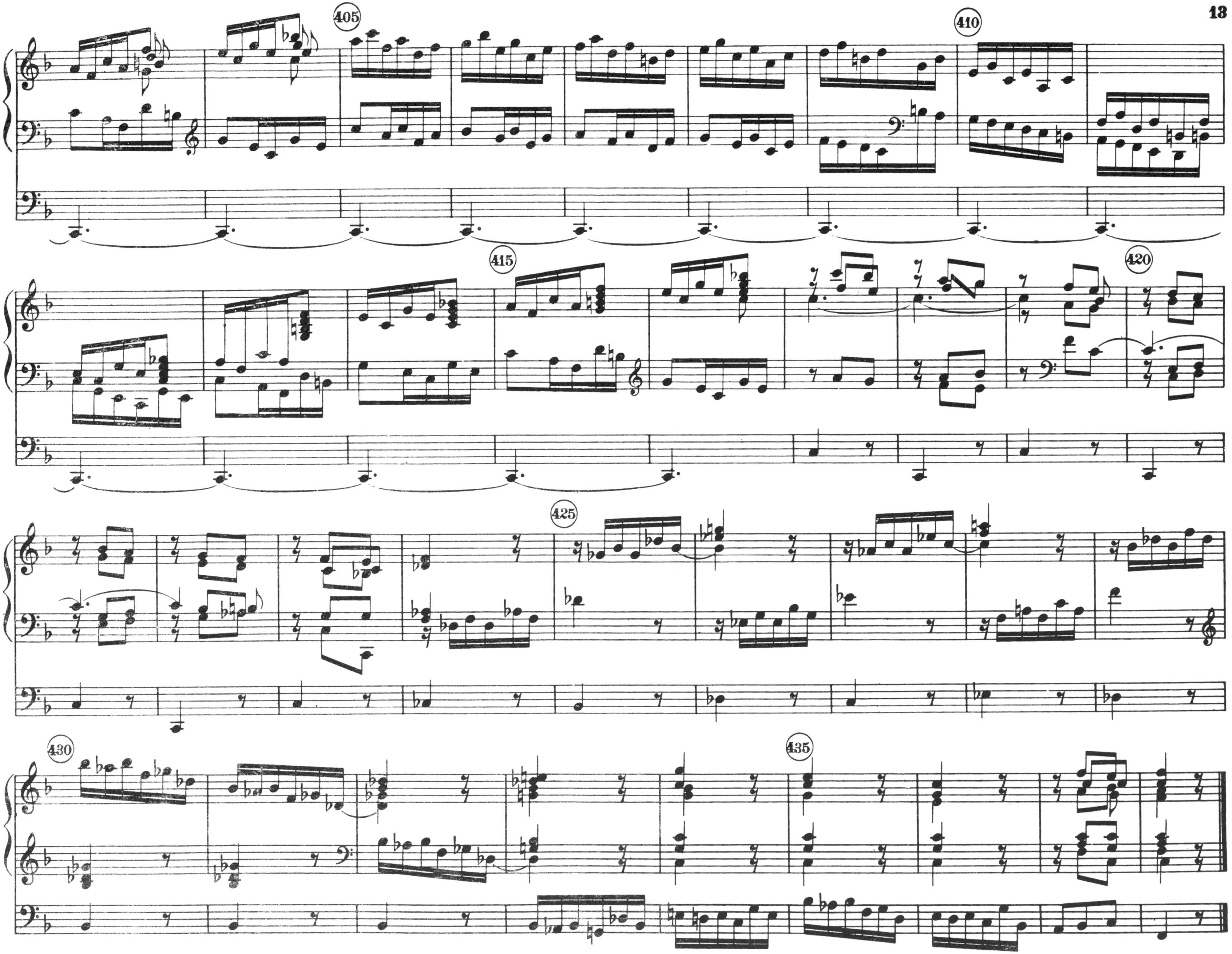
405
410
415
420
425
430
435

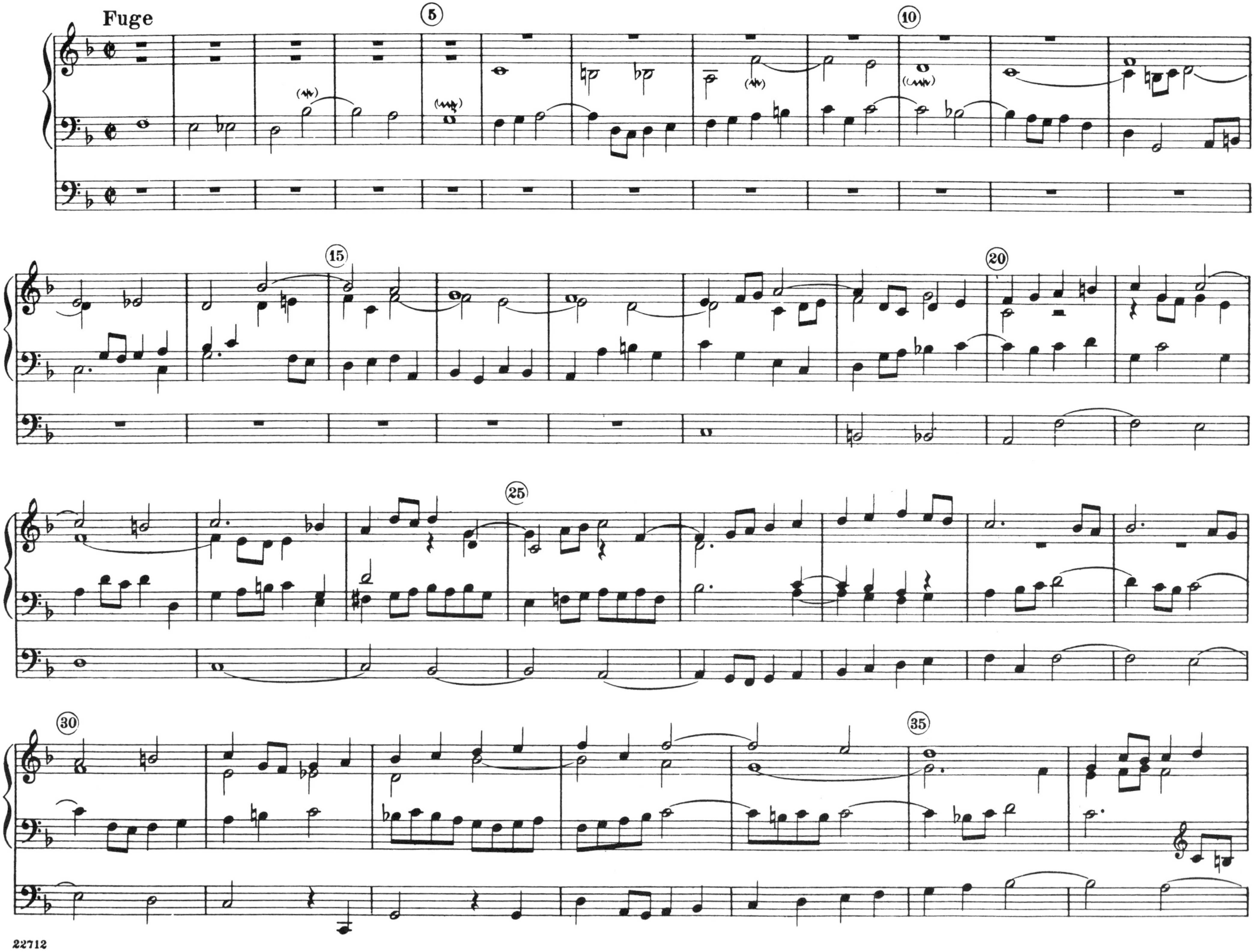
Fuge
5
10
15
20
25
30
35

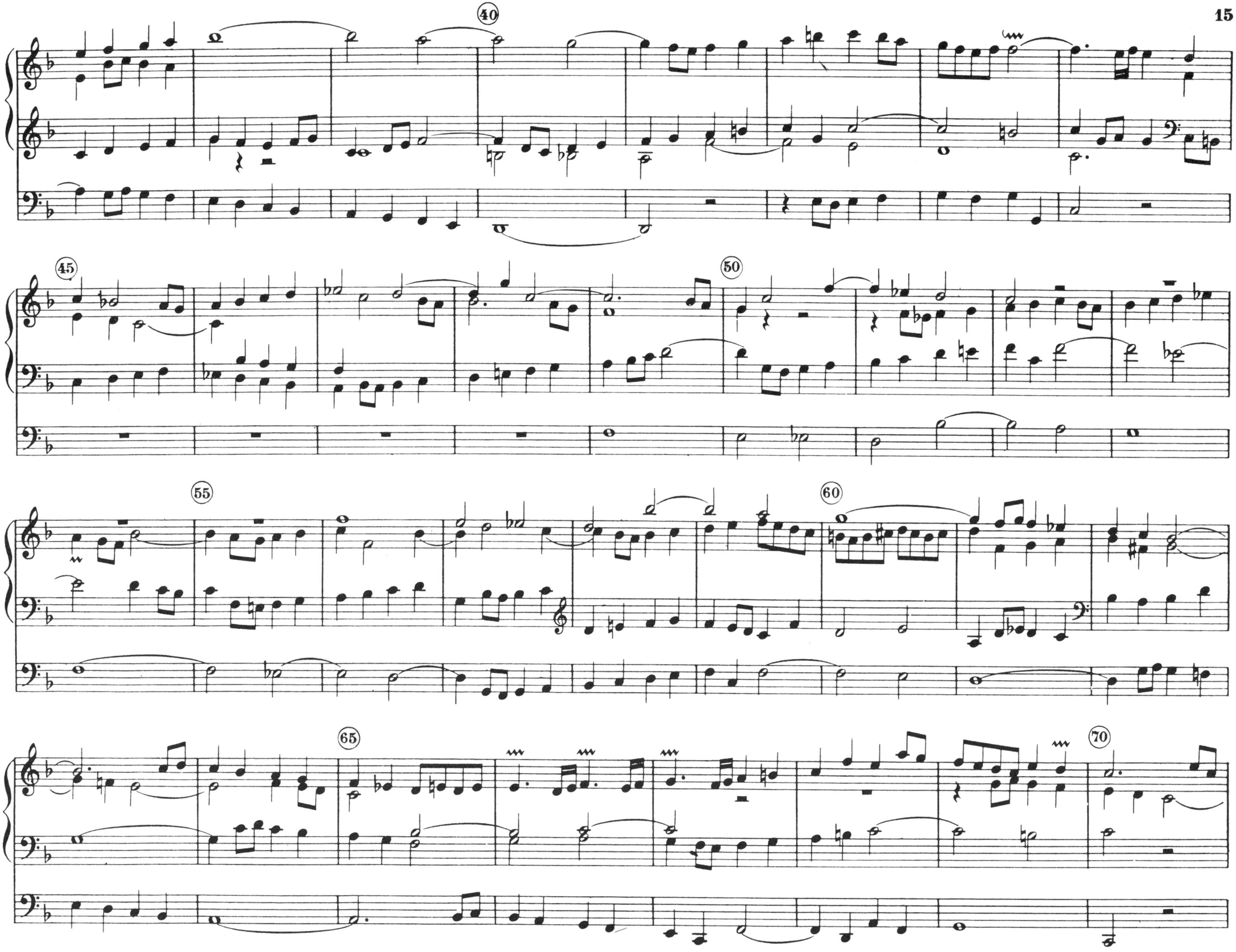
40
45
50
55
60
65
70

16

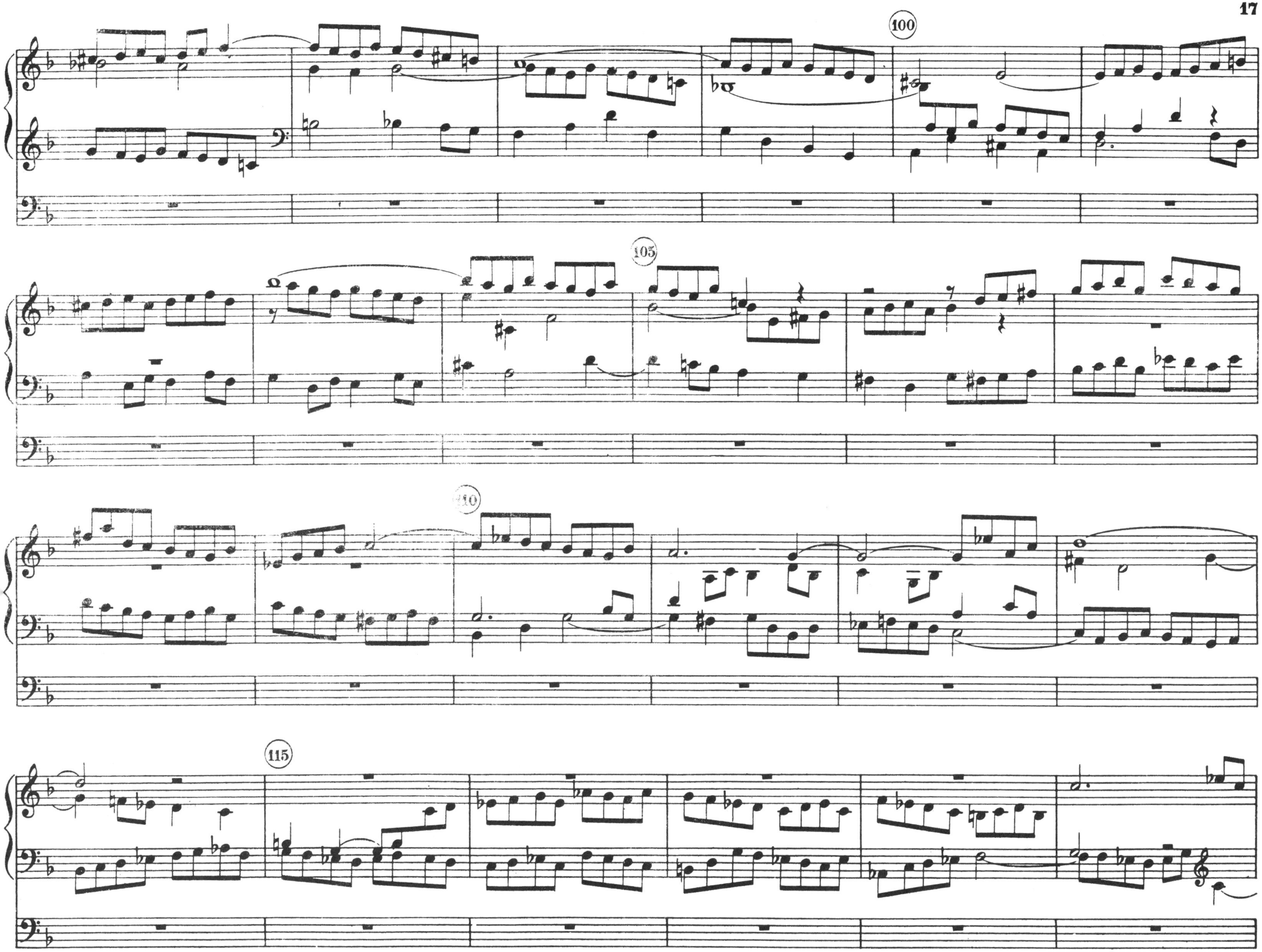
100
105
110
115

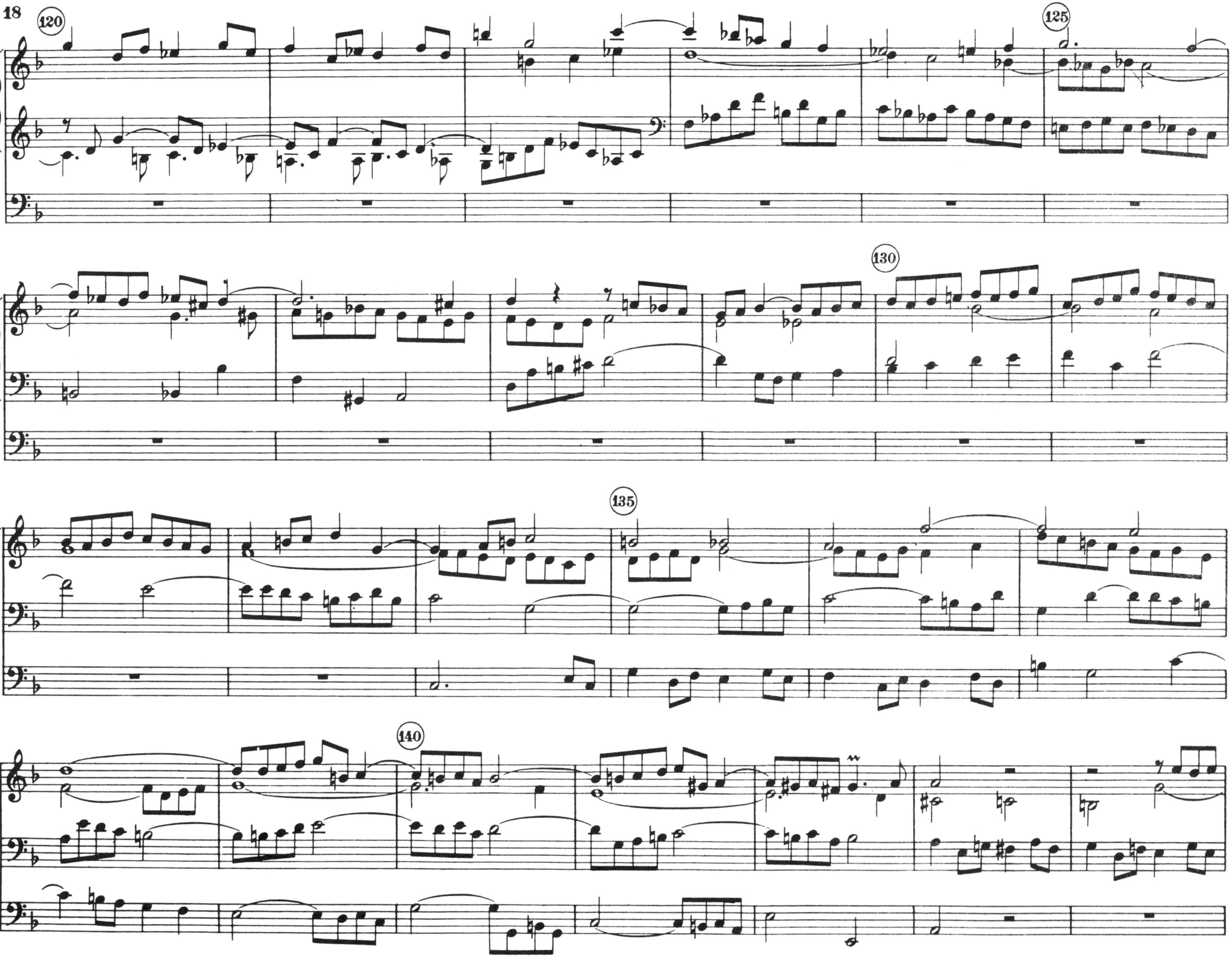
120
125
130
135
140

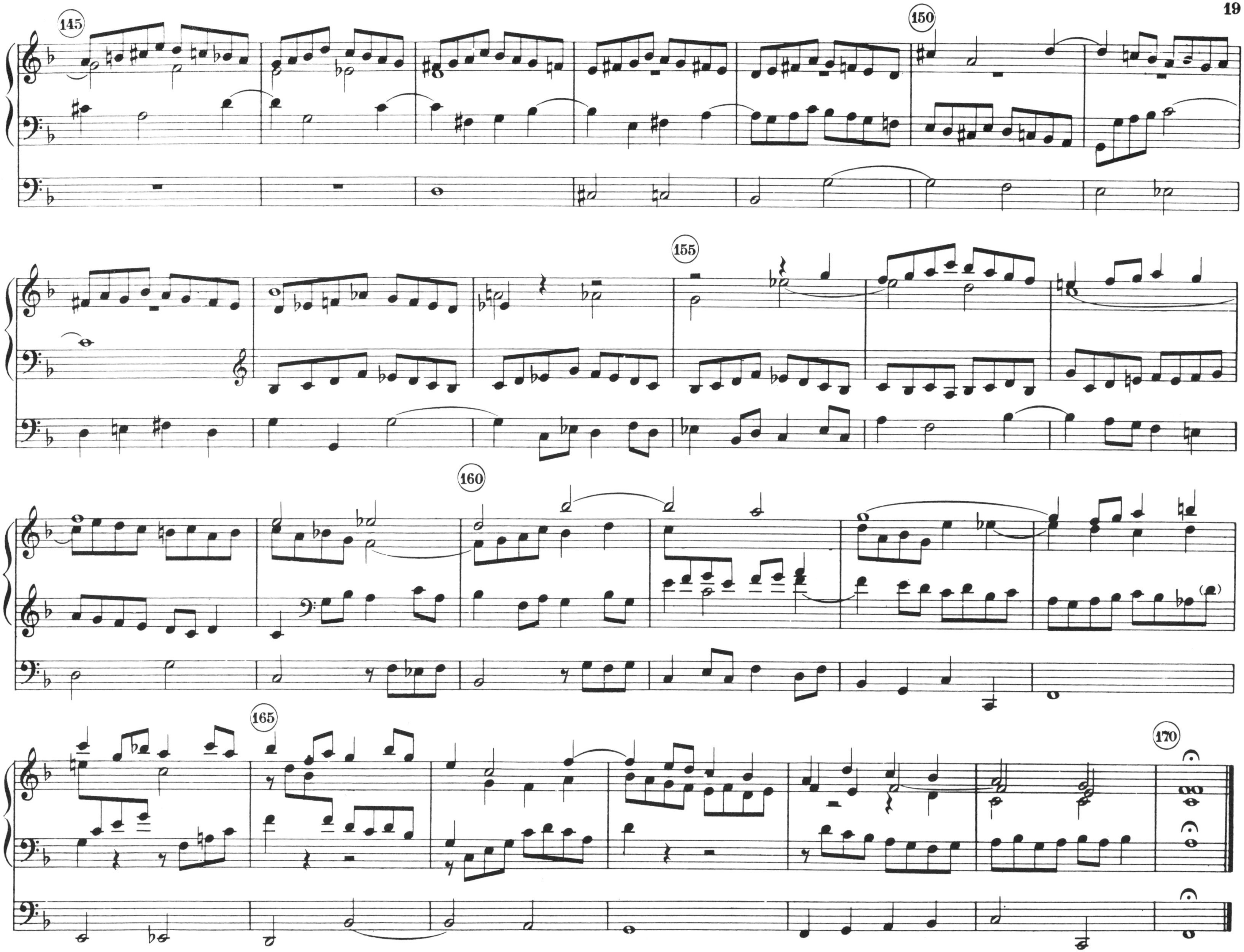
145
150
155
160
165
170

II
Praeludium und Fuge in F-Moll

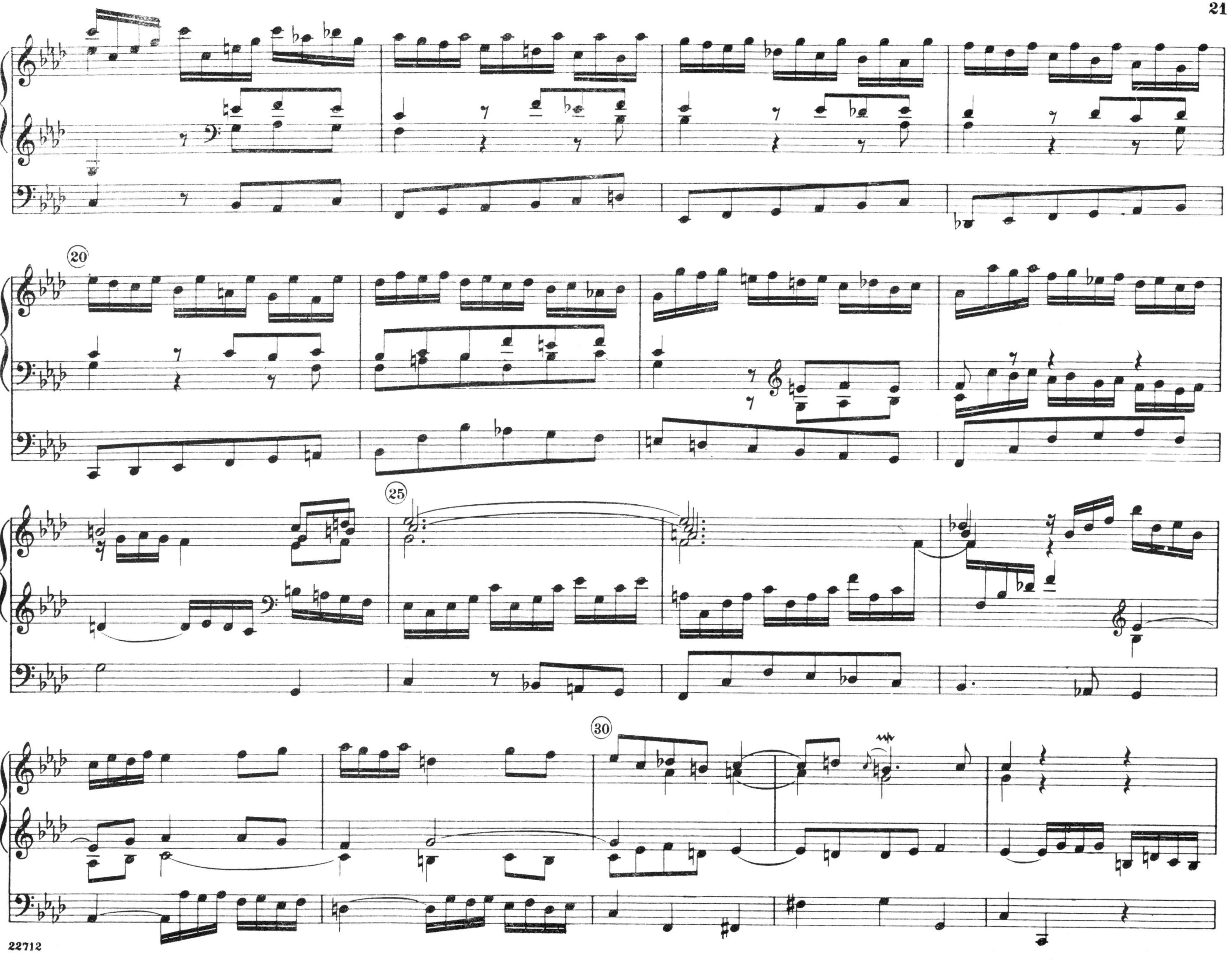
20
25
30

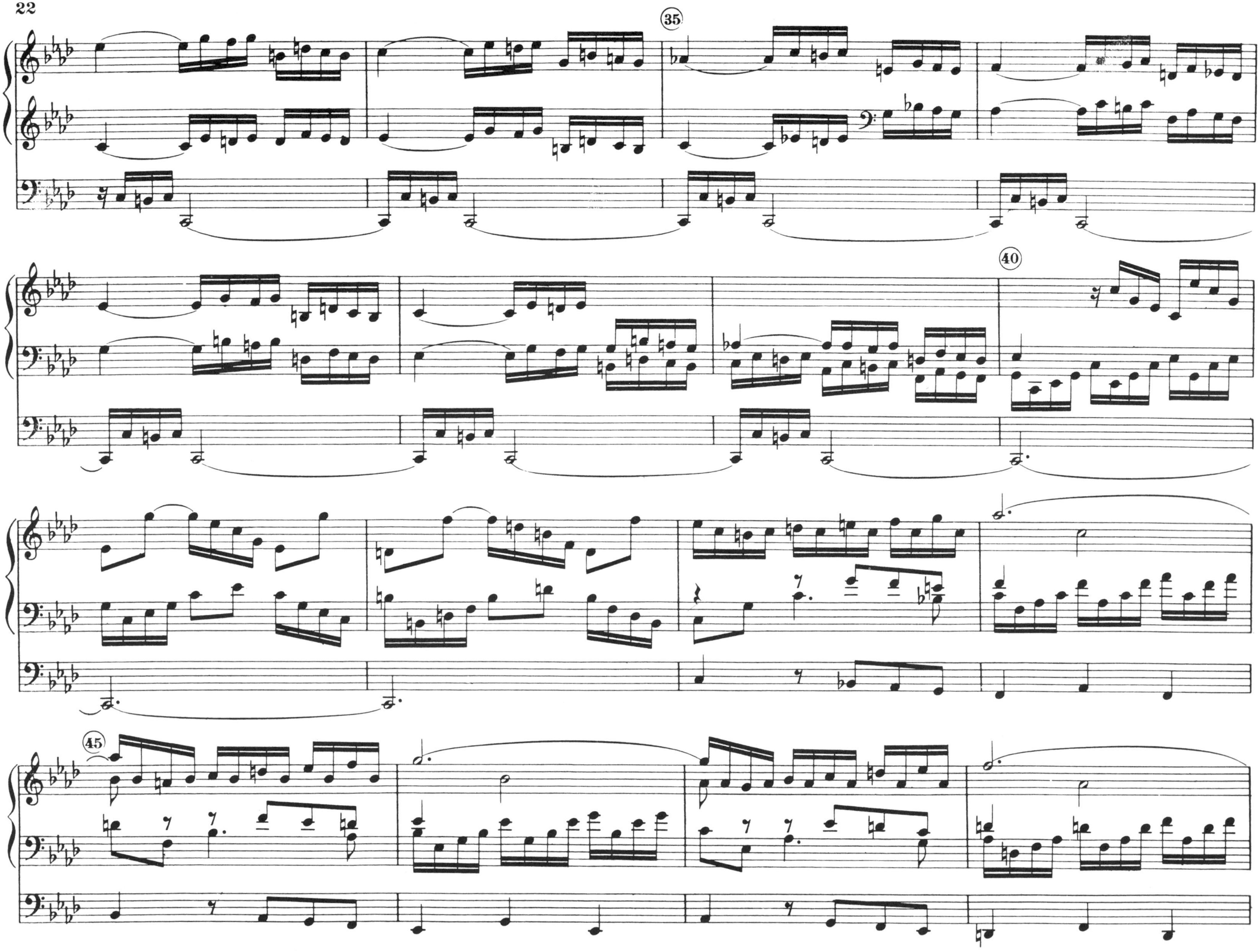
35
40
45

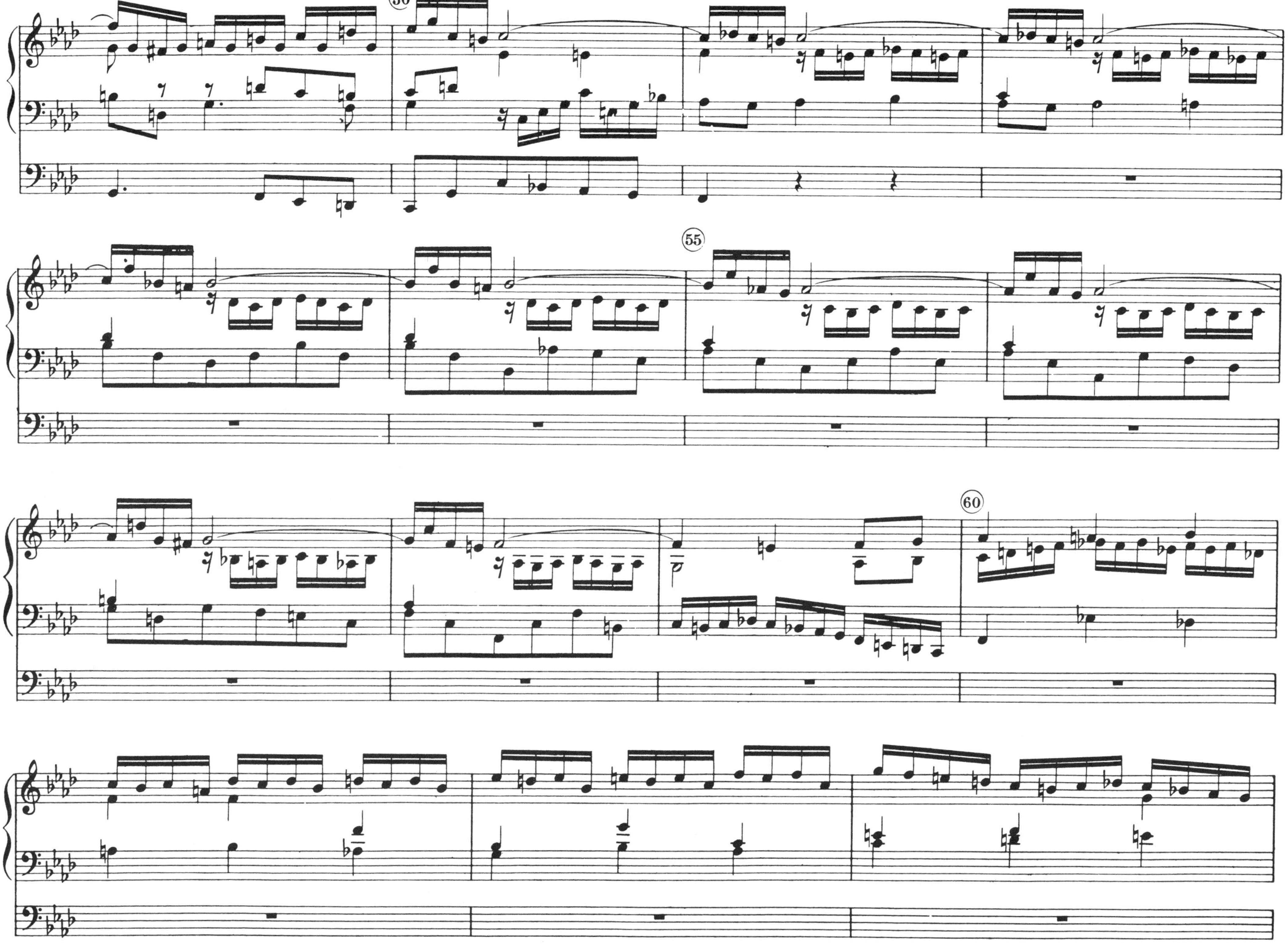
50
55
60

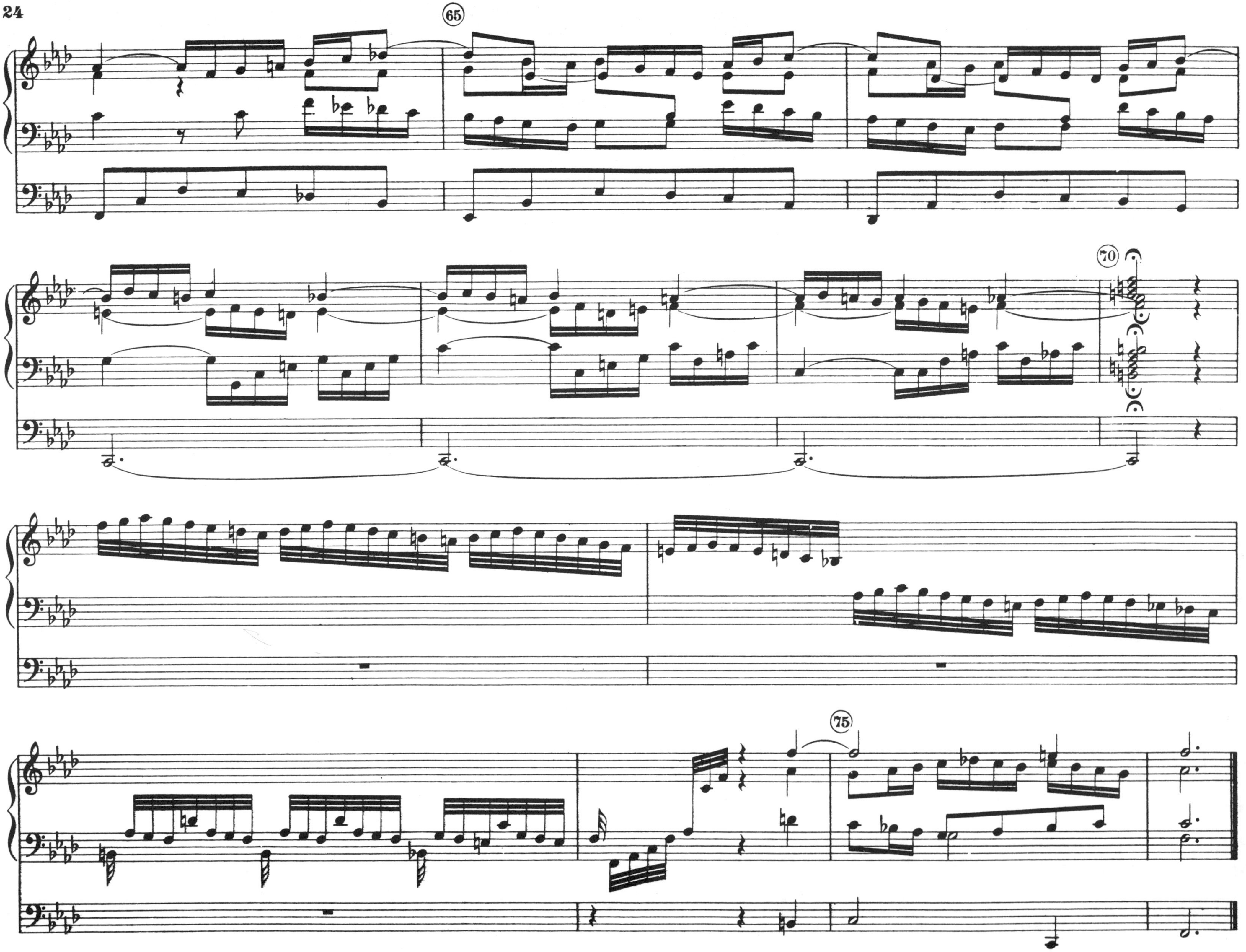
65
70
75

Fuge

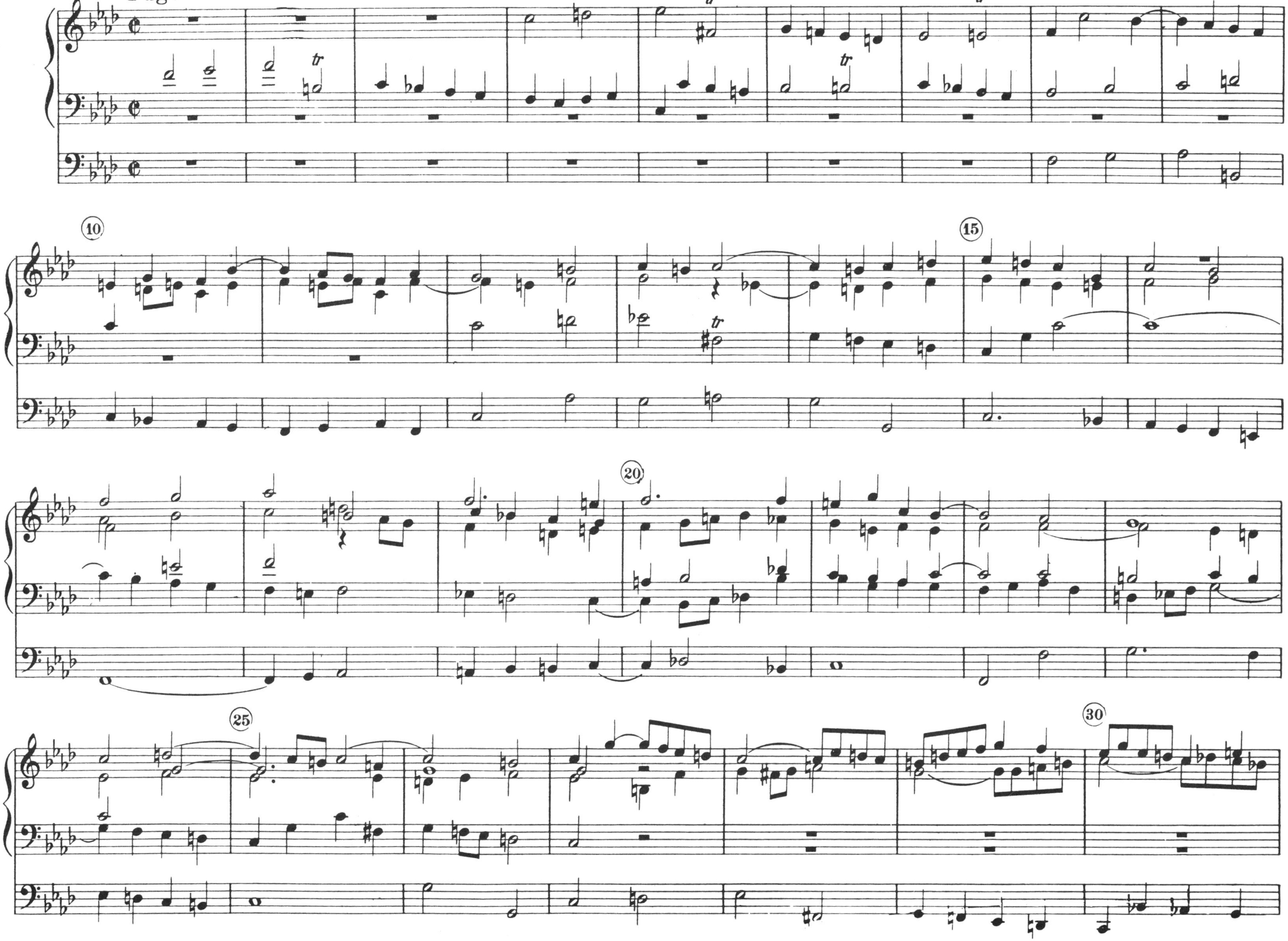

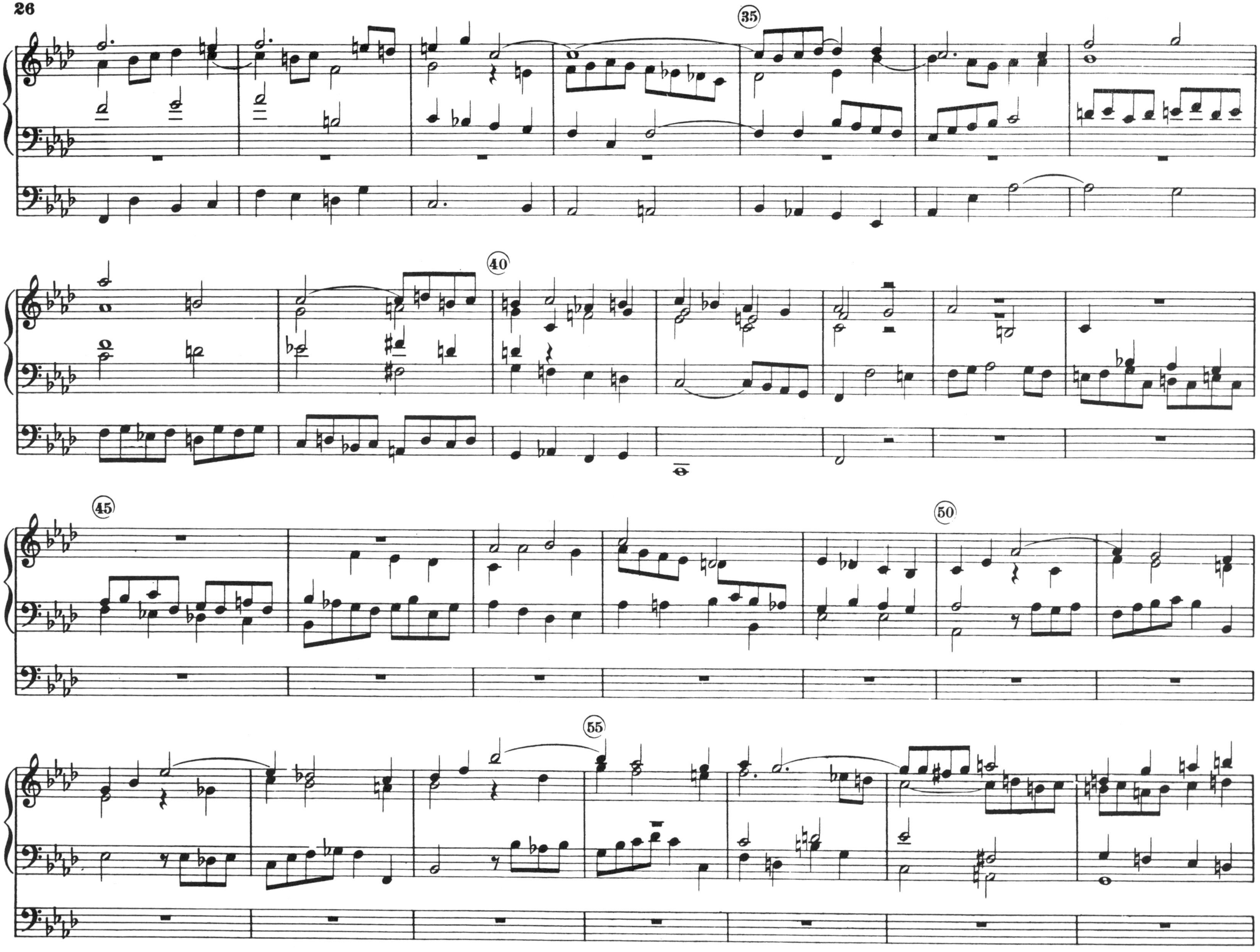
35
40
45
50
55

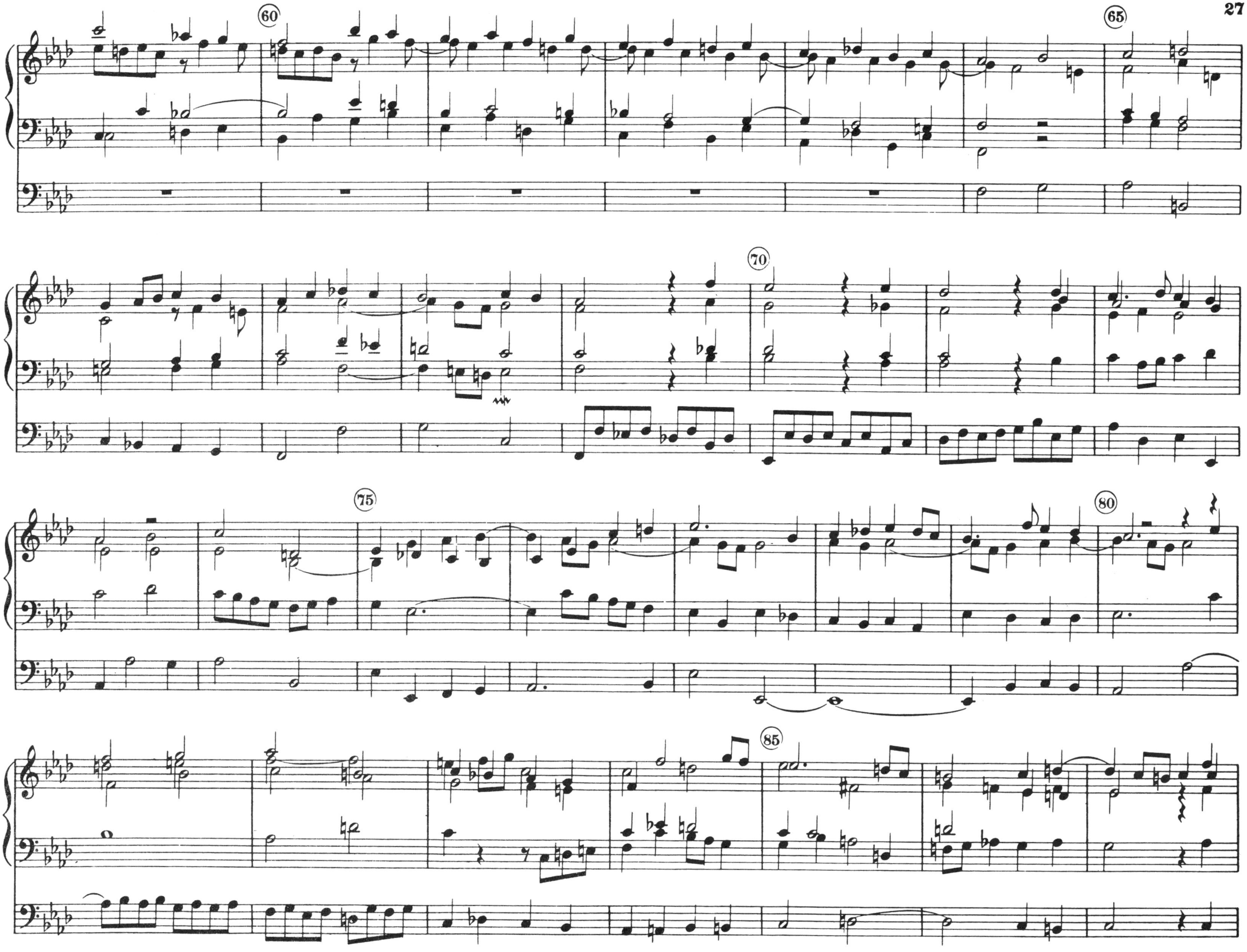
60
65
70
75
80
85

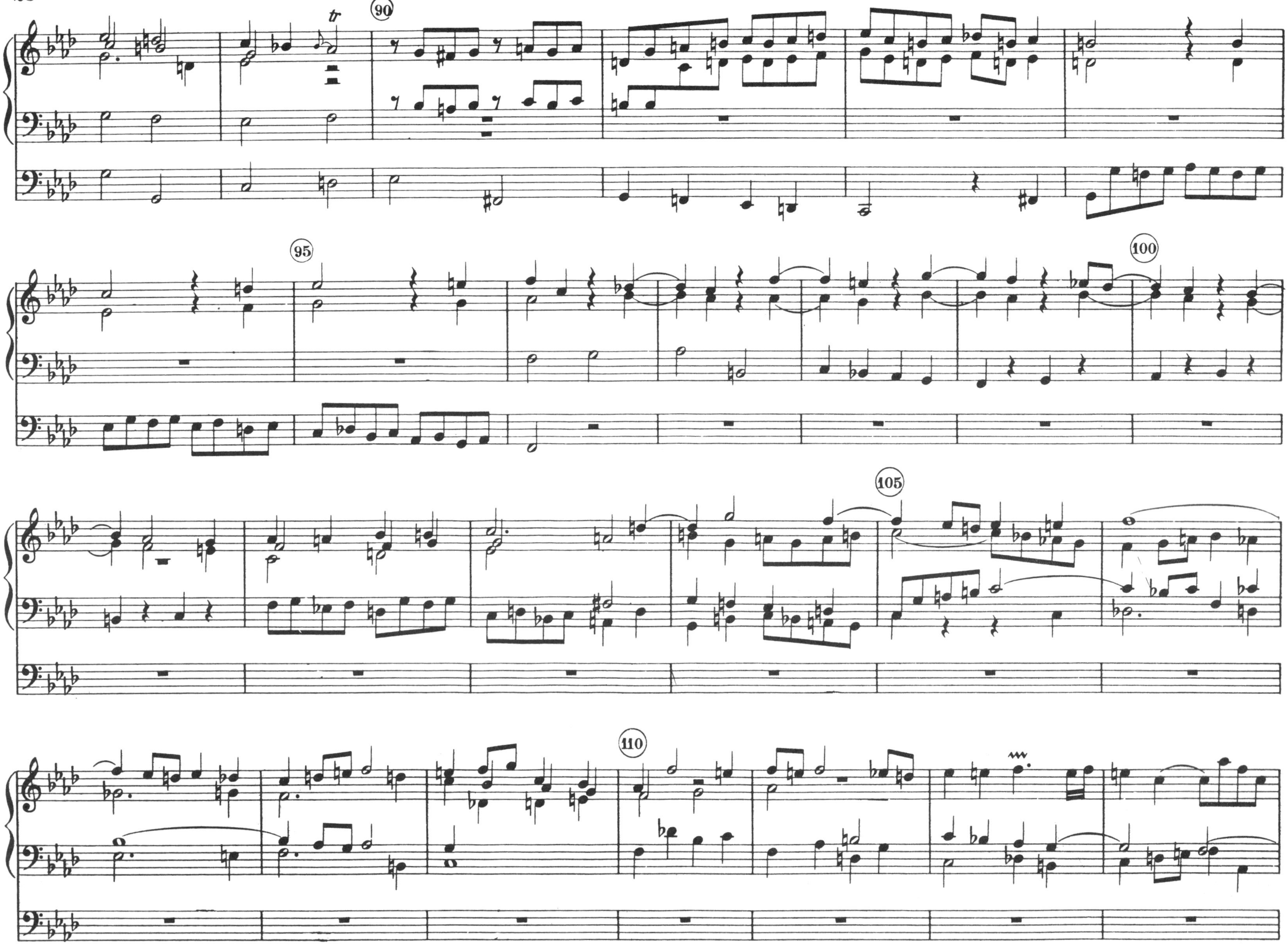
tr
90
95
100
105
110

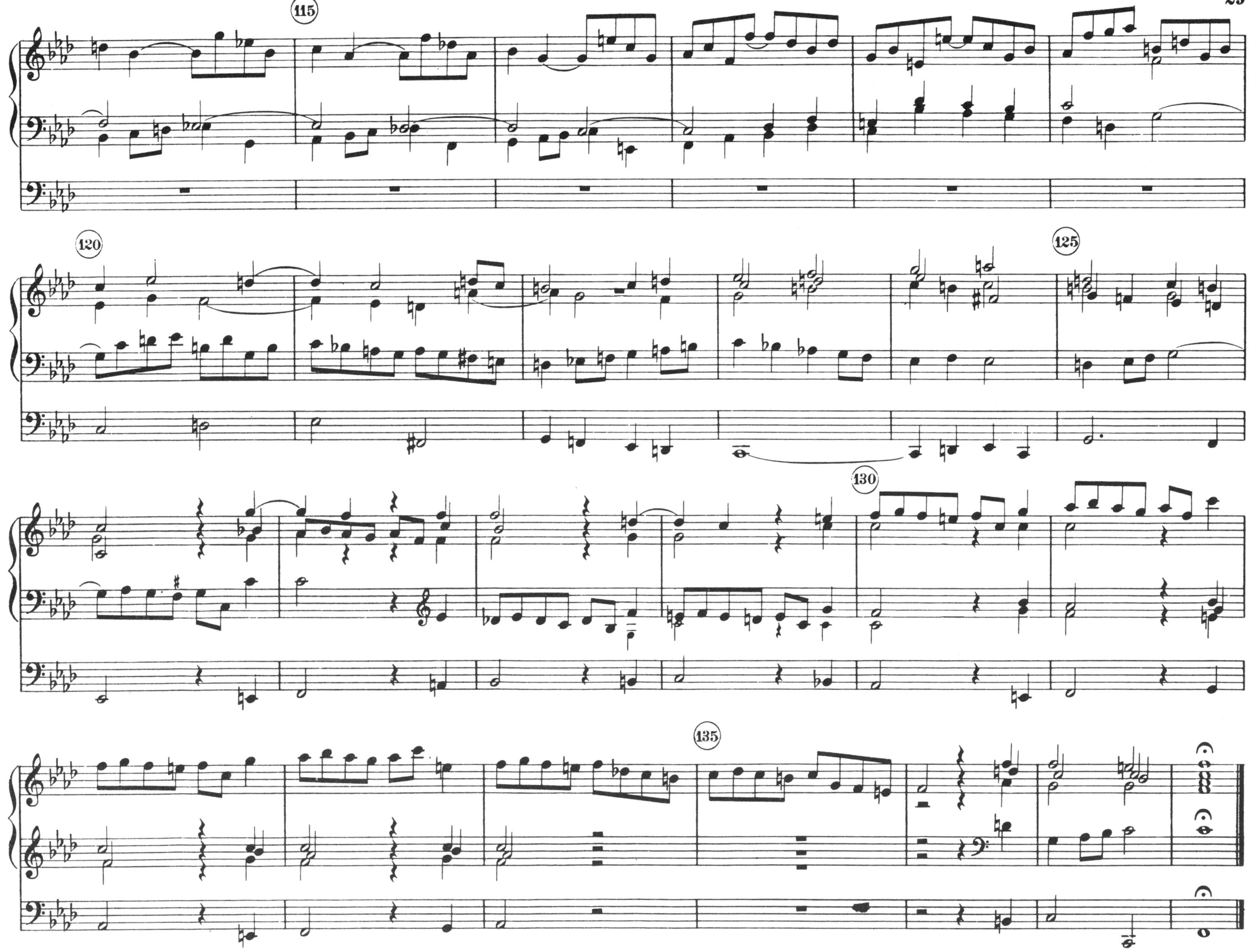
115
120
125
130
135

III
Praeludium und Fuge in G-Dur

Praeludium
Vivace

Manual

Pedal

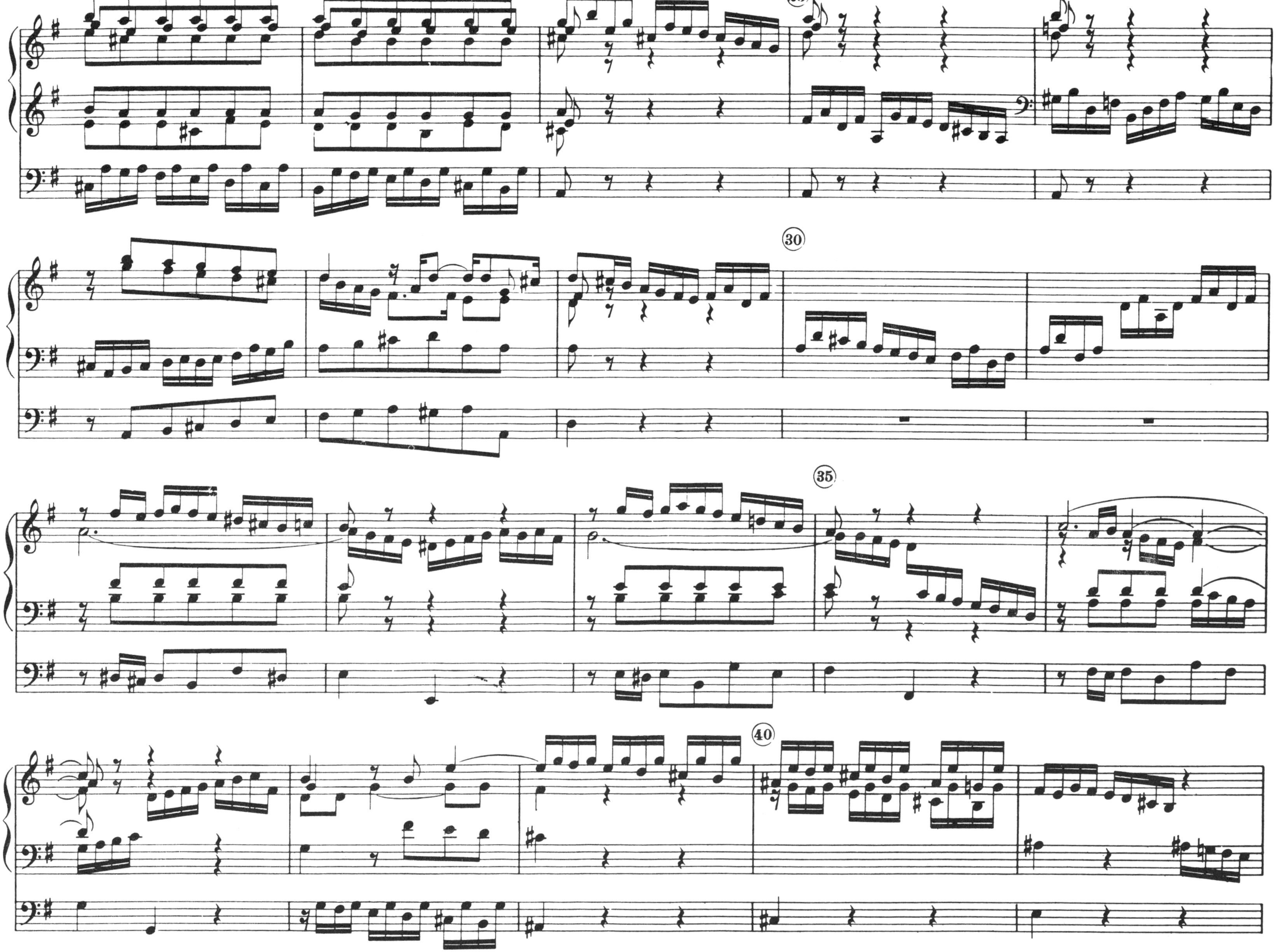
25
30
35
40

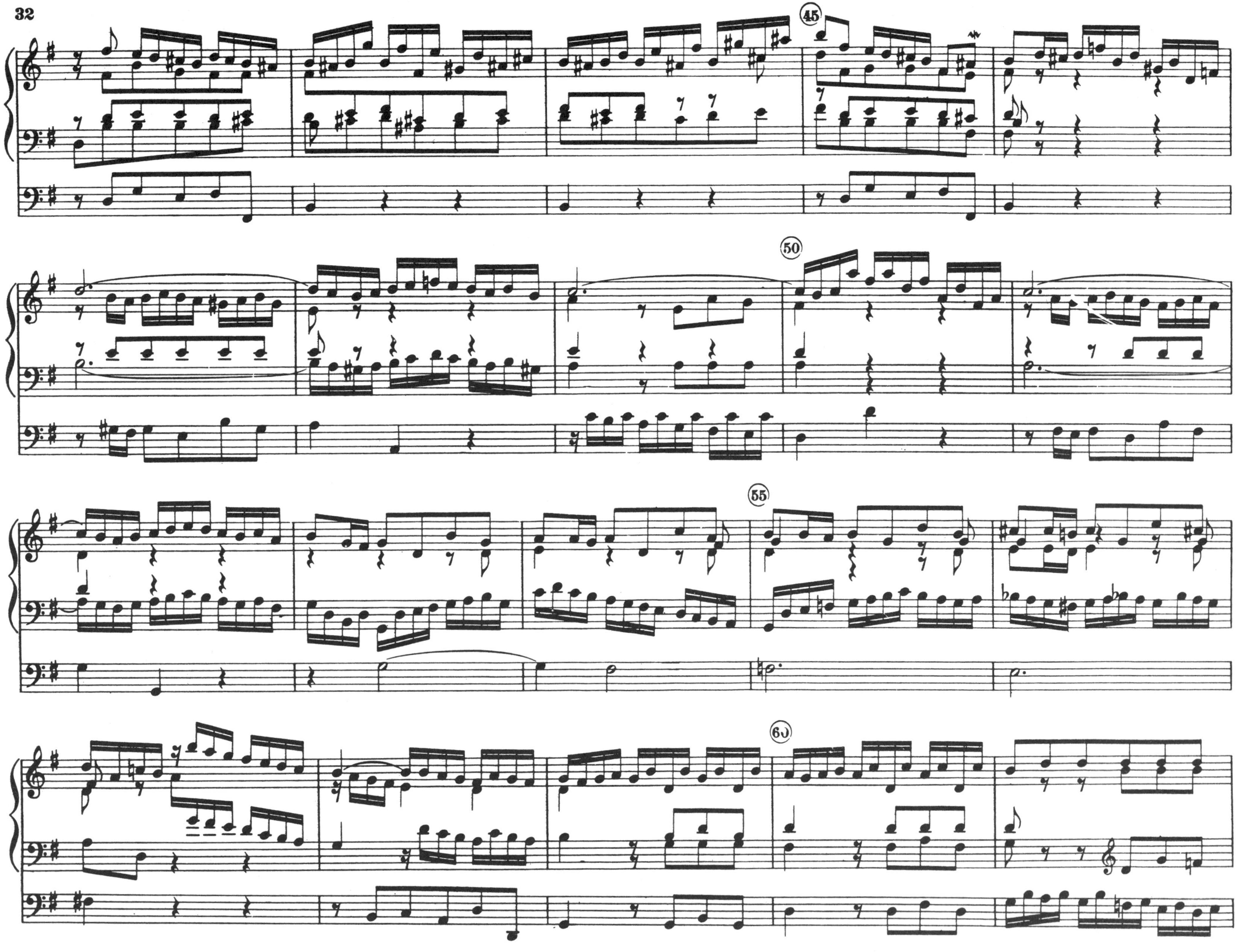
45
50
55
60

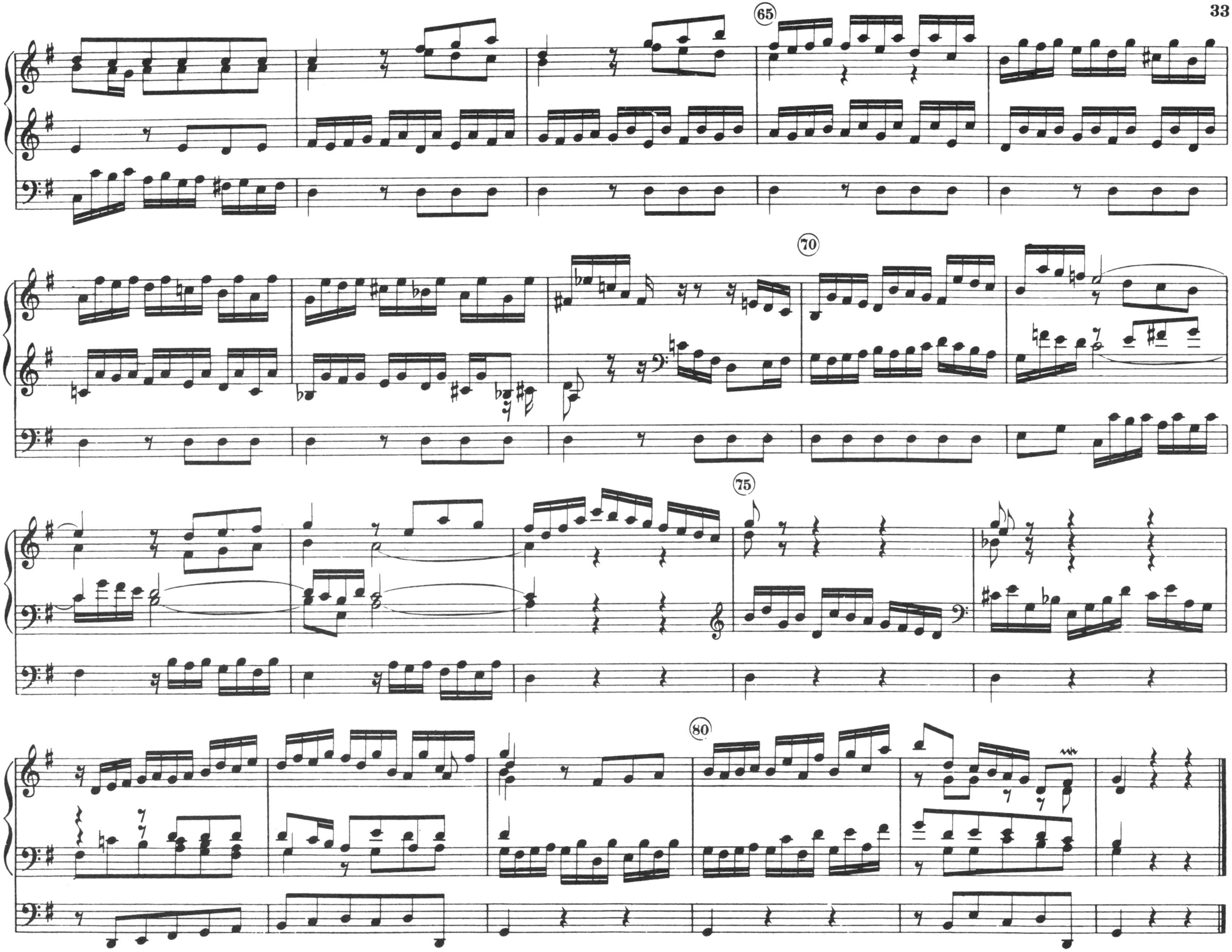
65
70
75
80

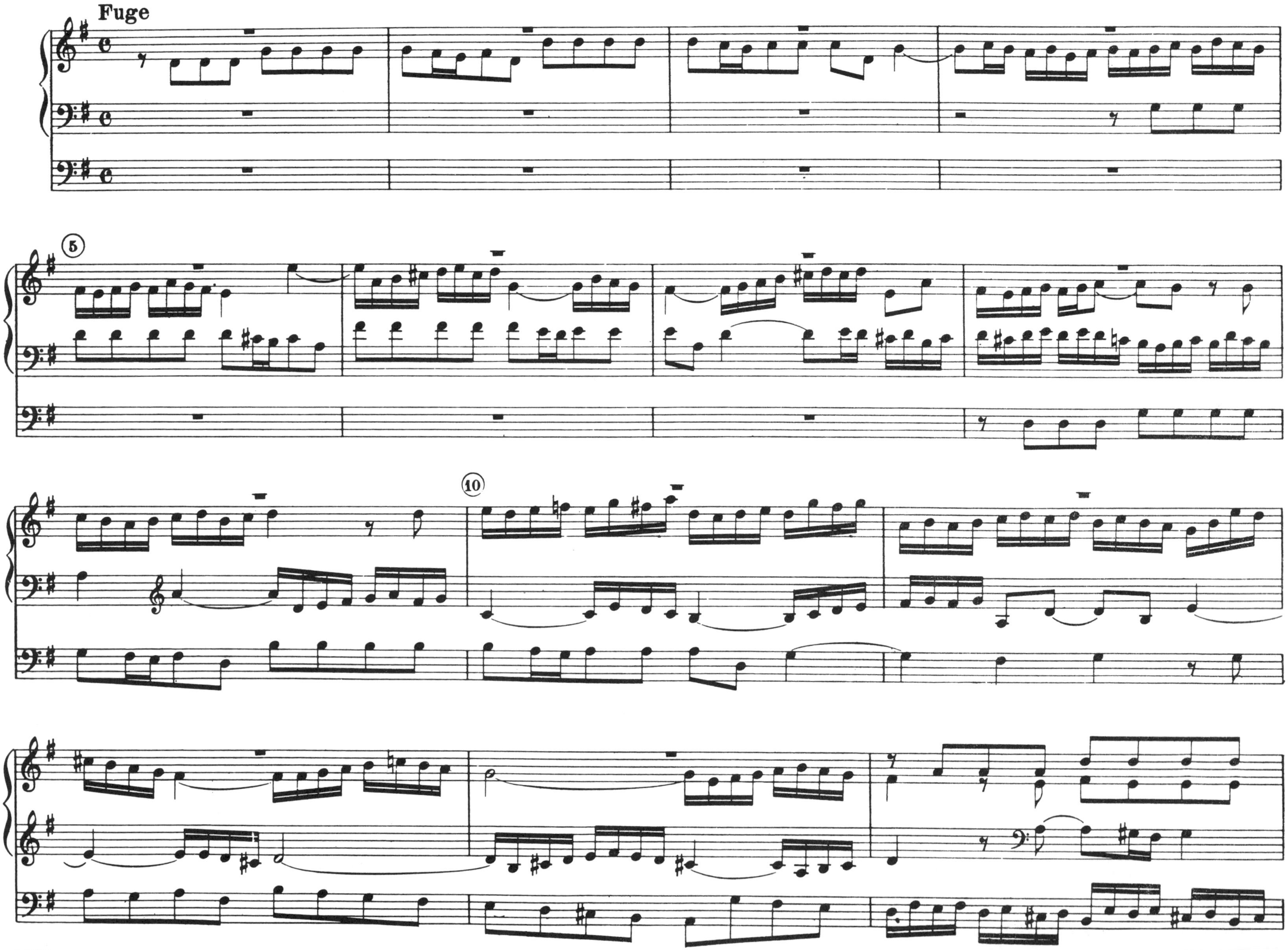
Fuge
5
10

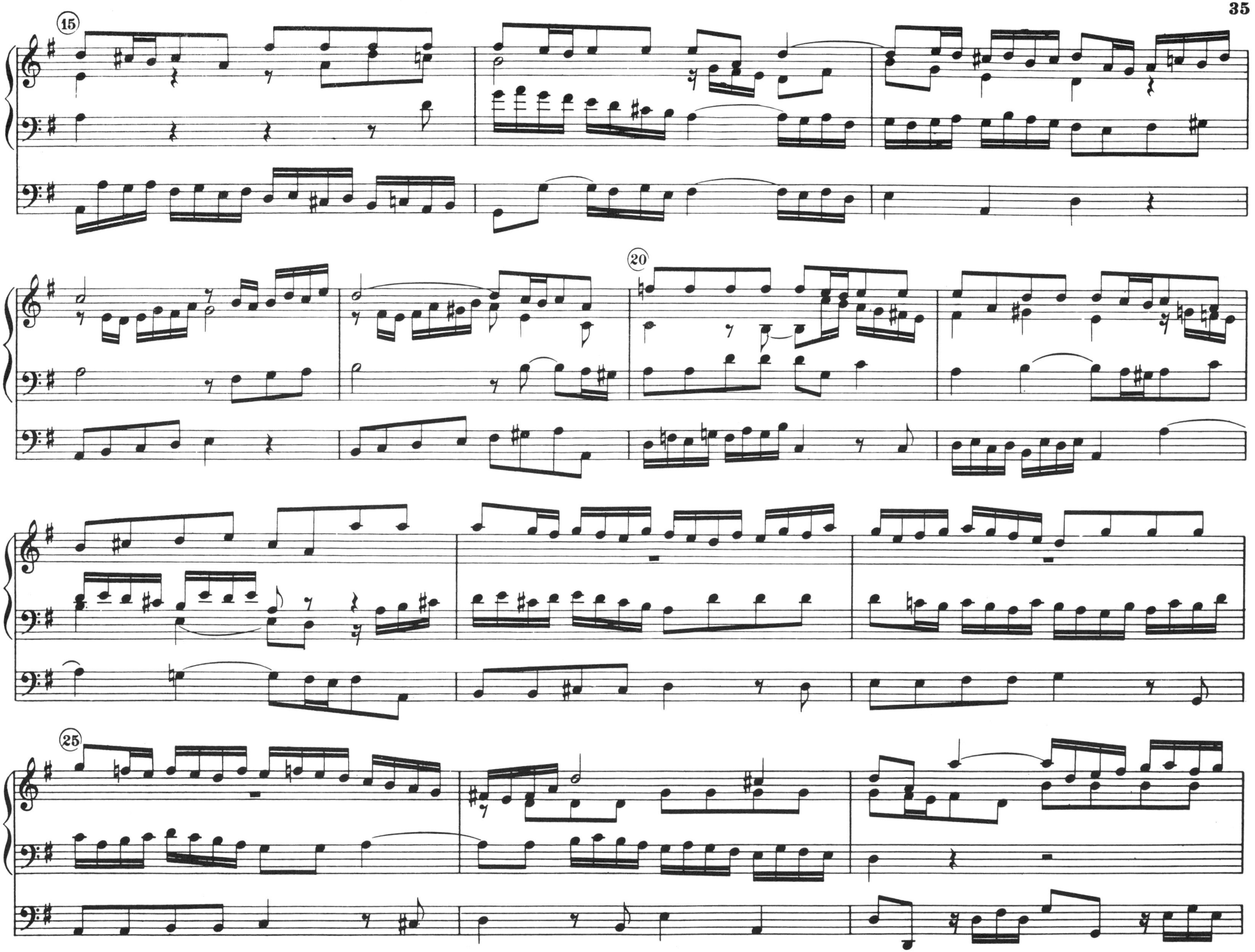
15
20
25

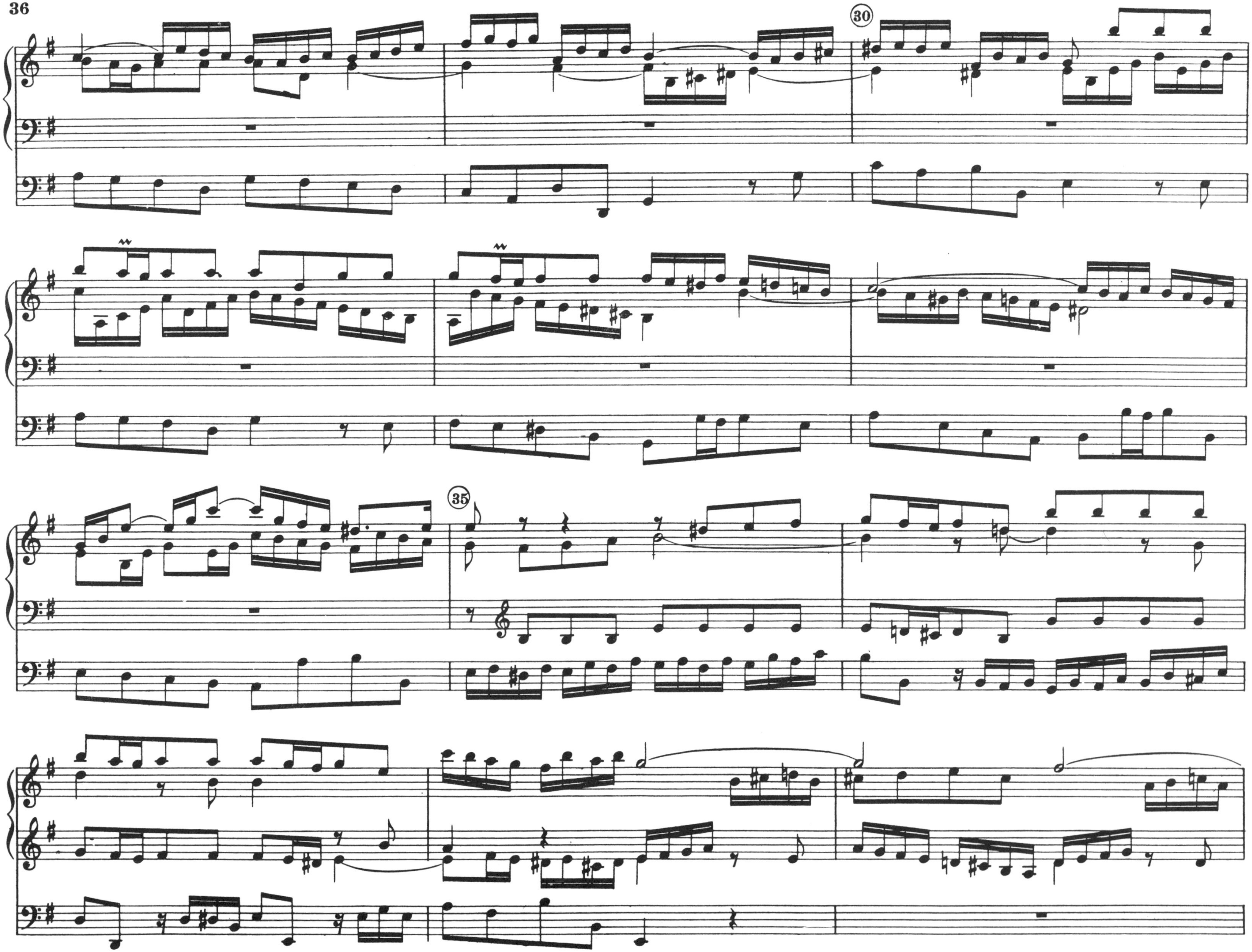
30
35

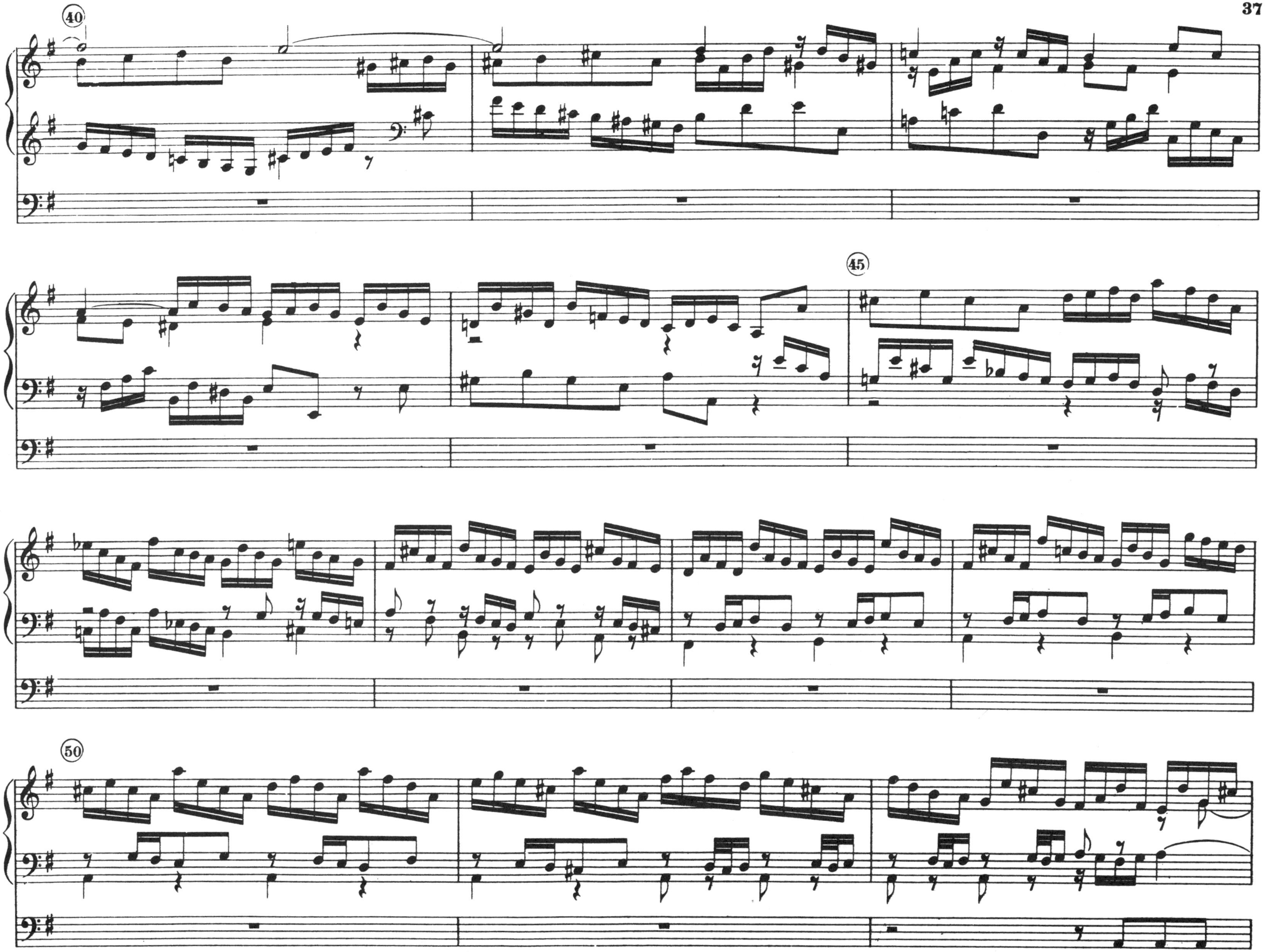
40
45
50

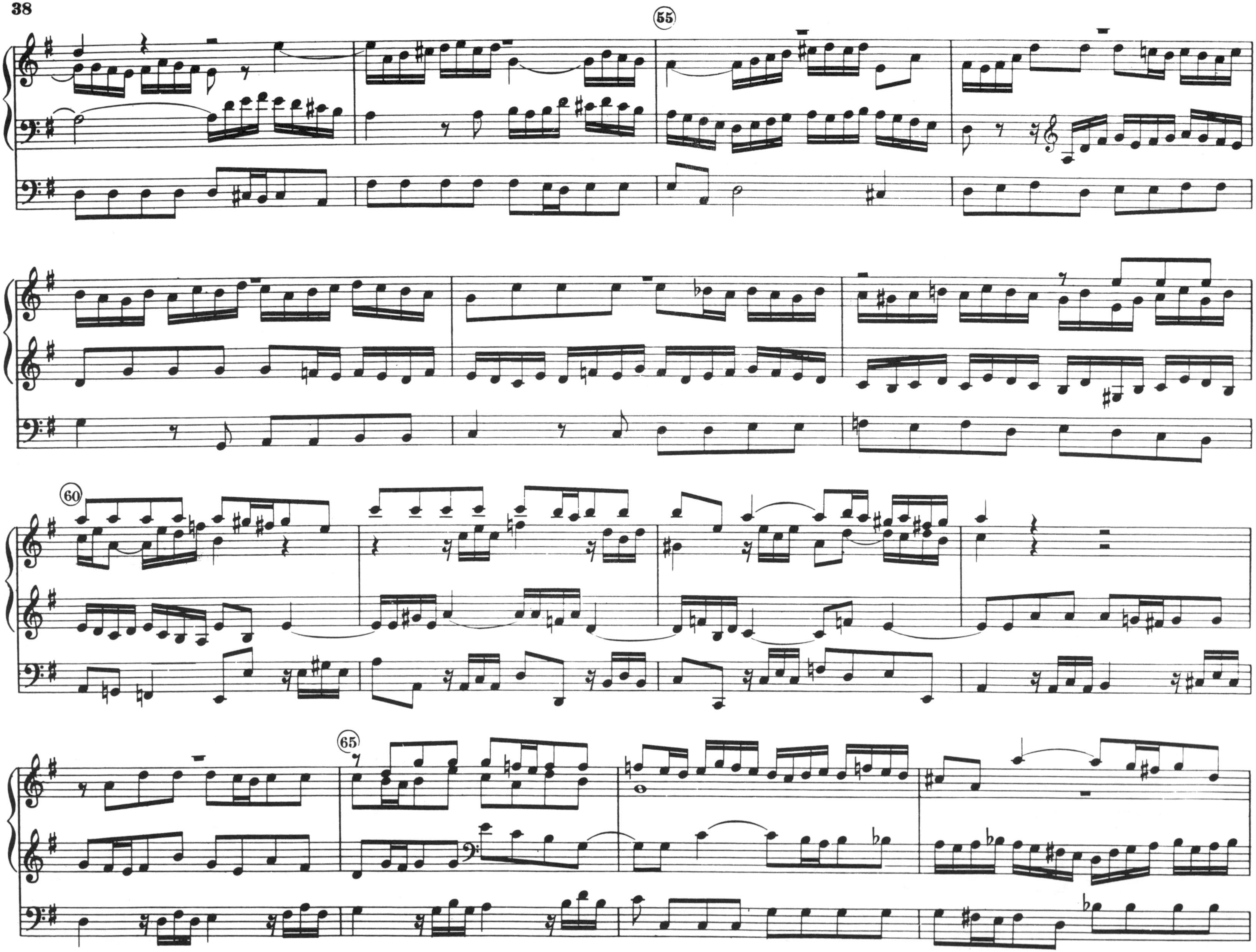
55
60
65

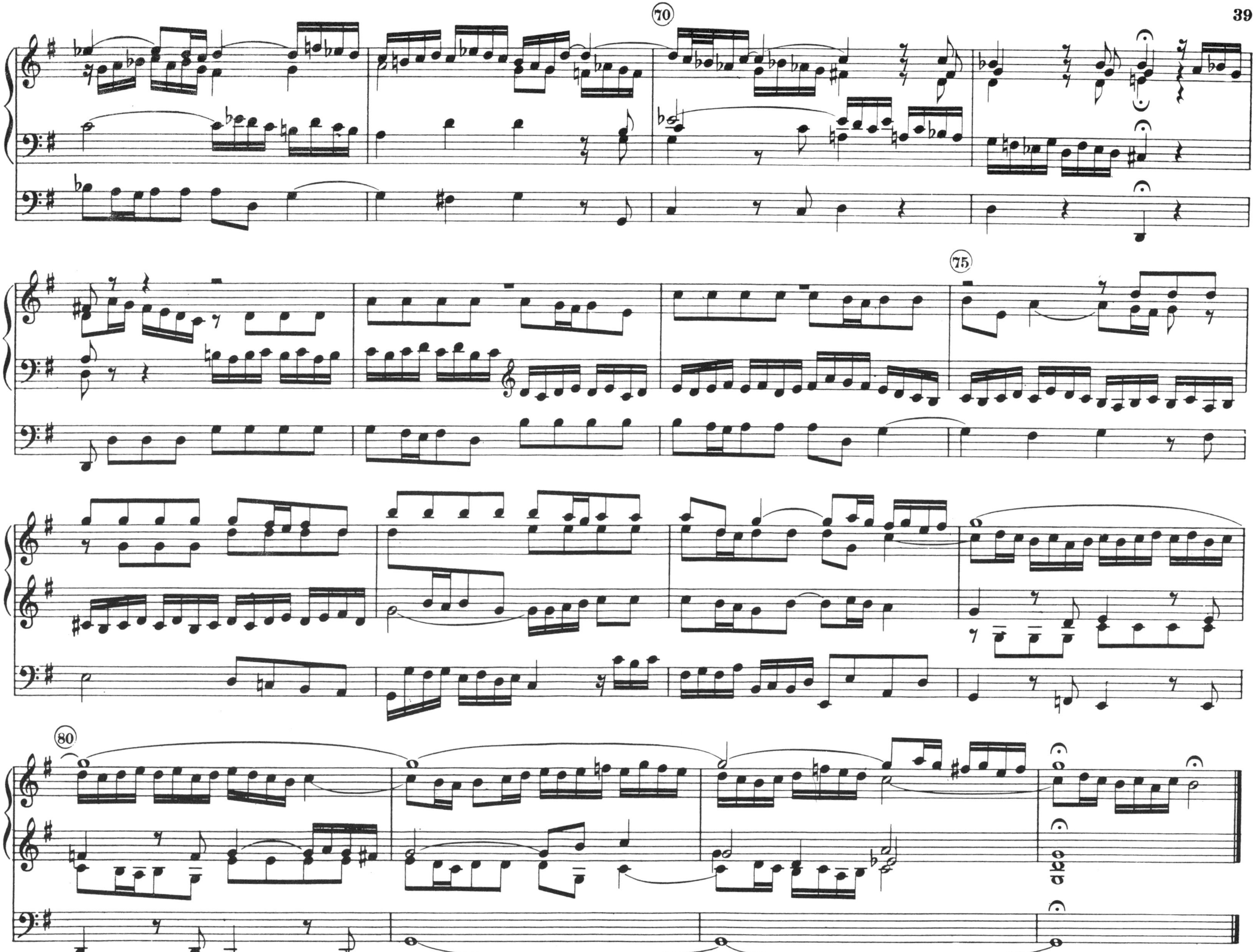
70
75
80

IV
Praeludium und Fuge in G-Moll

Praeludium (Fantasia)

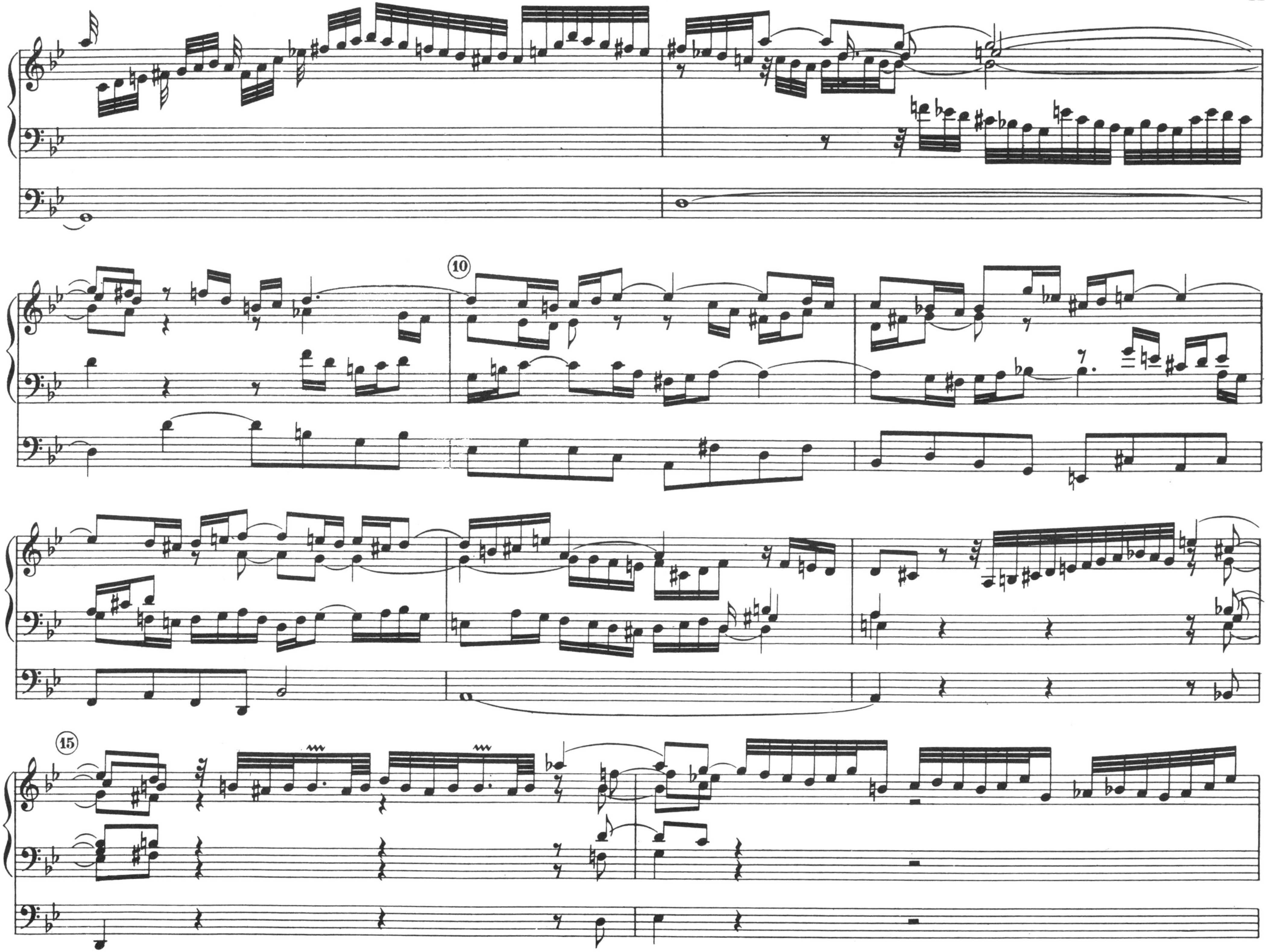
10
15

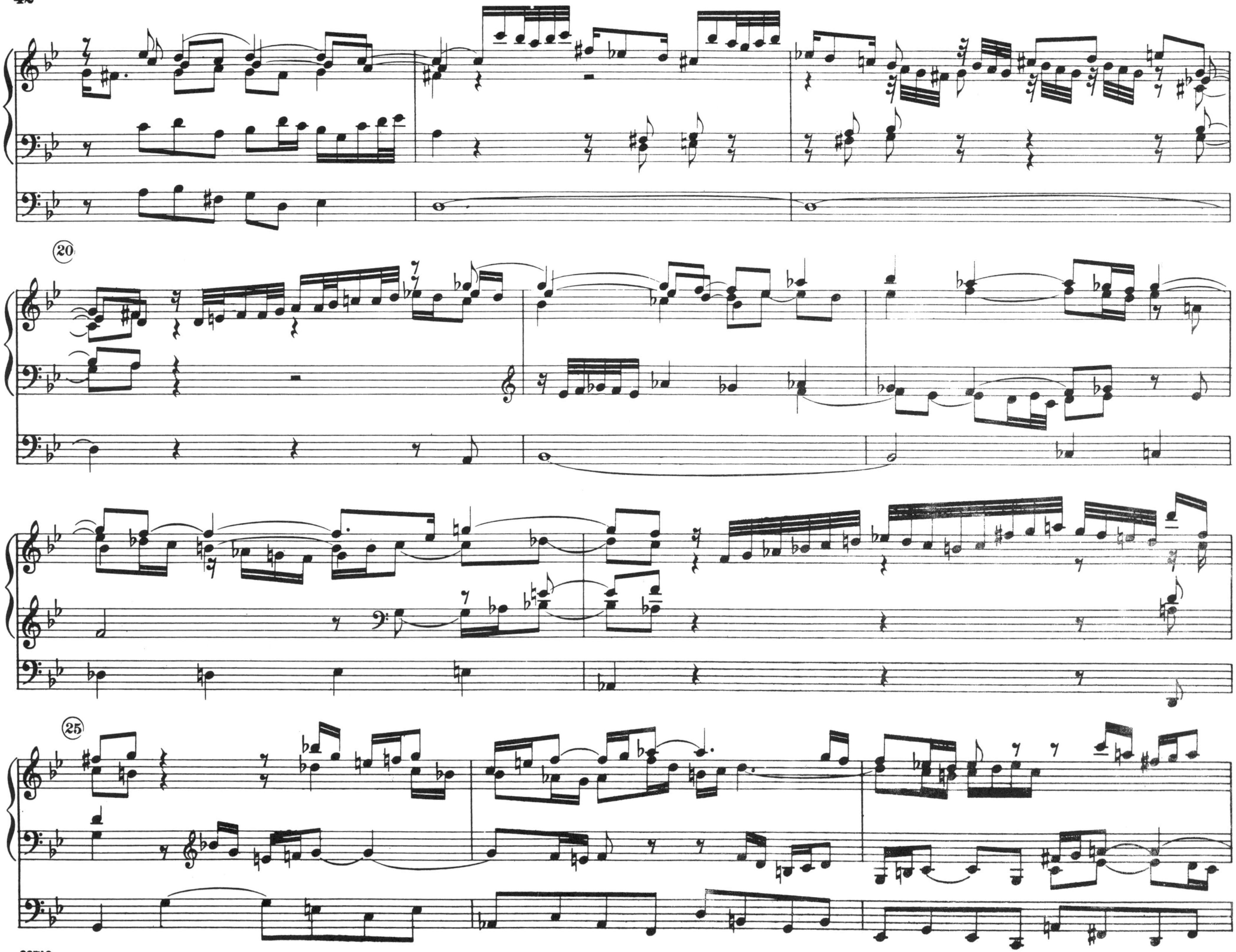
20
25

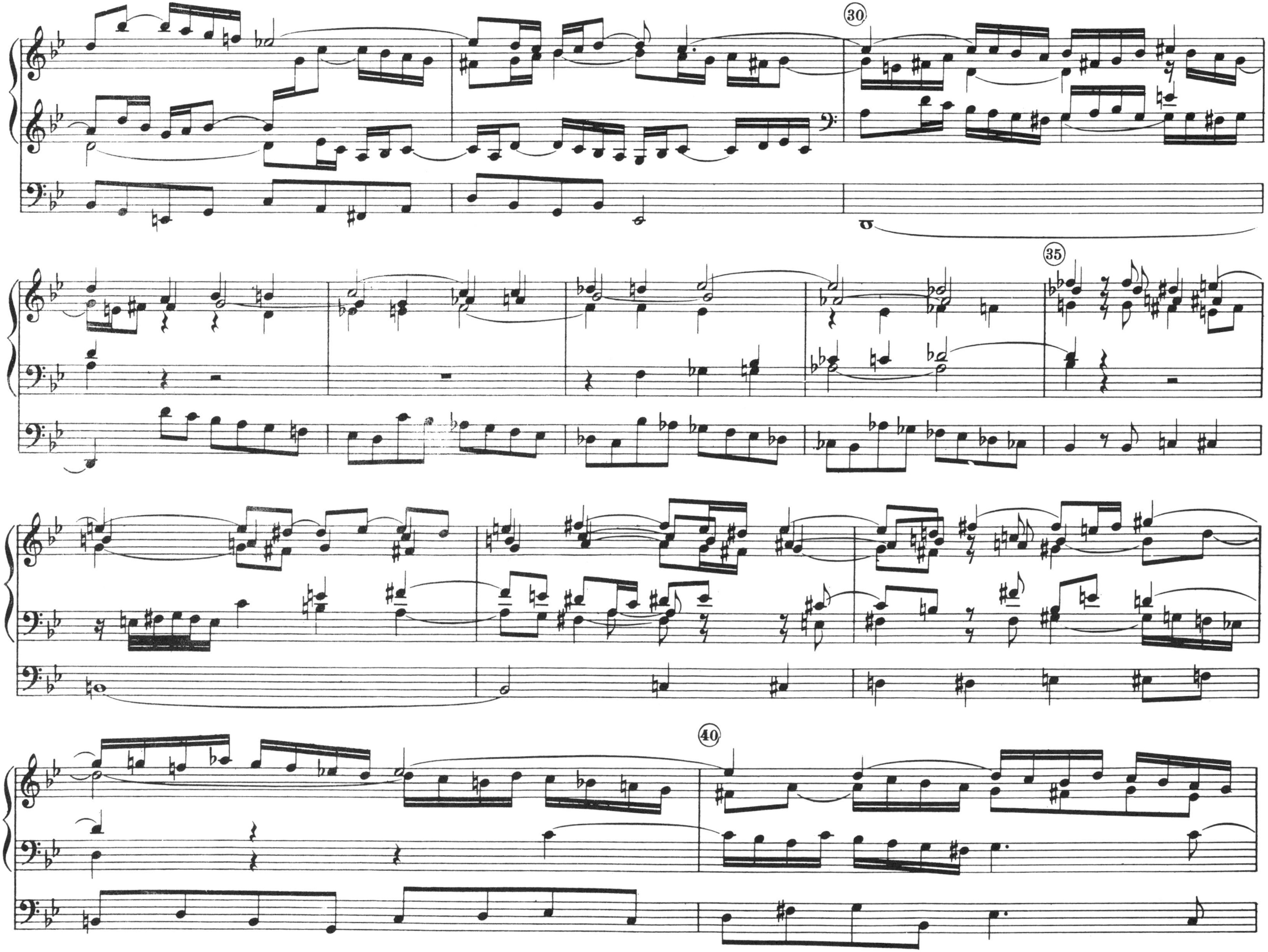
30
35
40

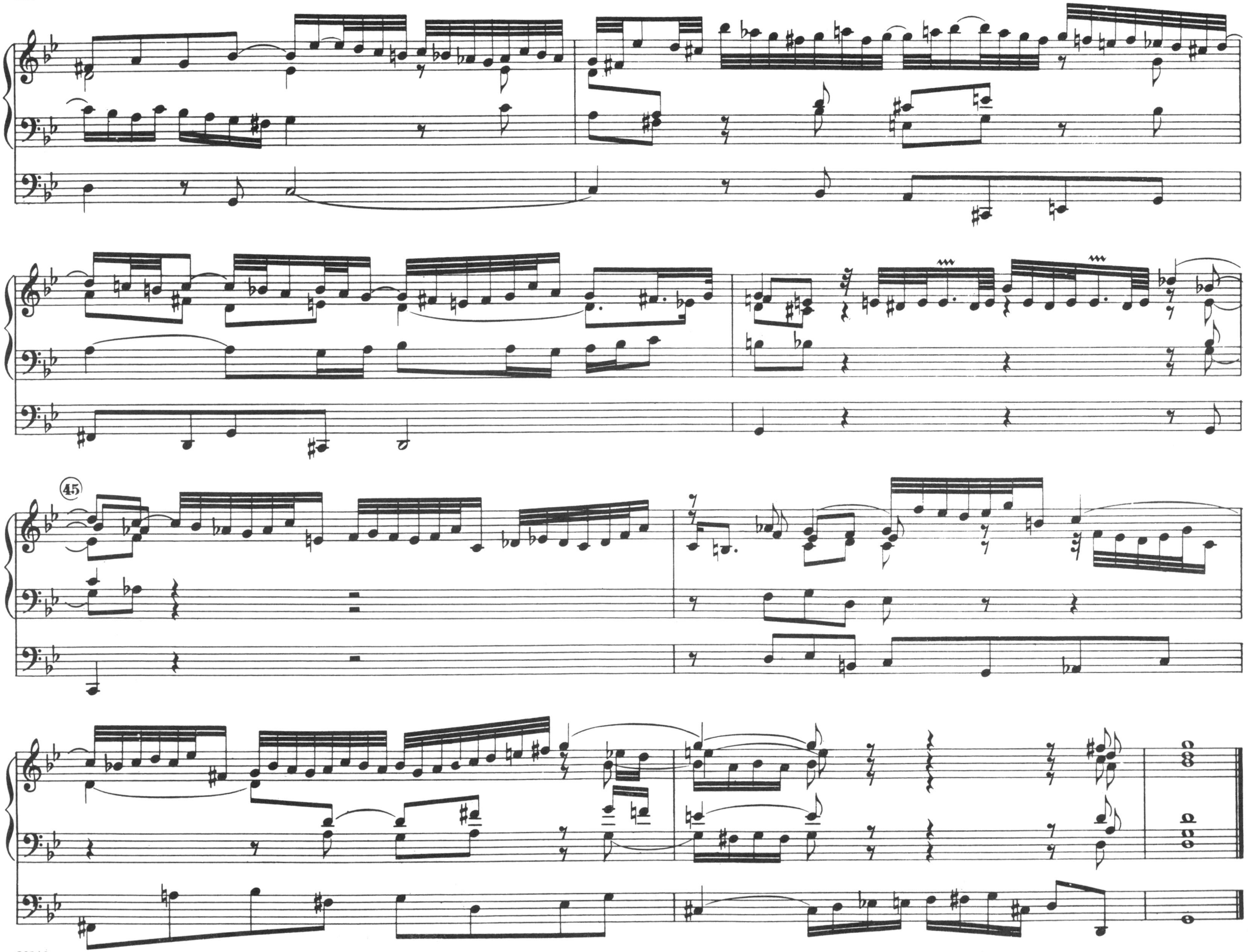
45

Fuge

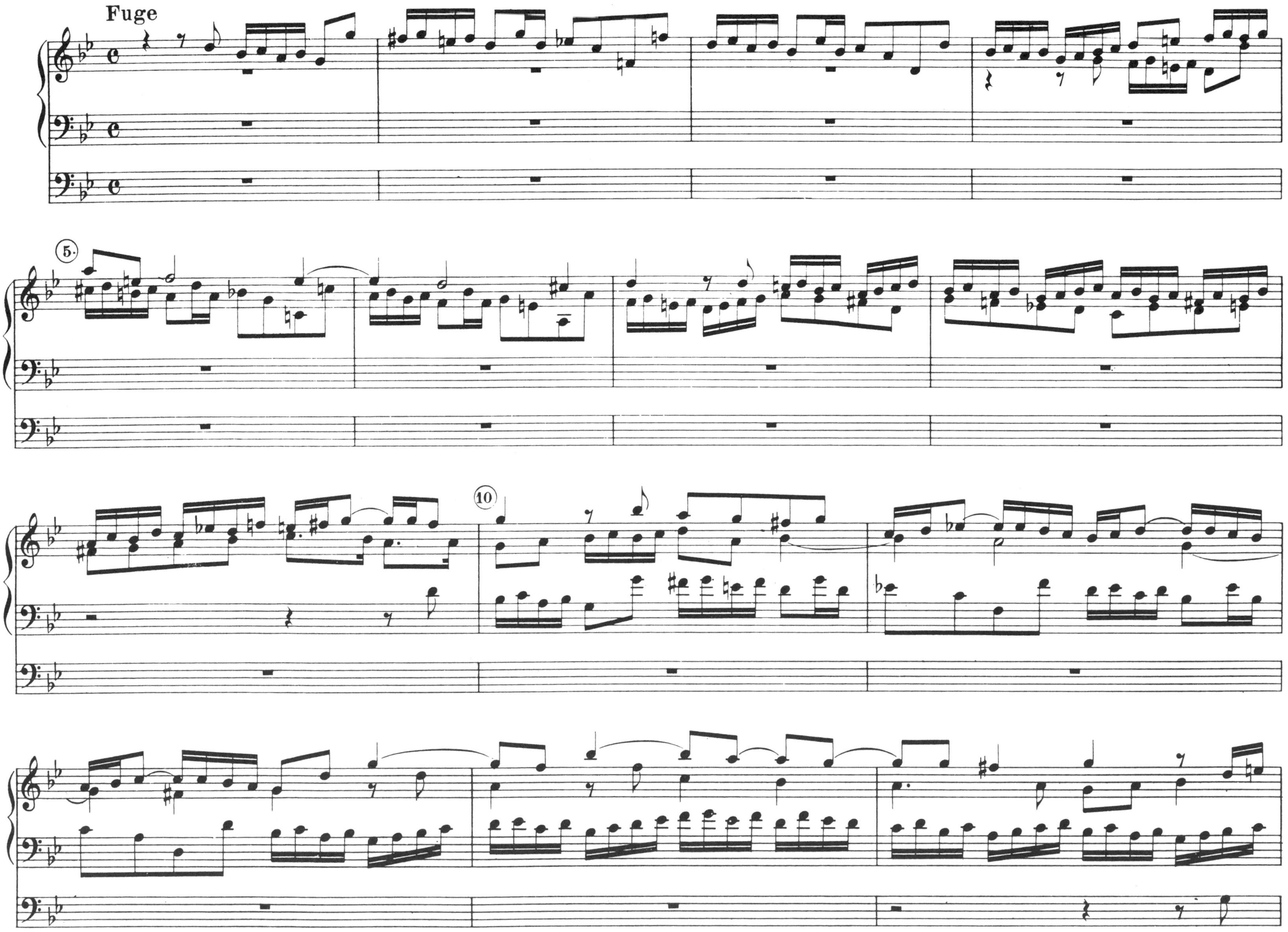

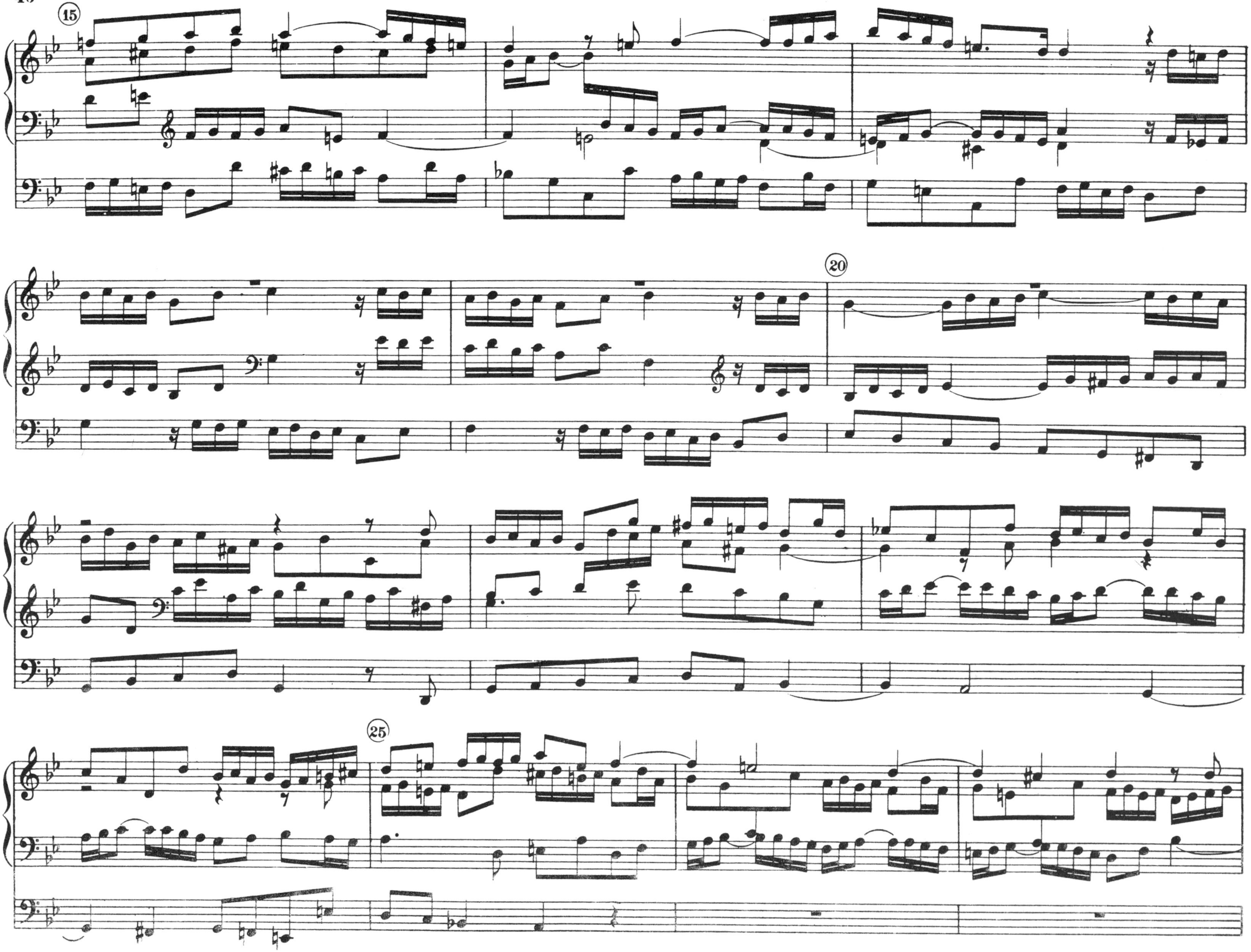
15
20
25

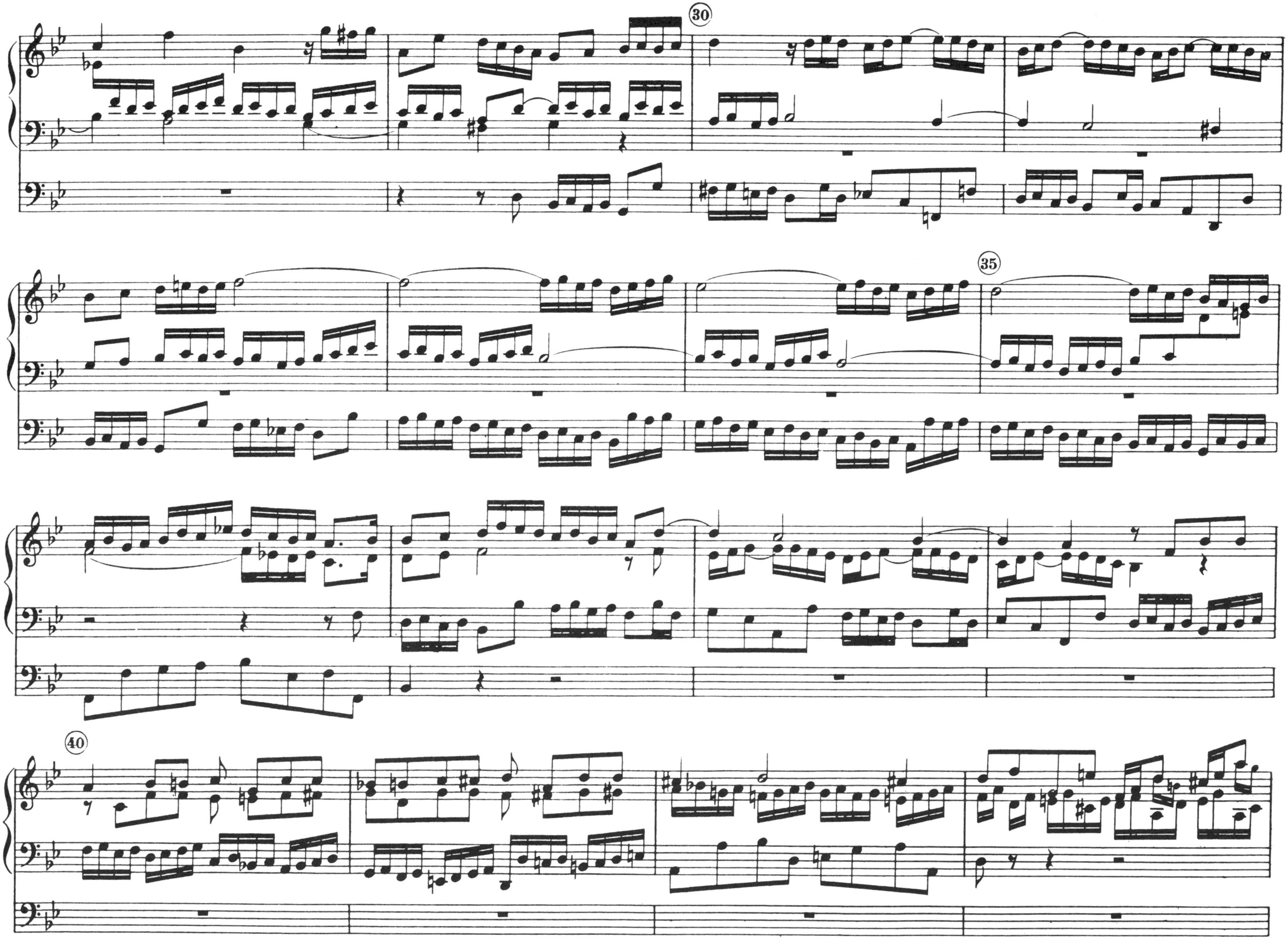
30
35
40

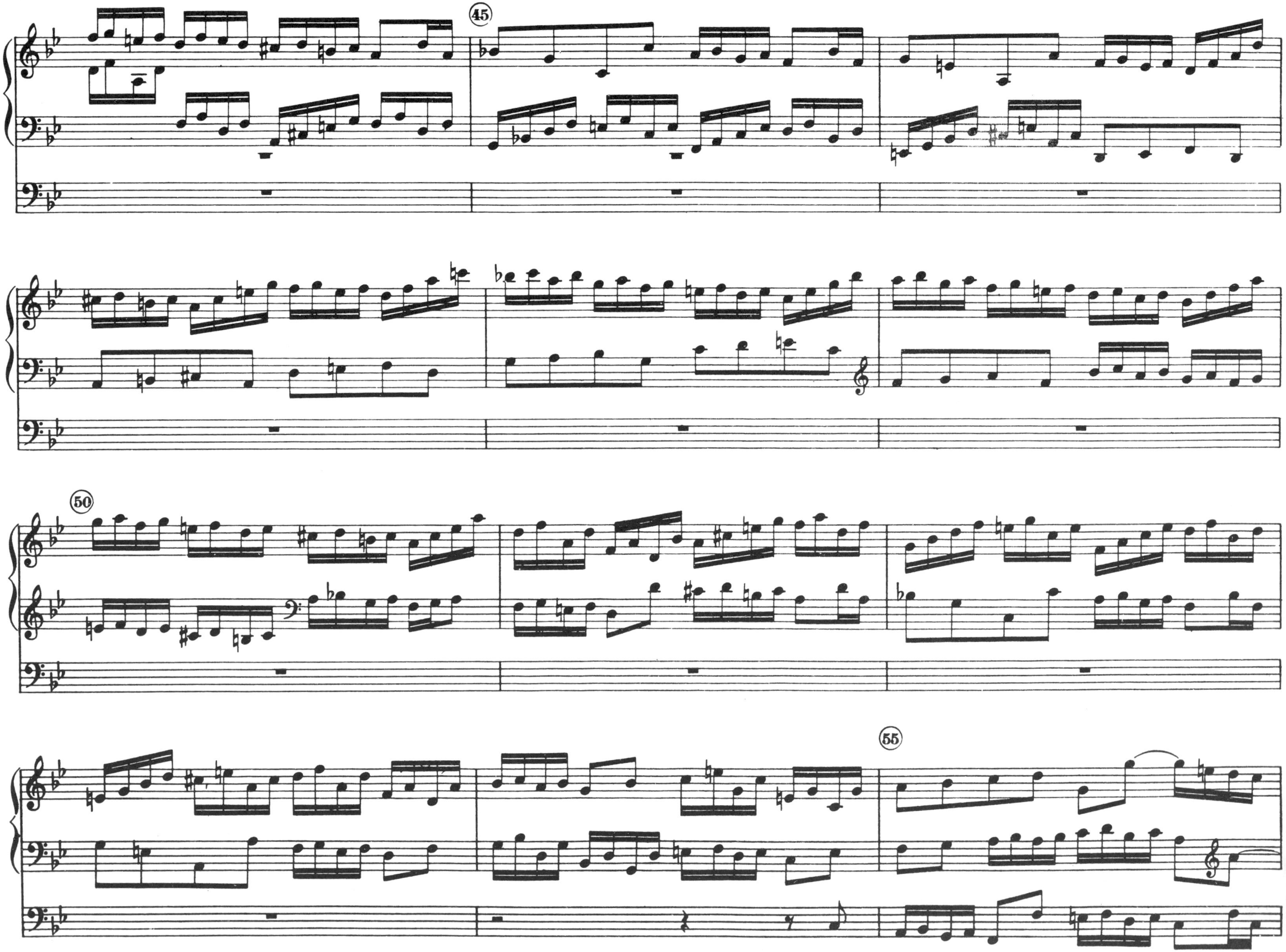
45
50
55

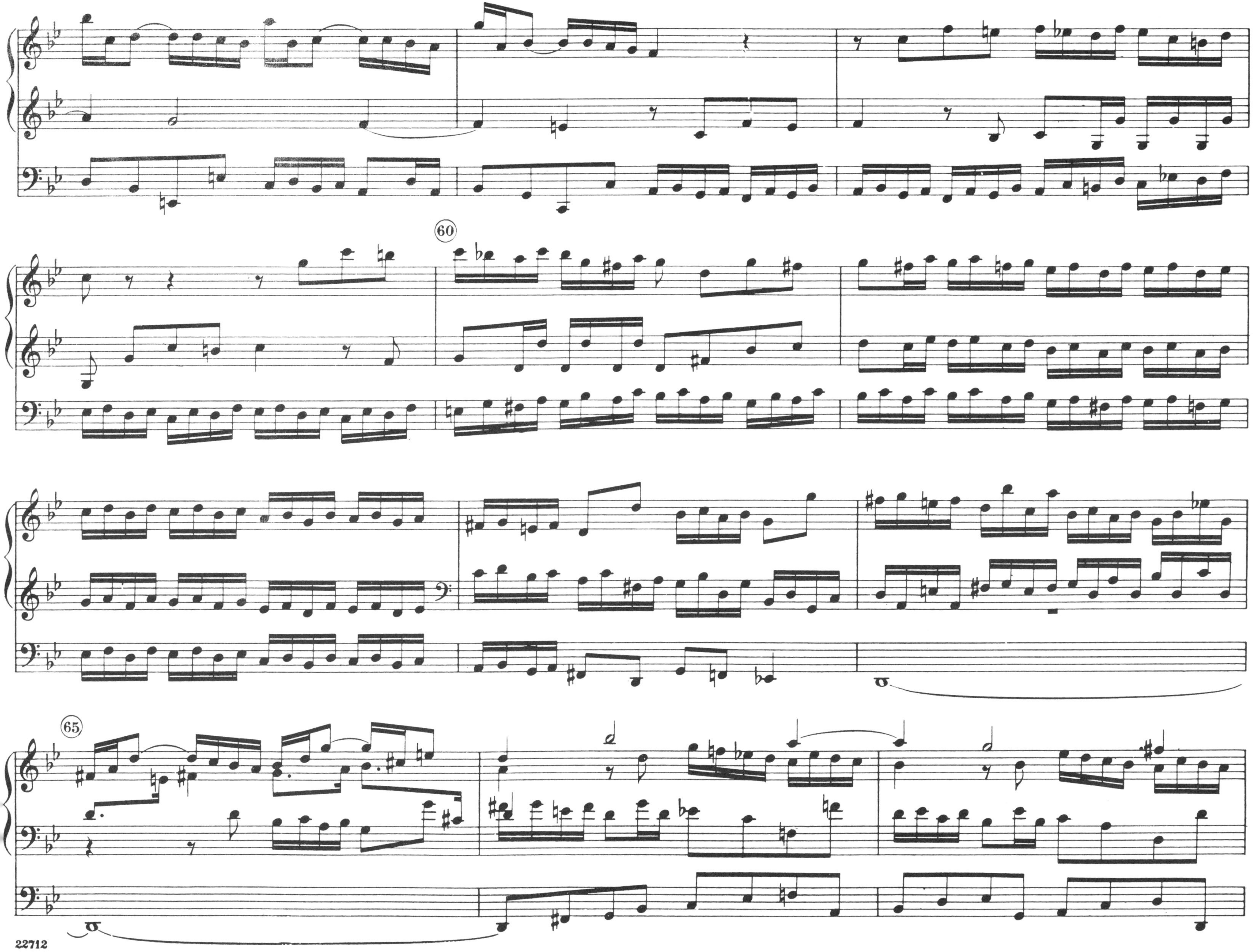
60
65

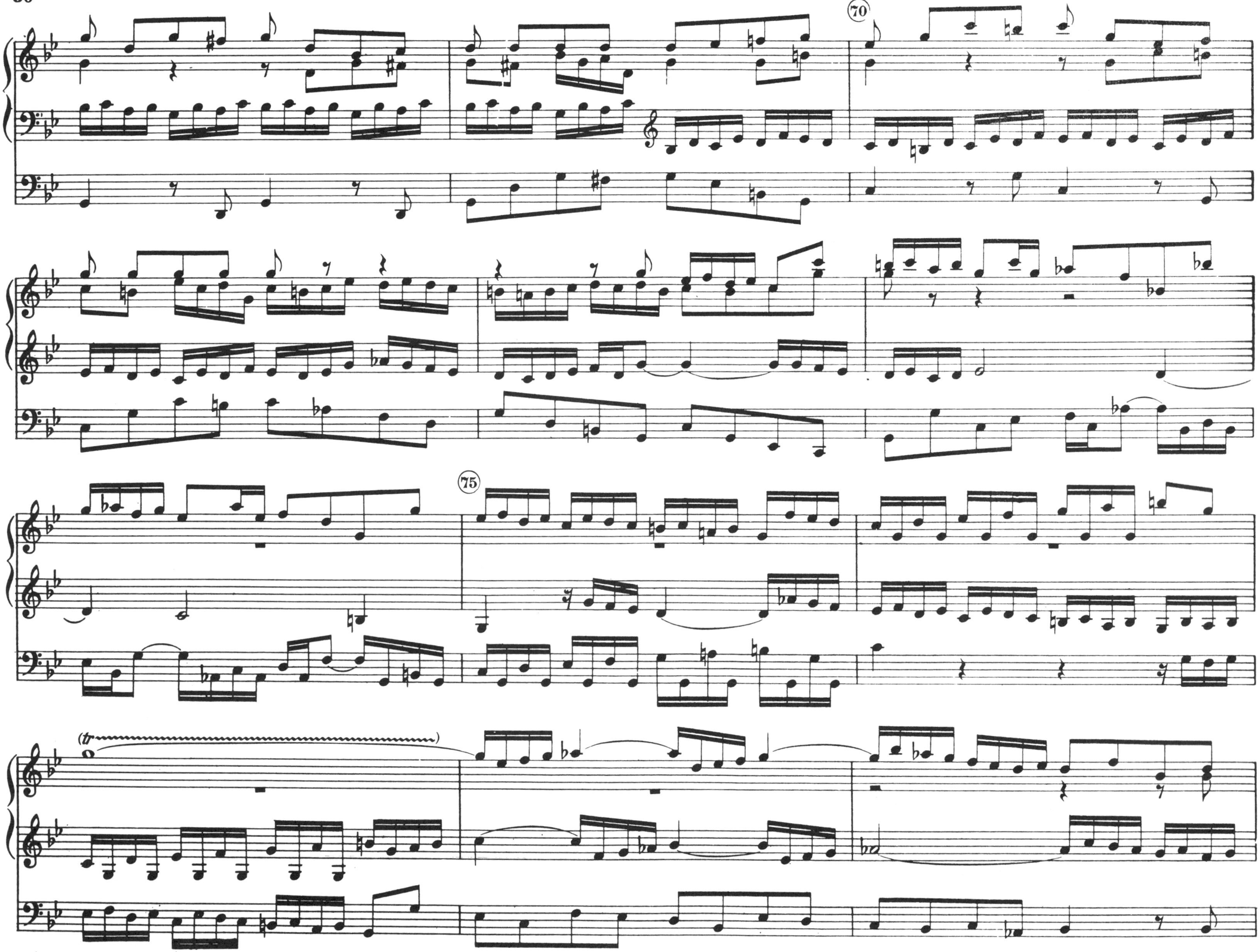
70
75
(tr

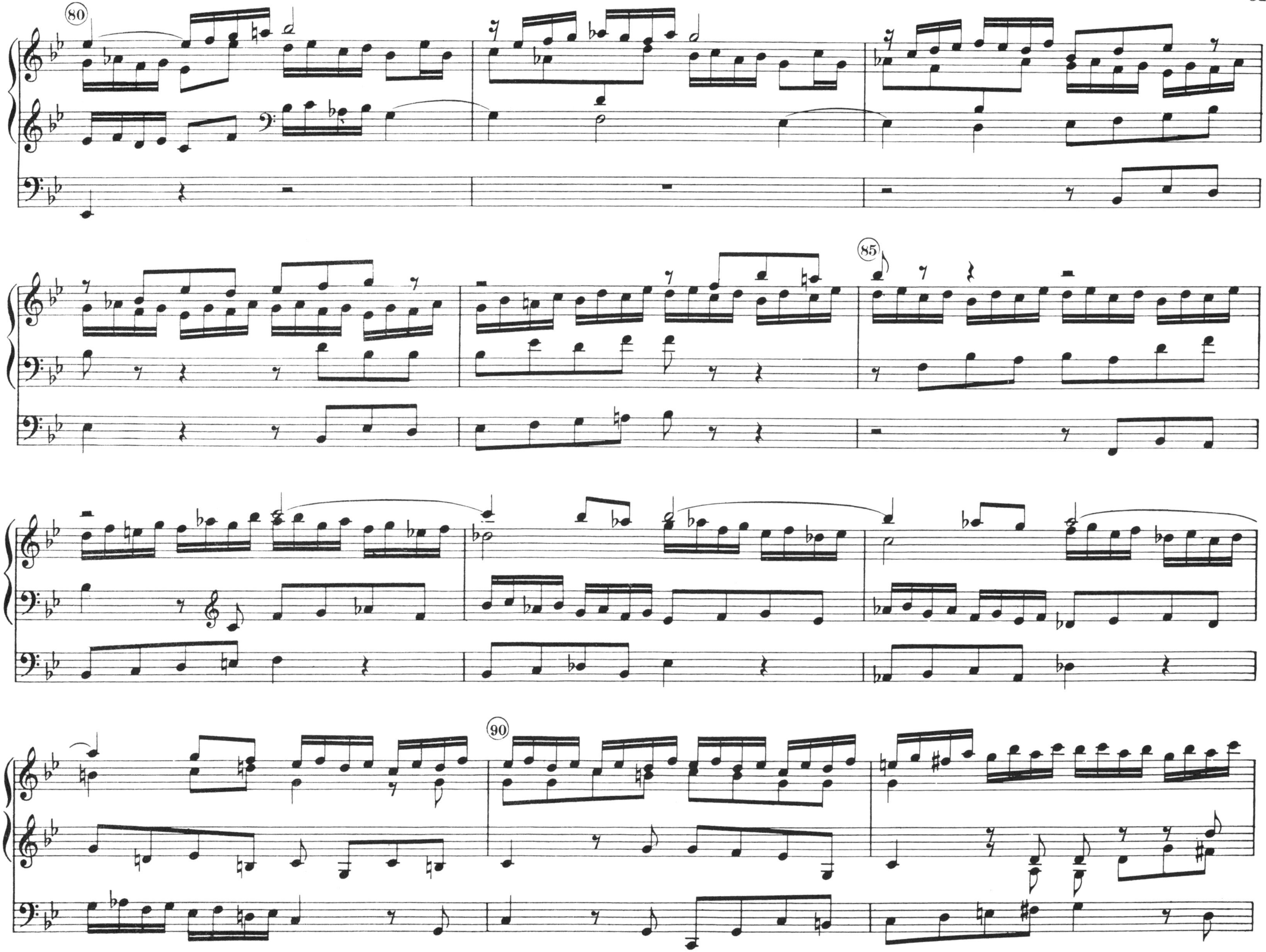
80
85
90

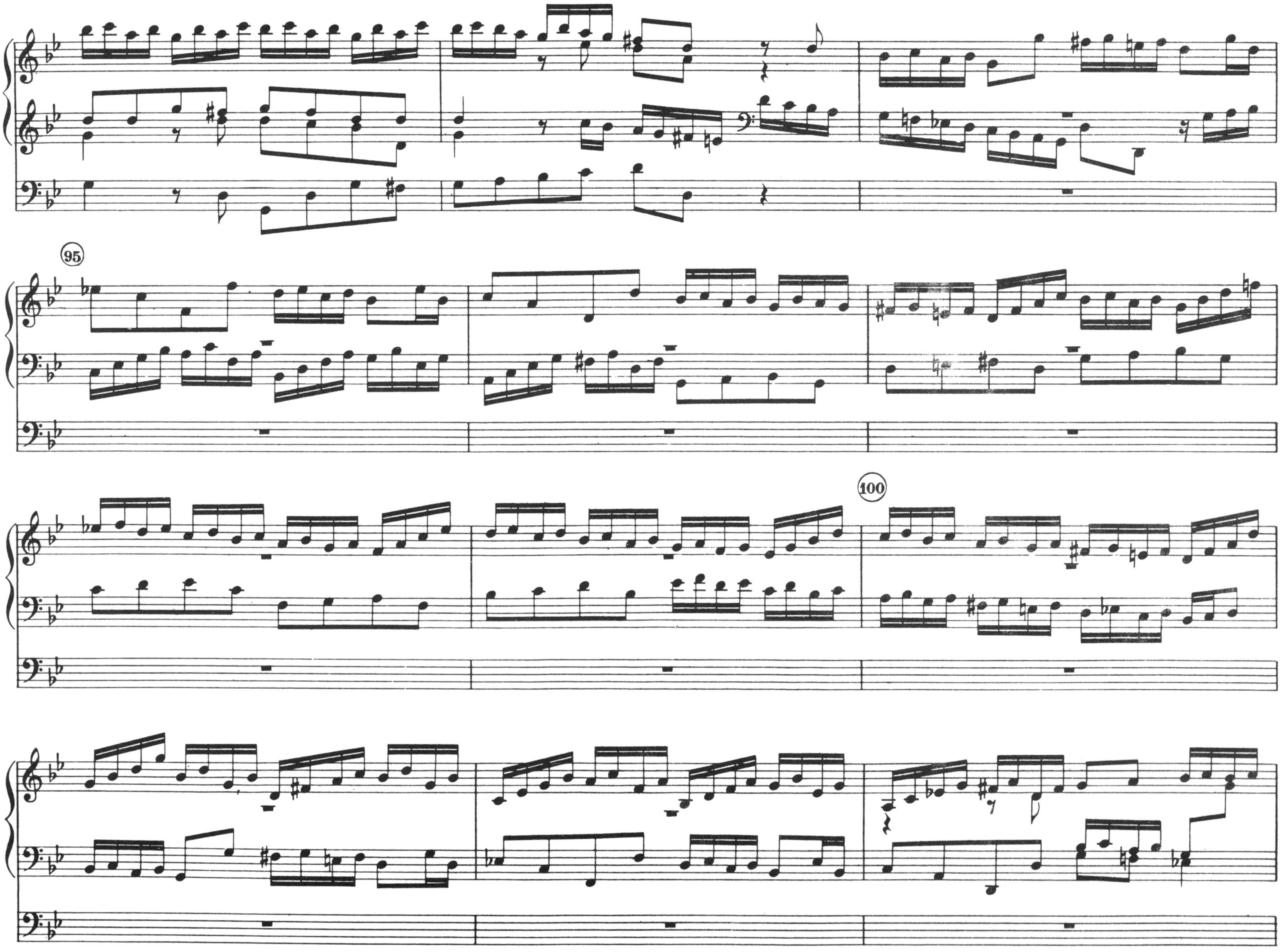
95
100

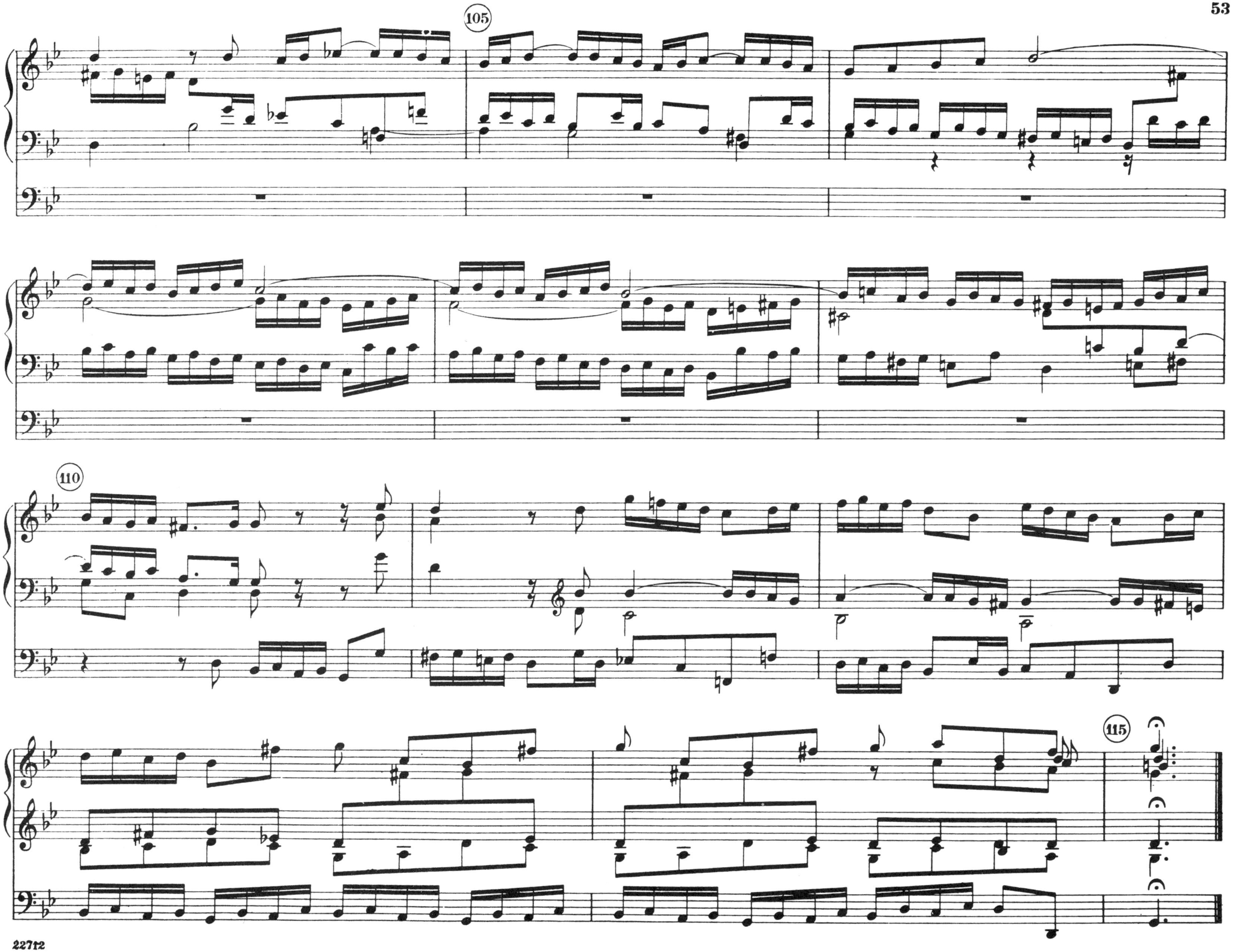
105
110
115

V
Praeludium und Fuge in A-Dur

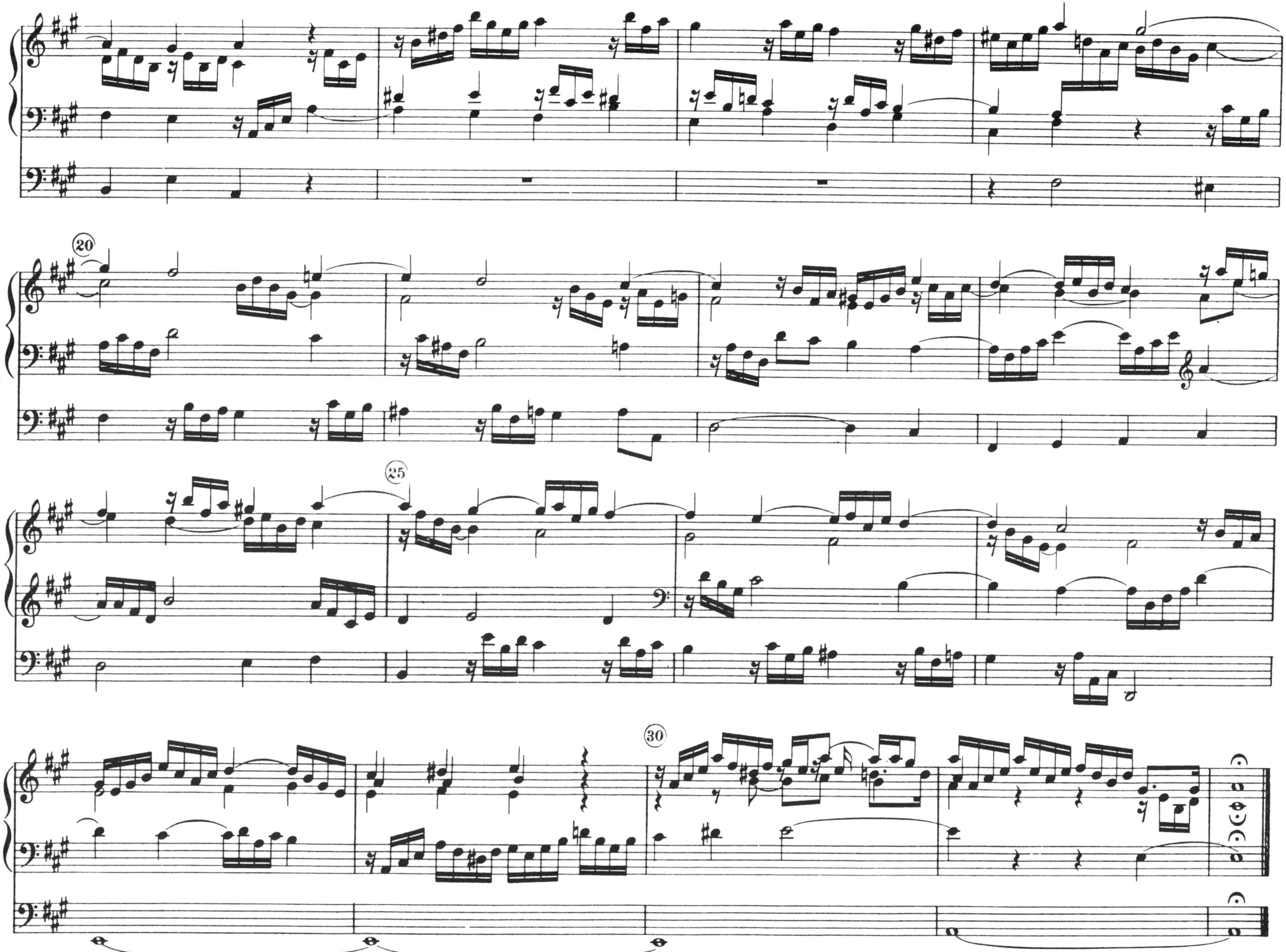
20
25
30

Fuge

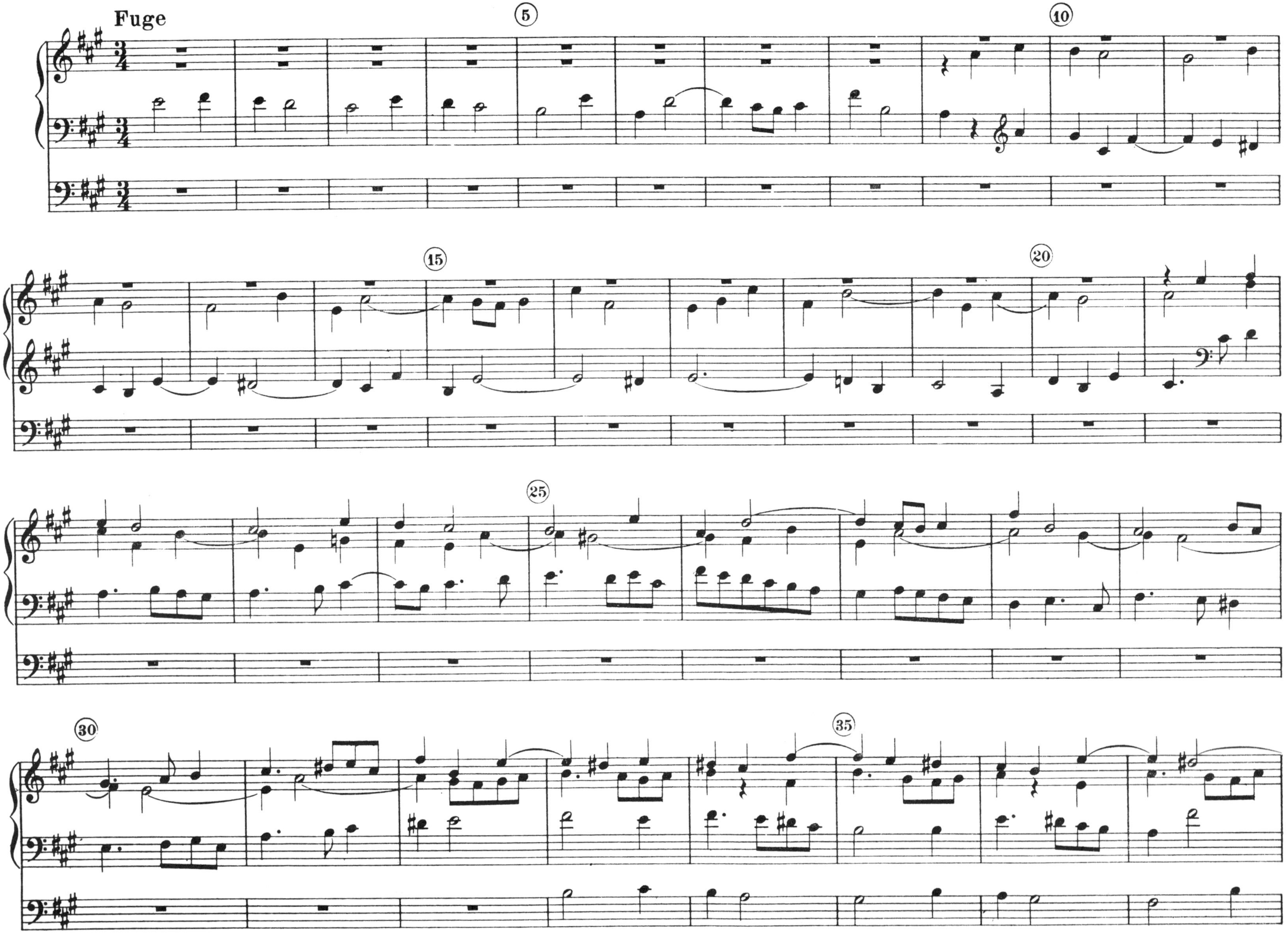

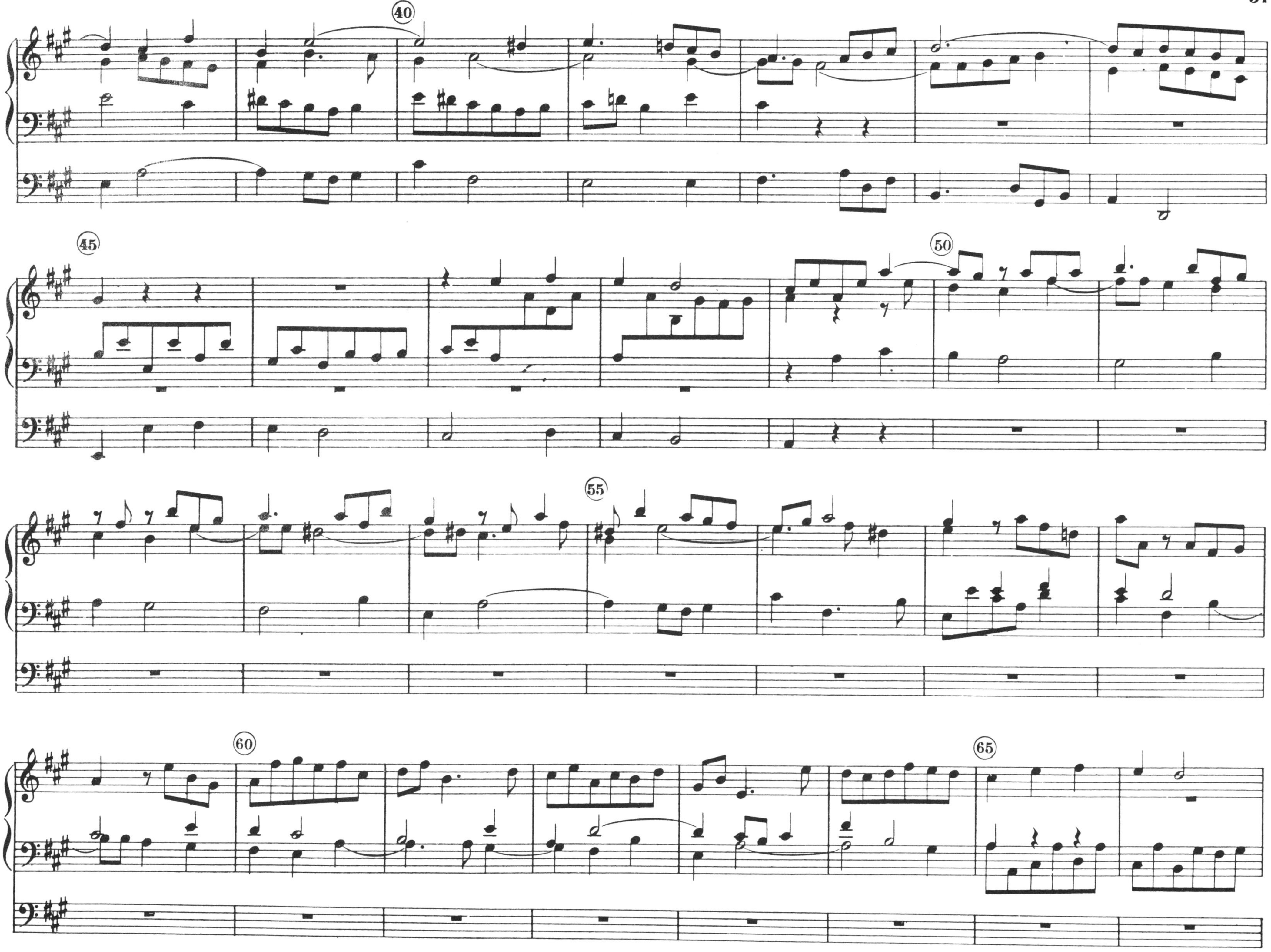
40
45
50
55
60
65

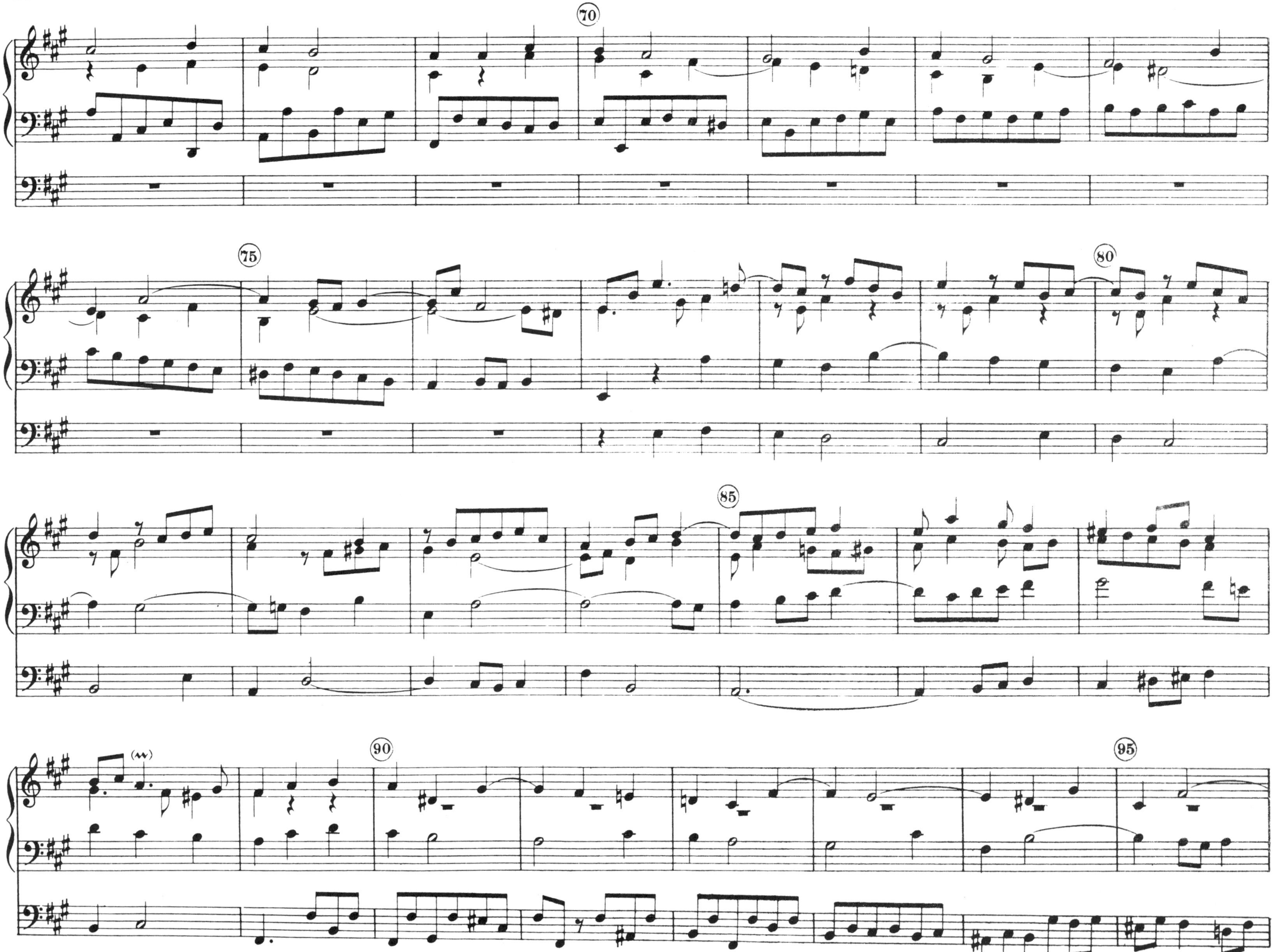
70
75
80
85
90
95

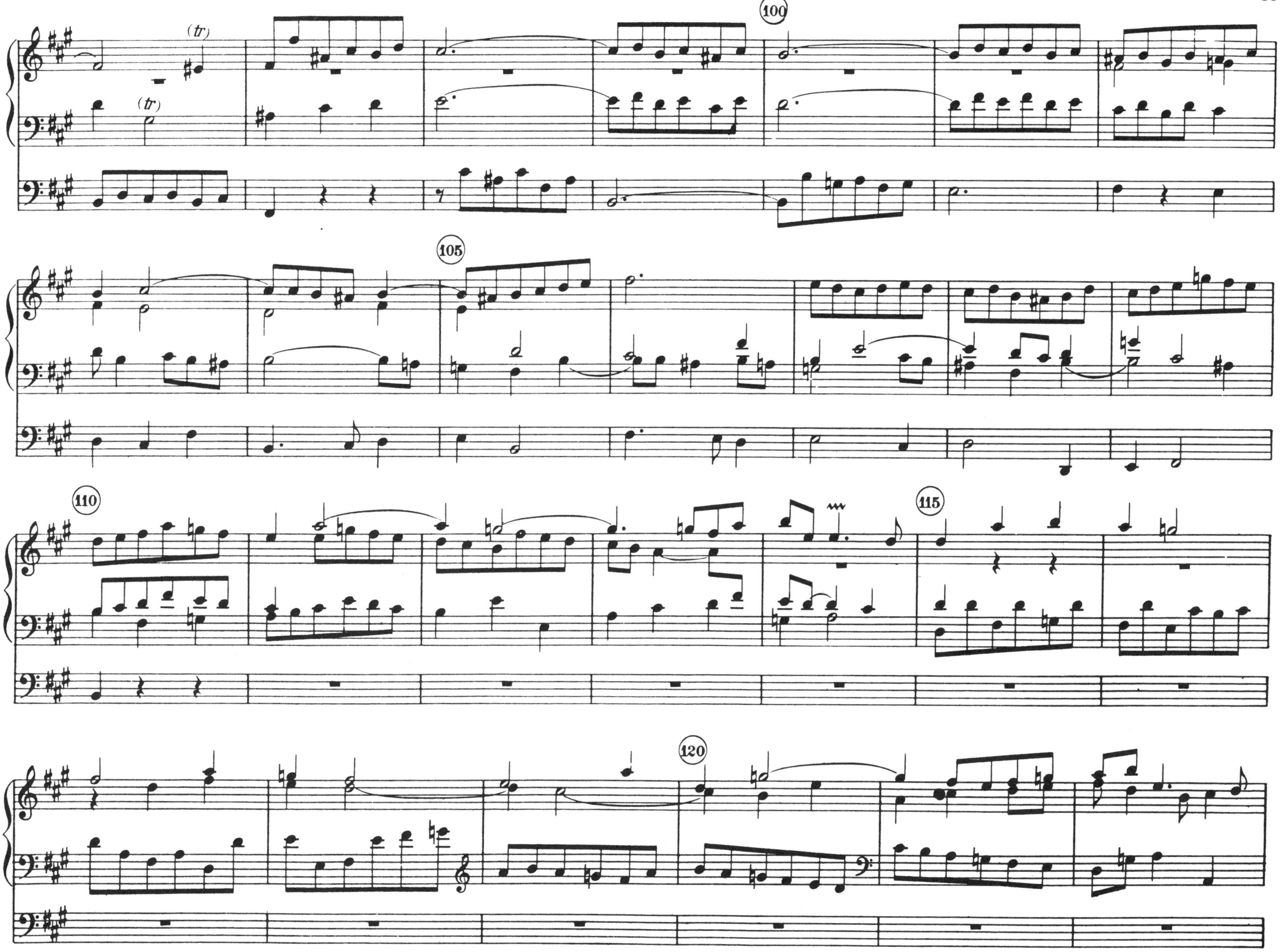
(tr)
(tr)
100
105
110
115
120

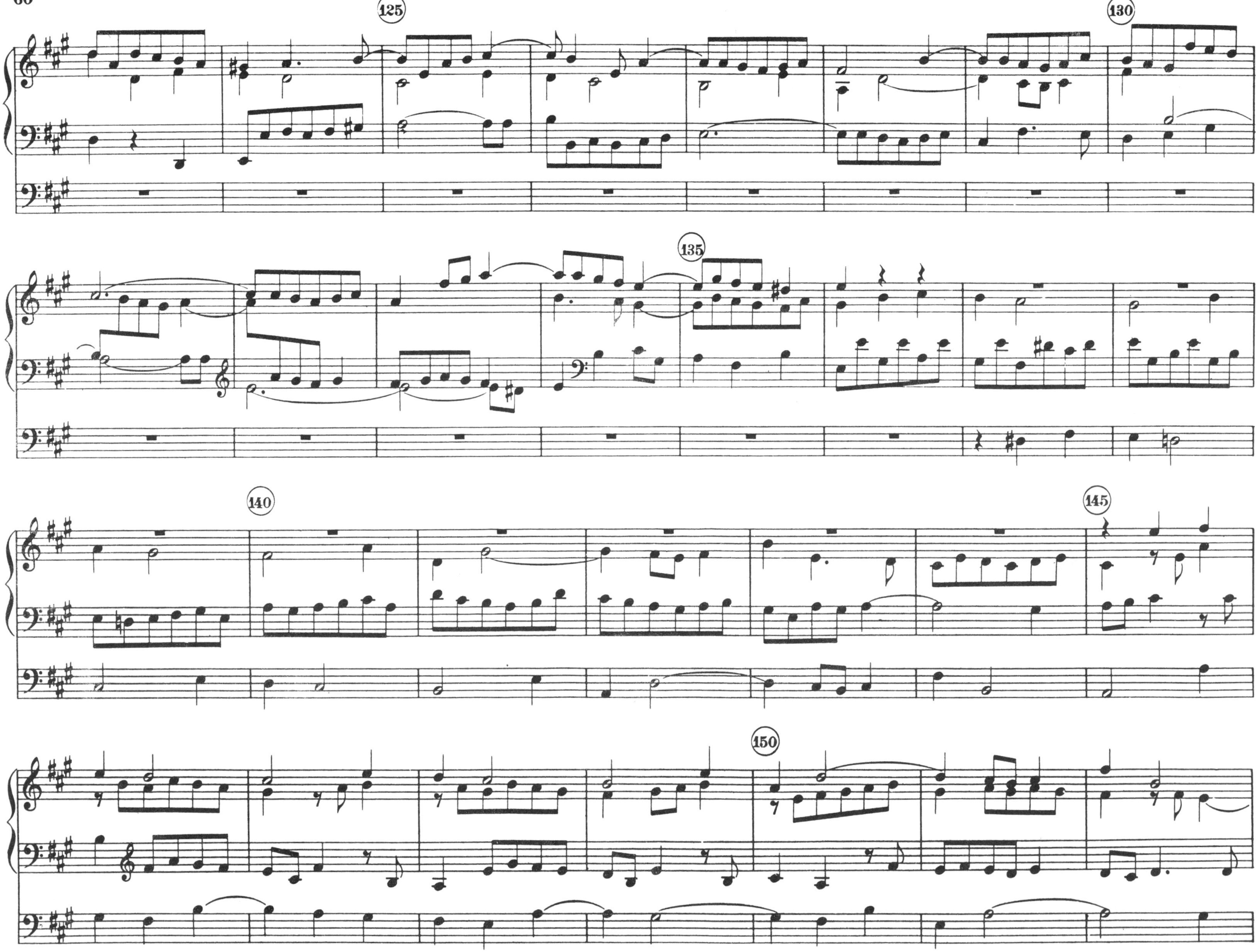
125
130
135
140
145
150

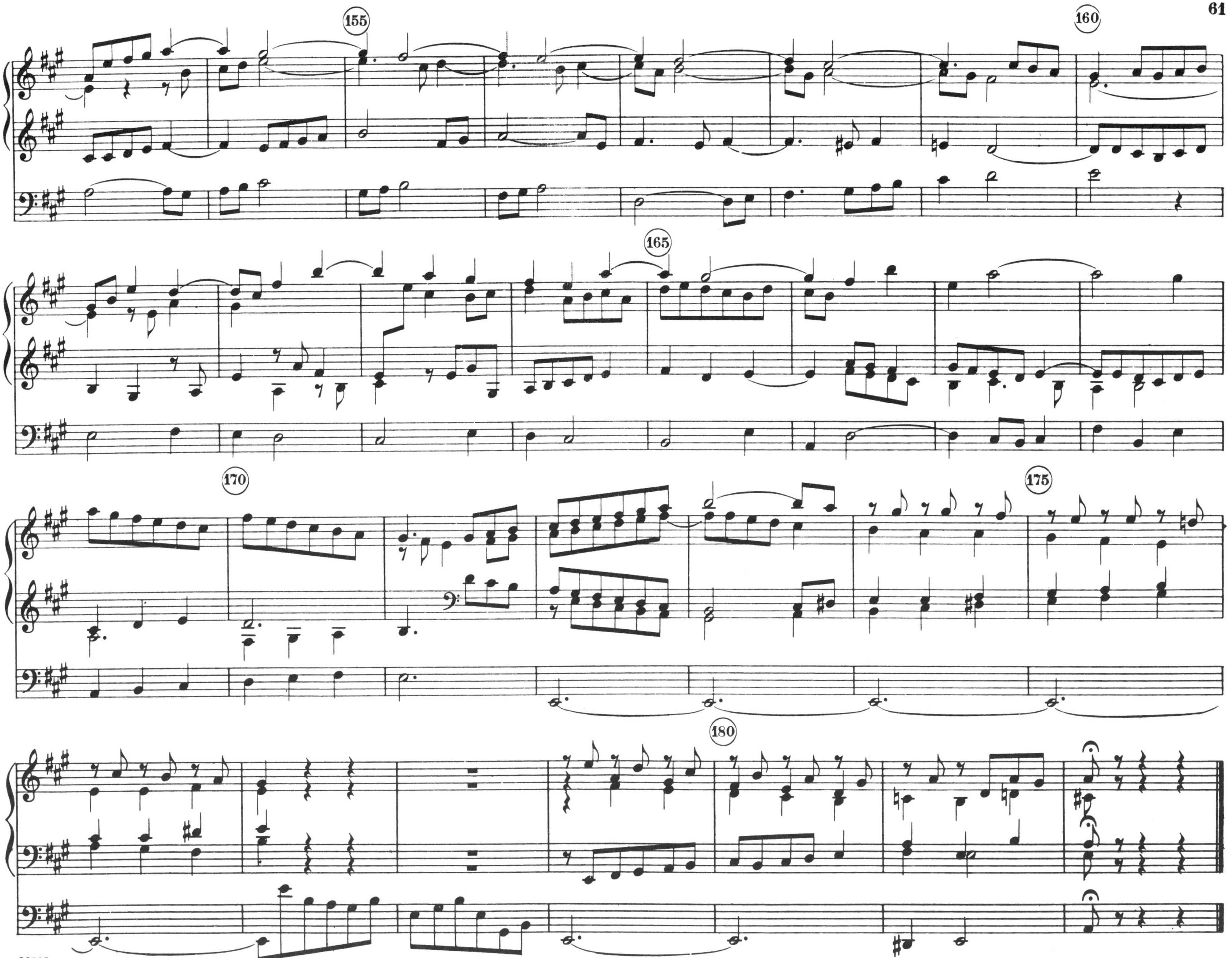
155
160
165
170
175
180

VI
Praeludium und Fuge in A-Moll

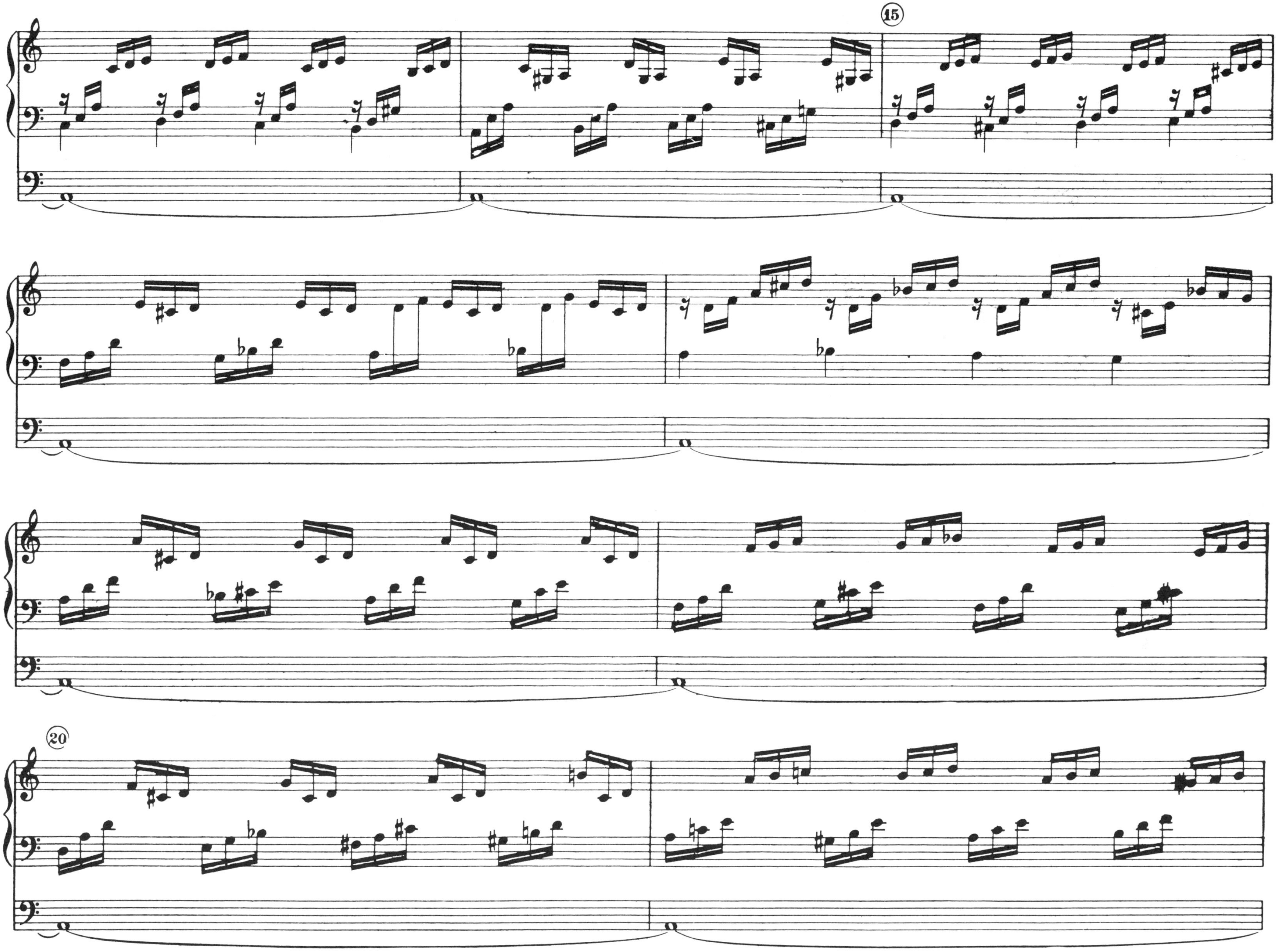
15
20

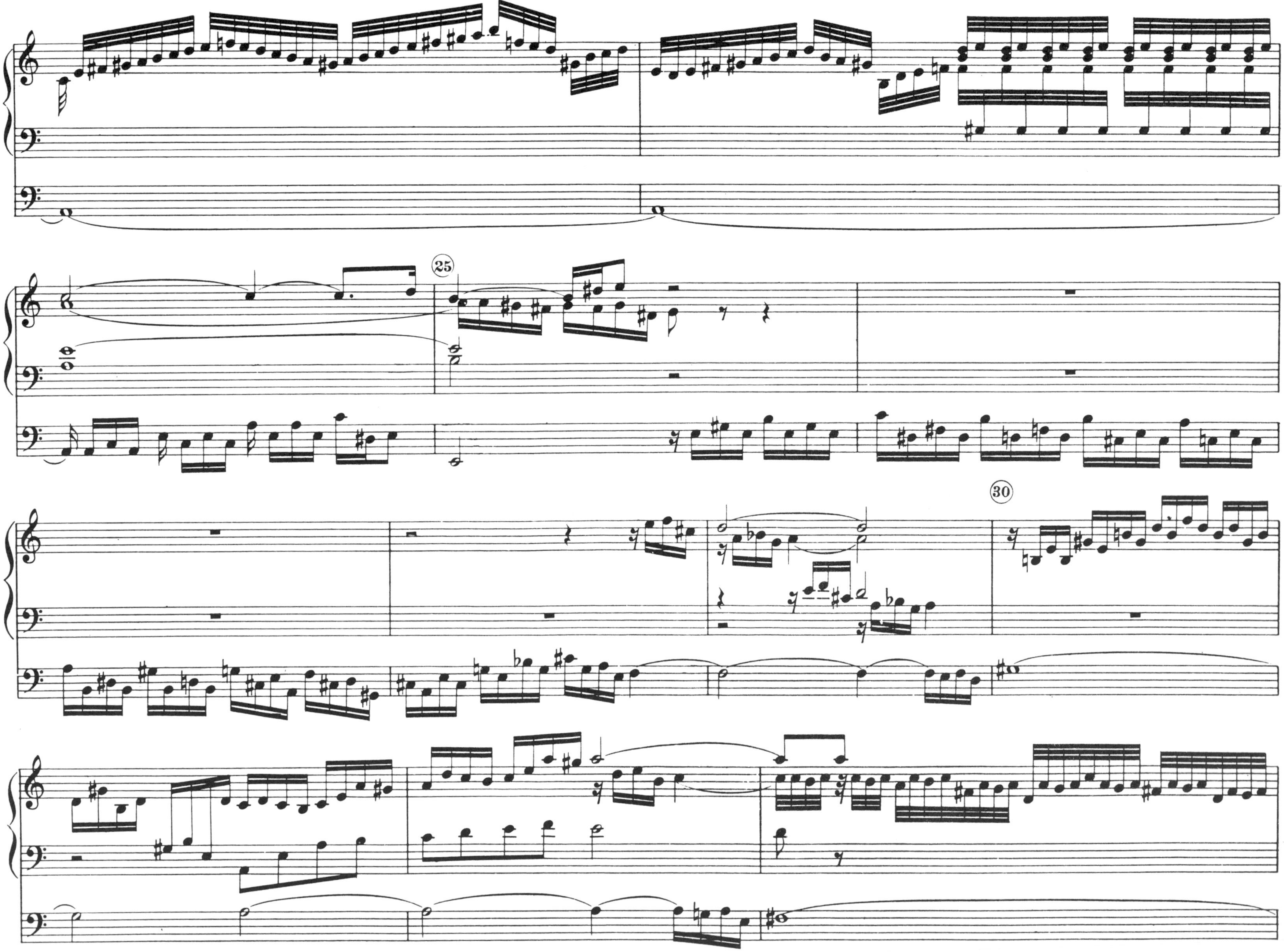
25
30

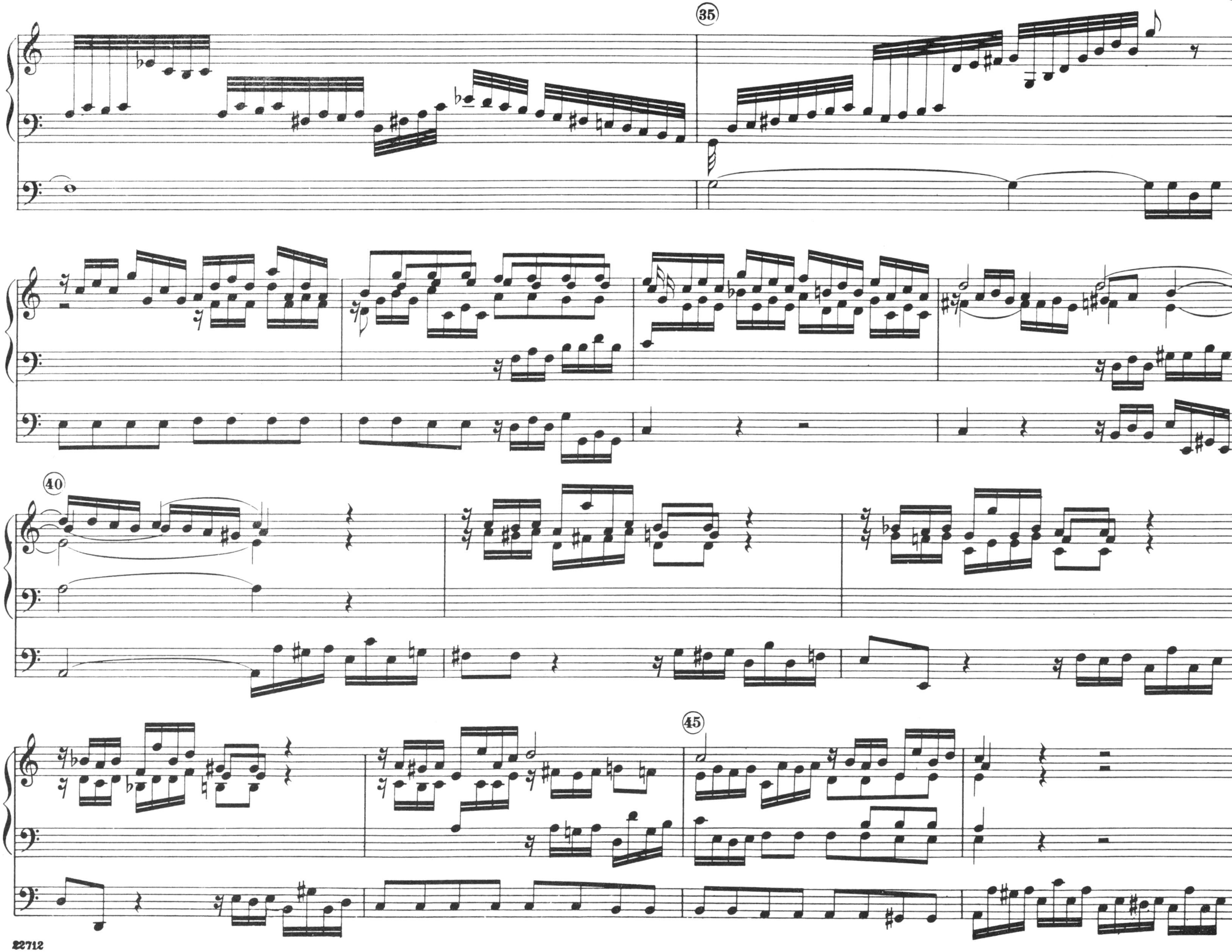
35
40
45

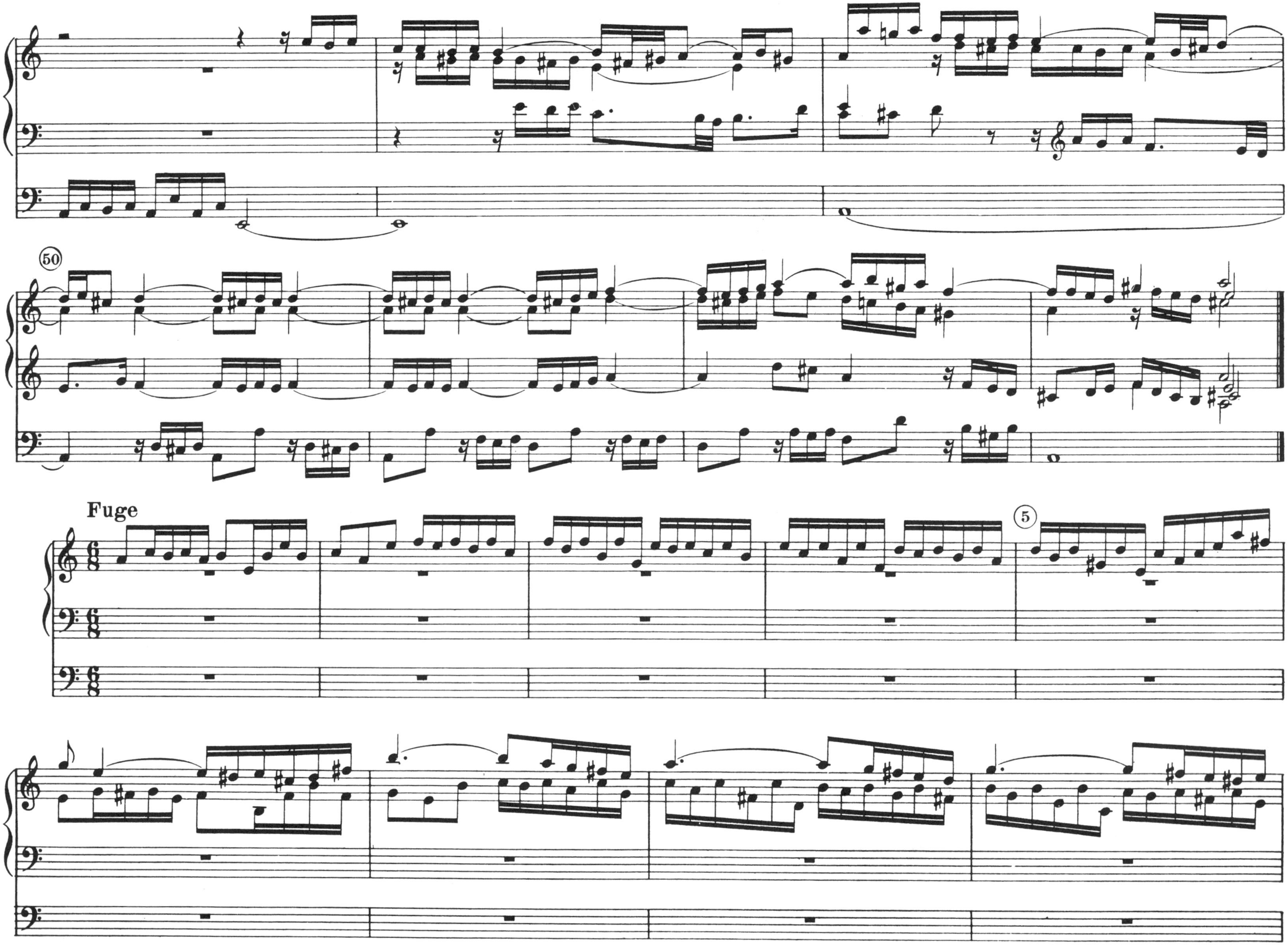
50
Fuge
5

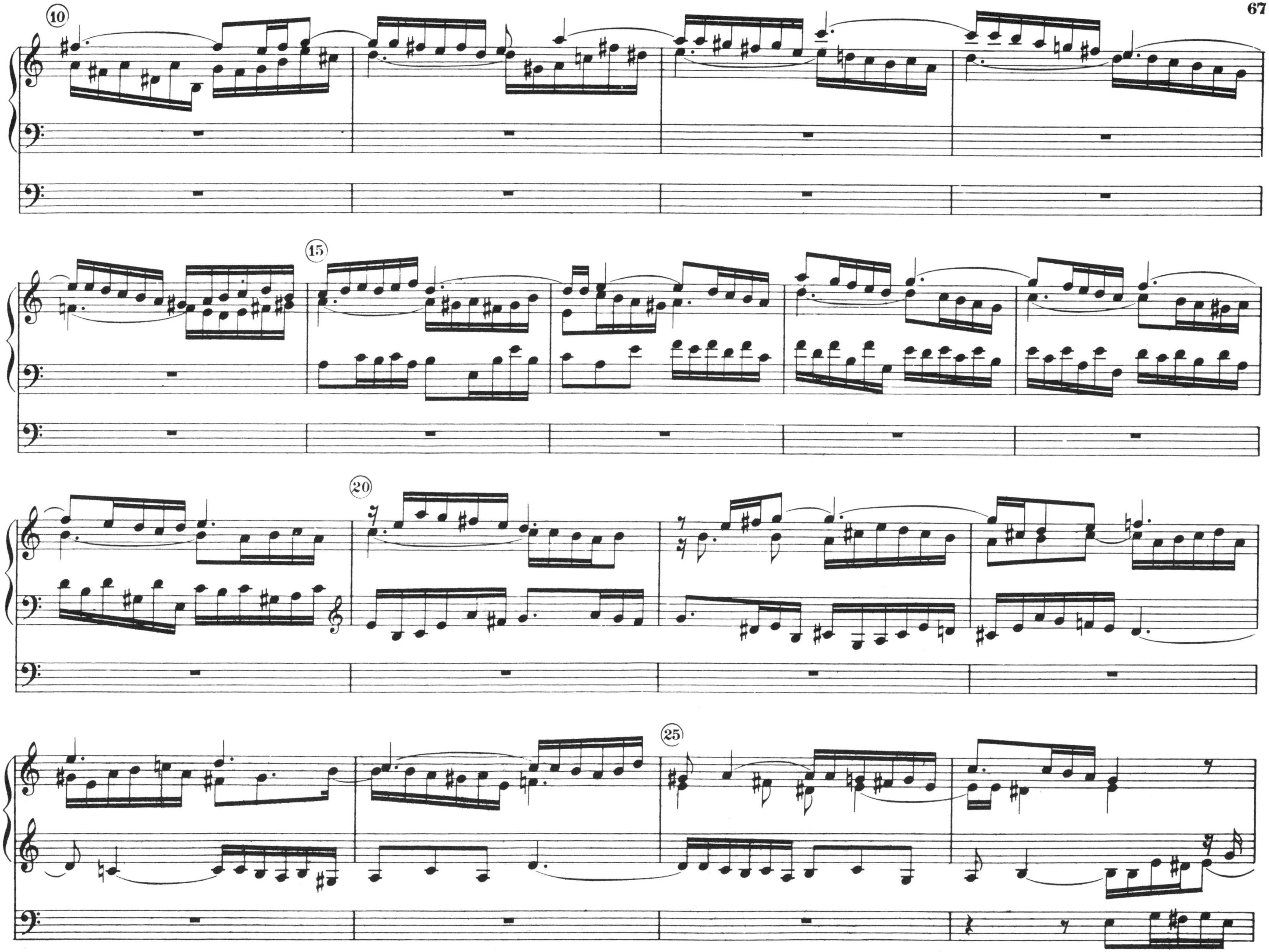
10
15
20
25

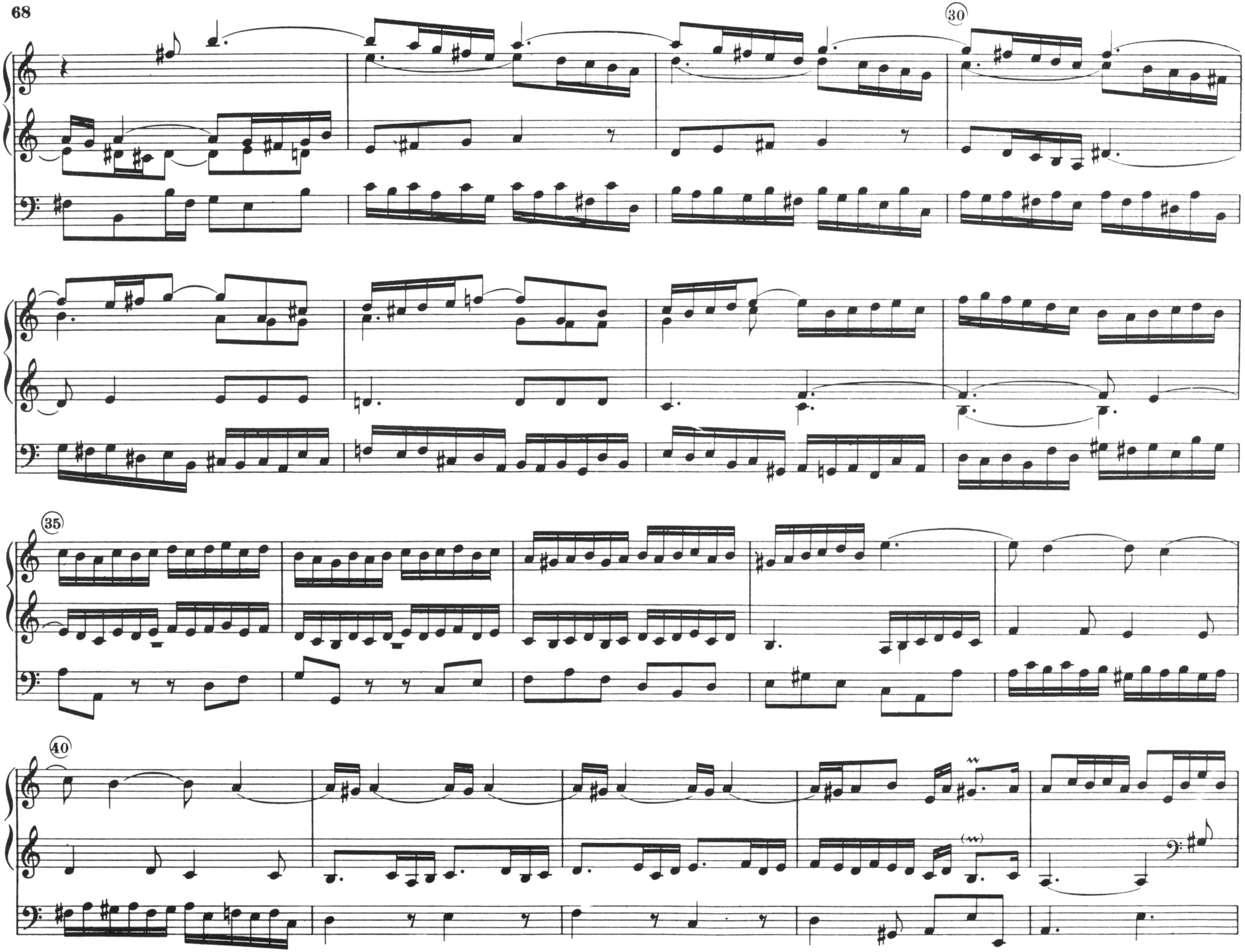
30
35
40

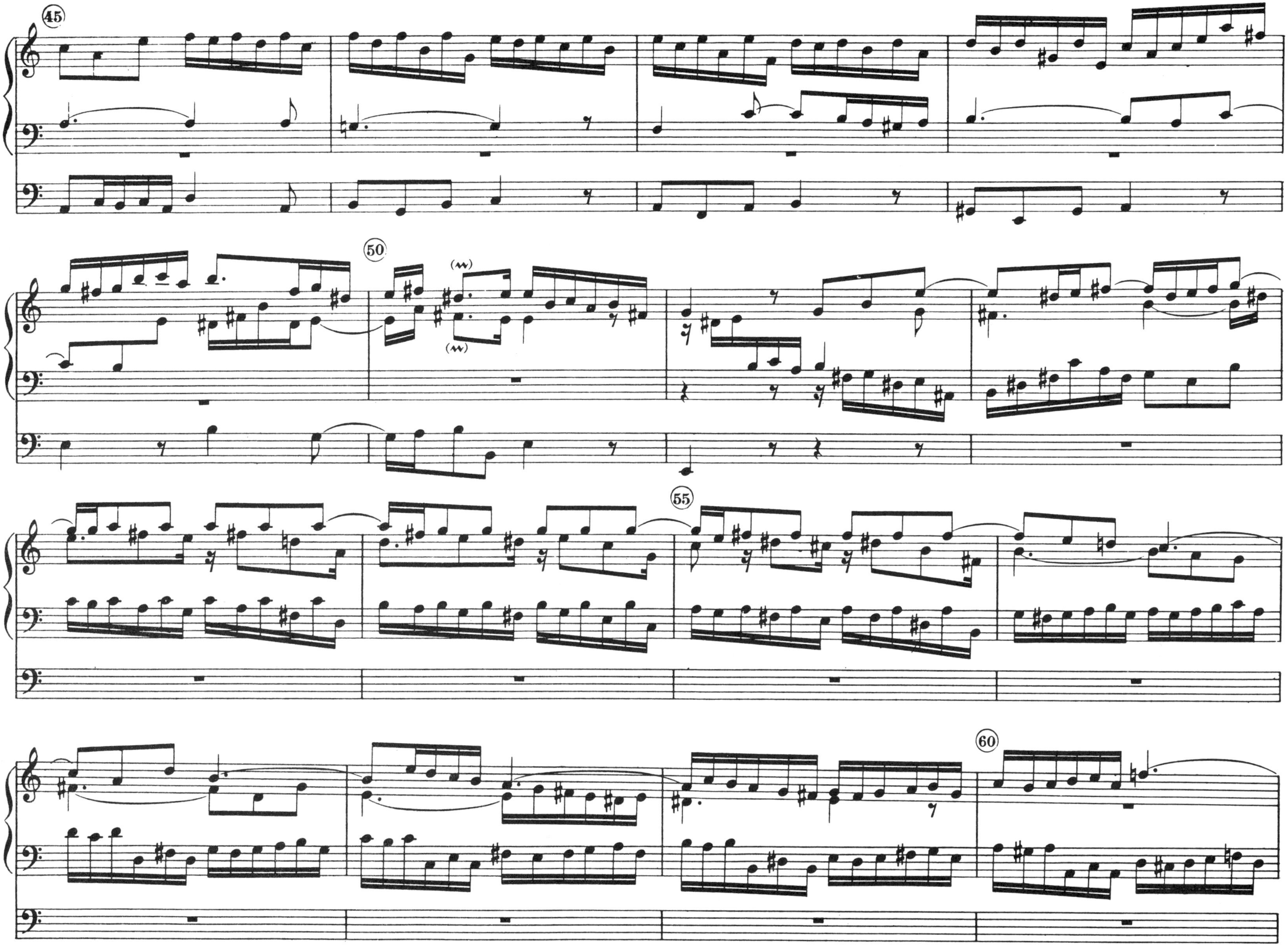
45
50
(w)
(w)
55
60

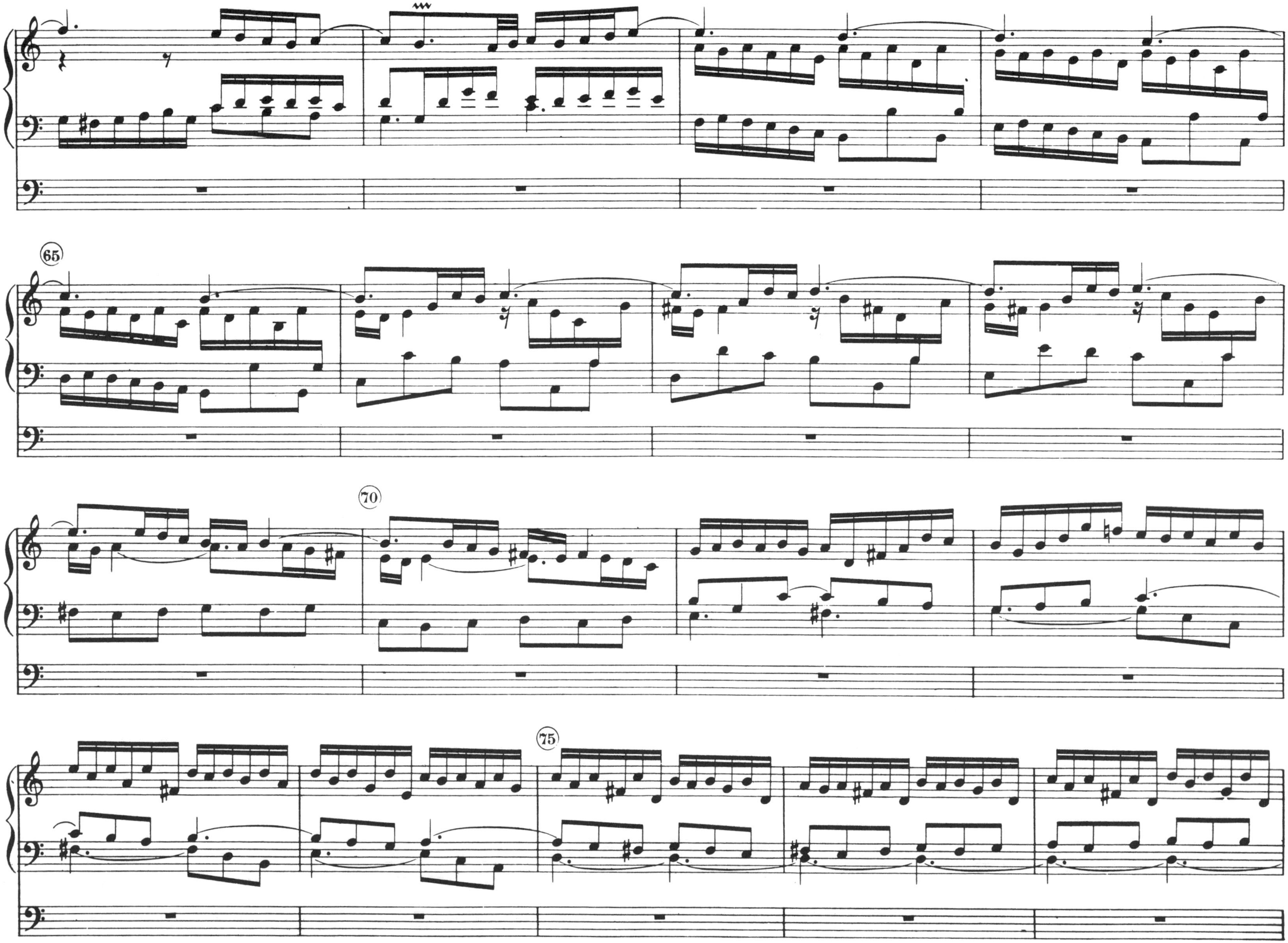
65
70
75

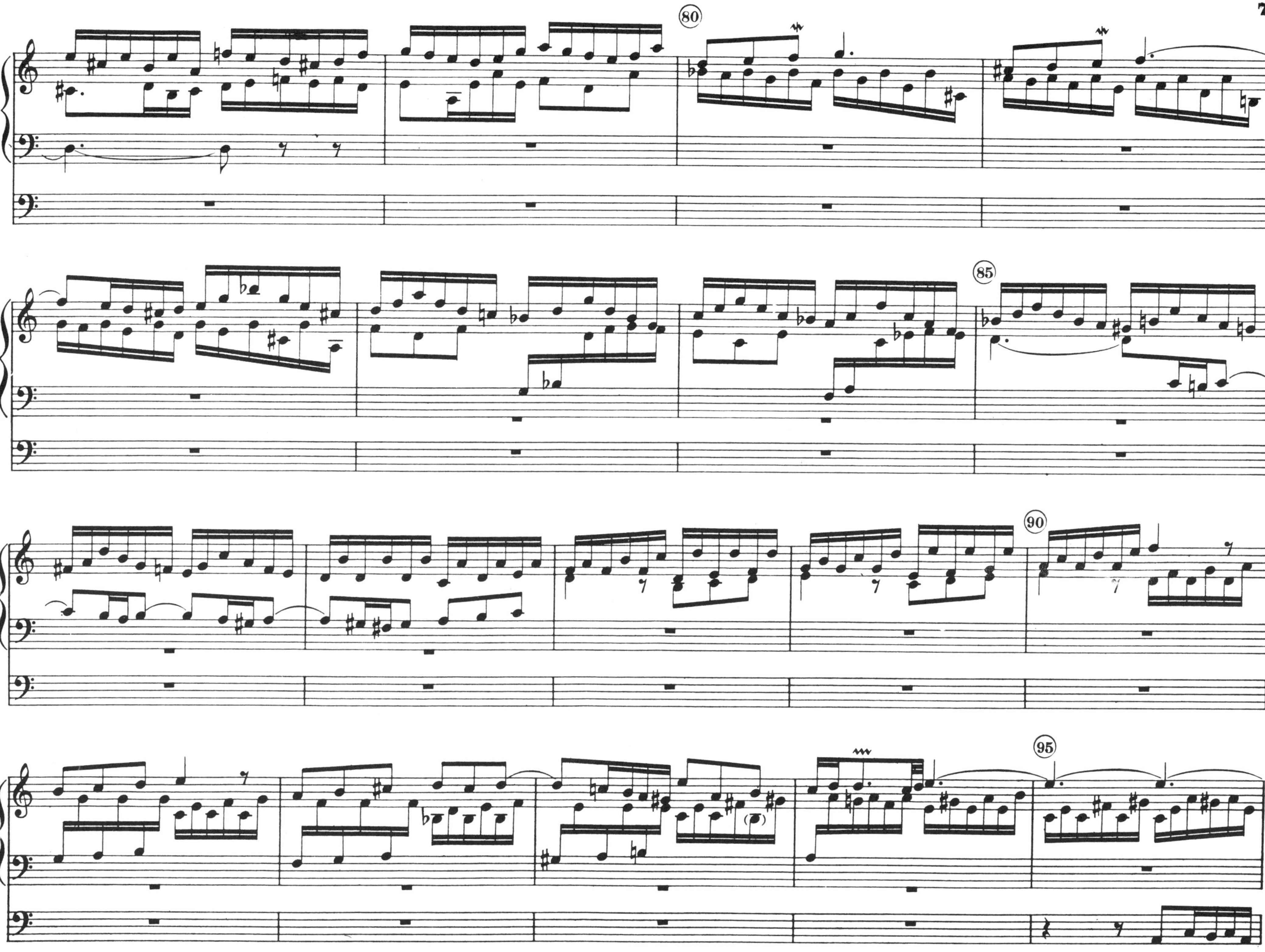
80
85
90
95

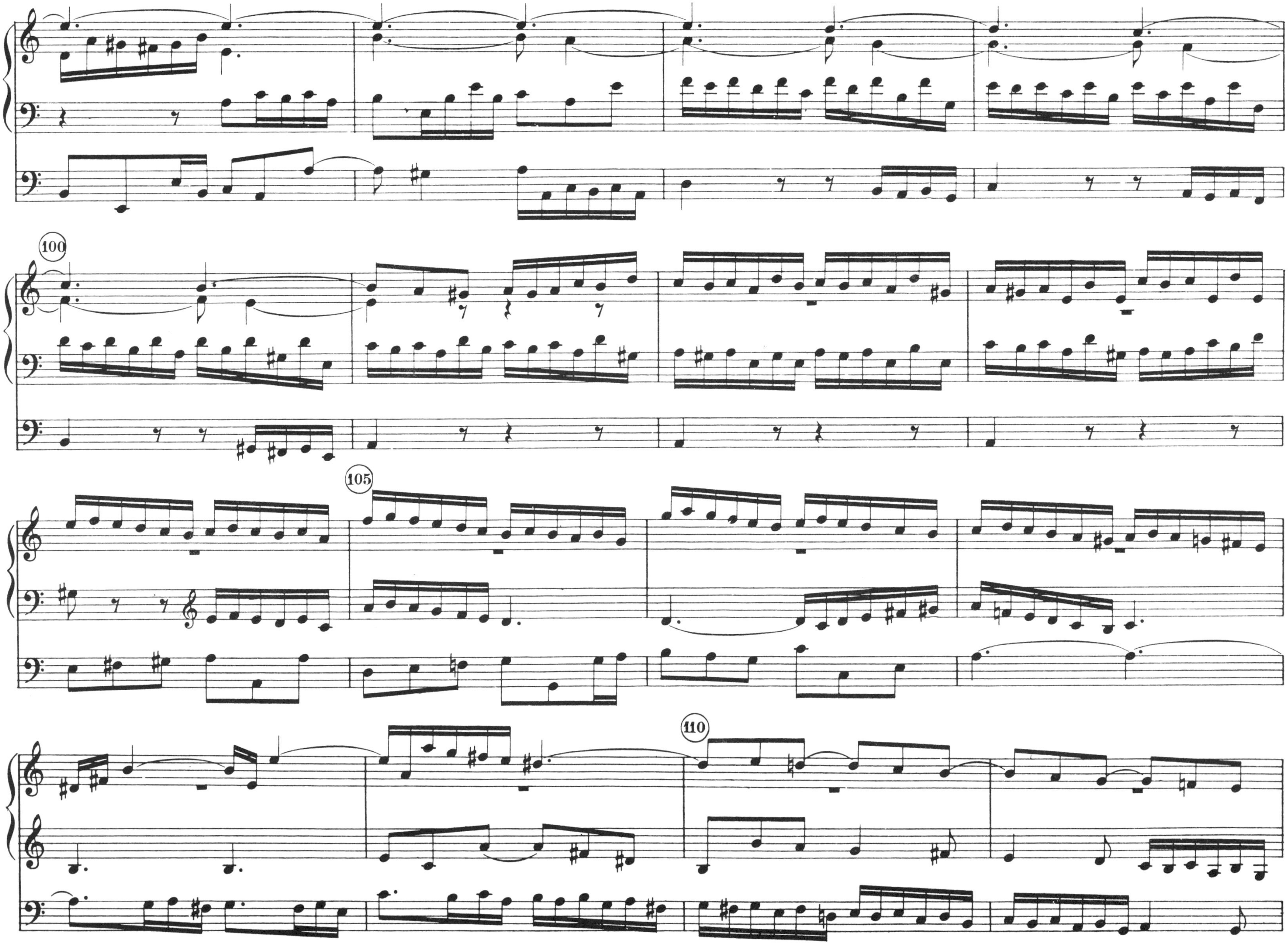
100
105
110

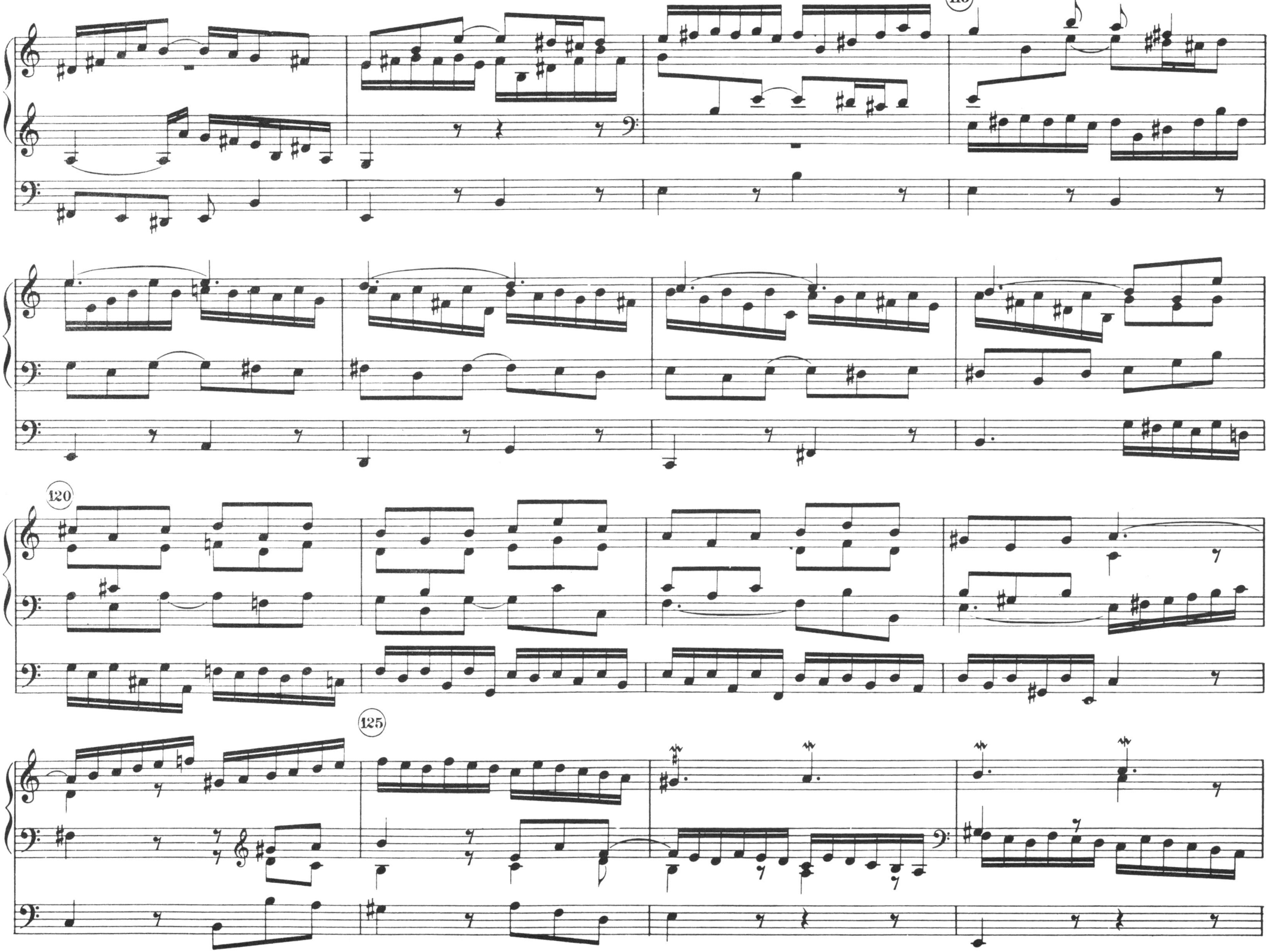
115
120
125

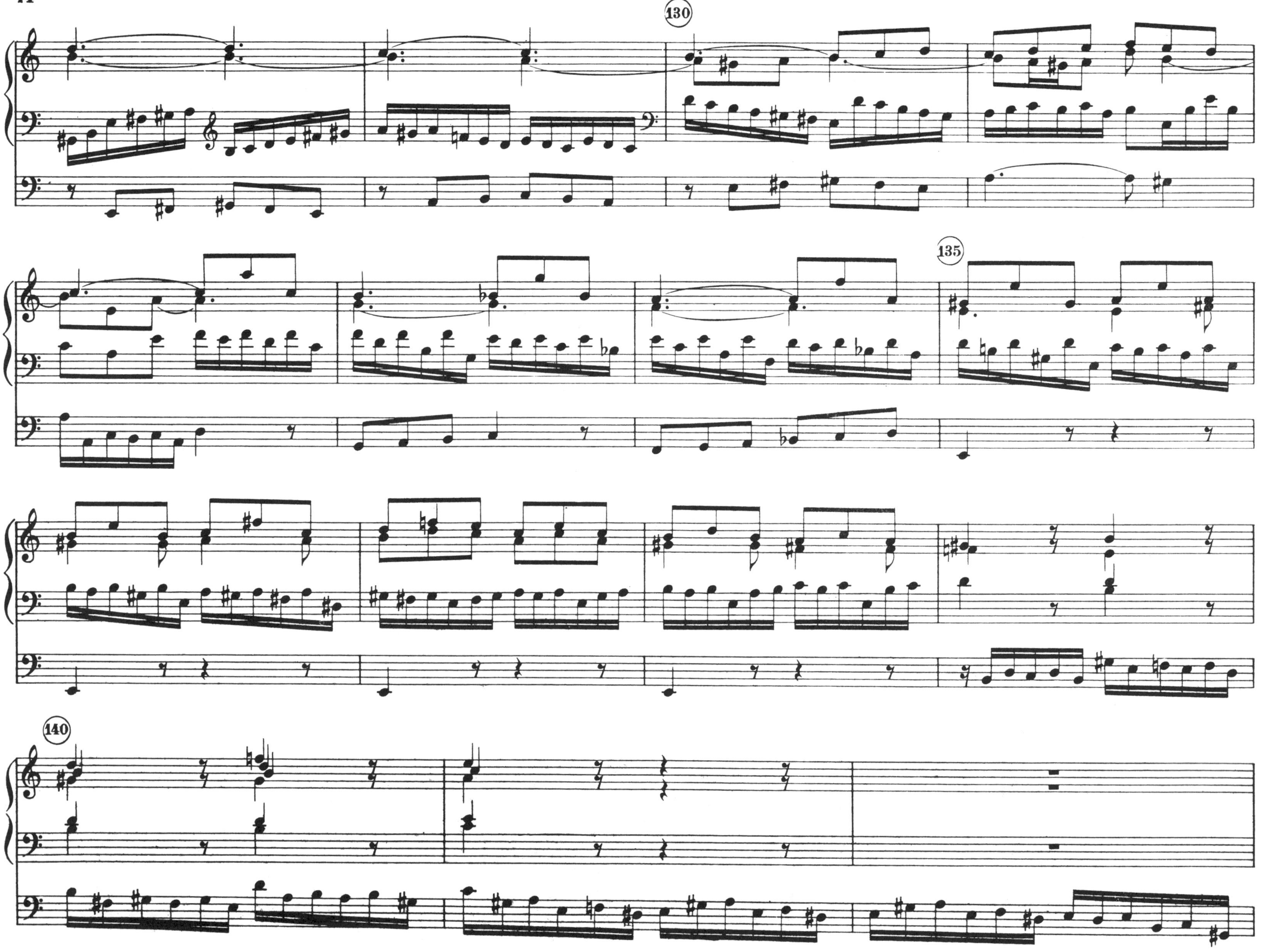
130
135
140

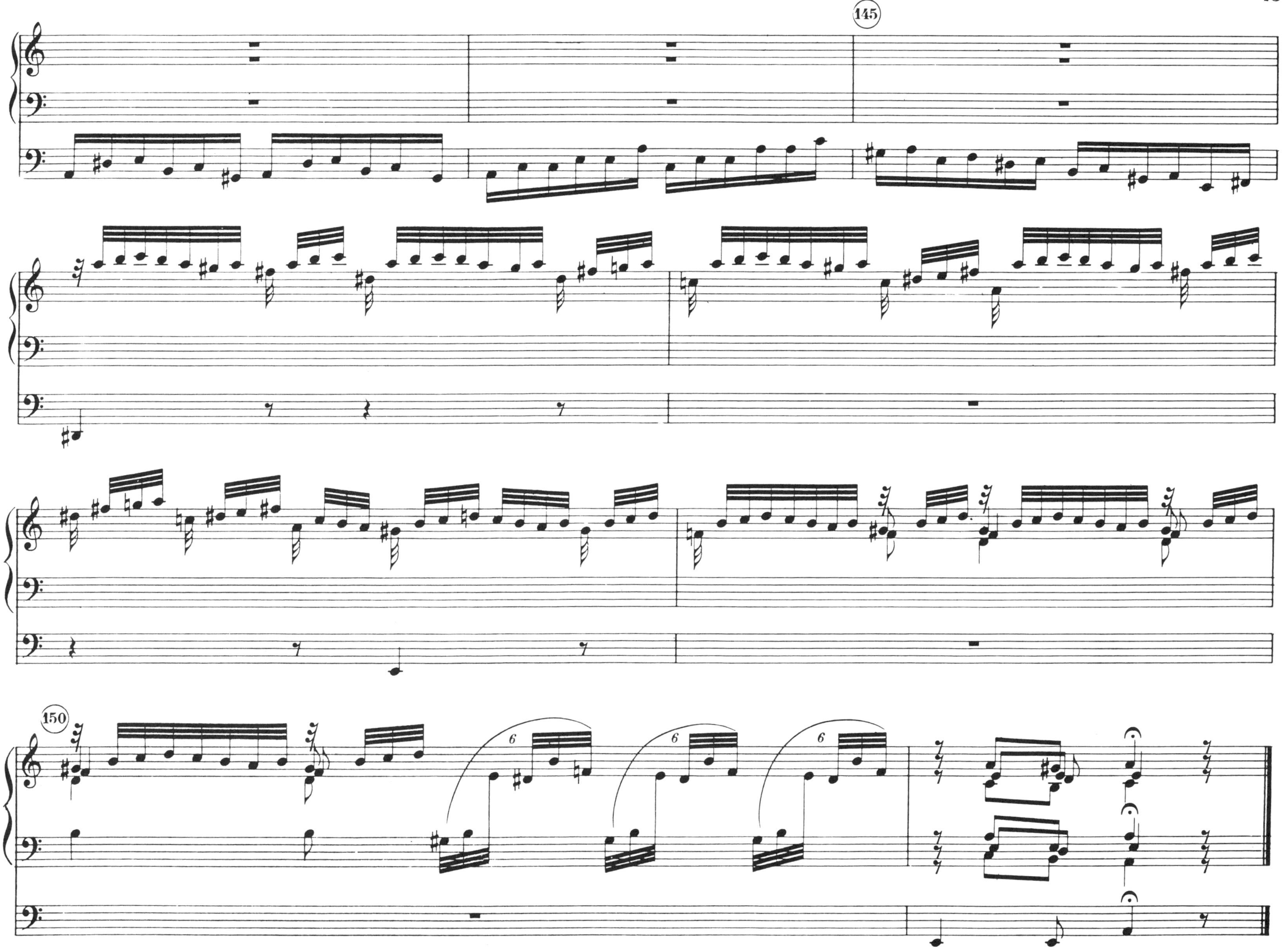
145
6
6
6
150

VII
Praeludium und Fuge in H-Moll

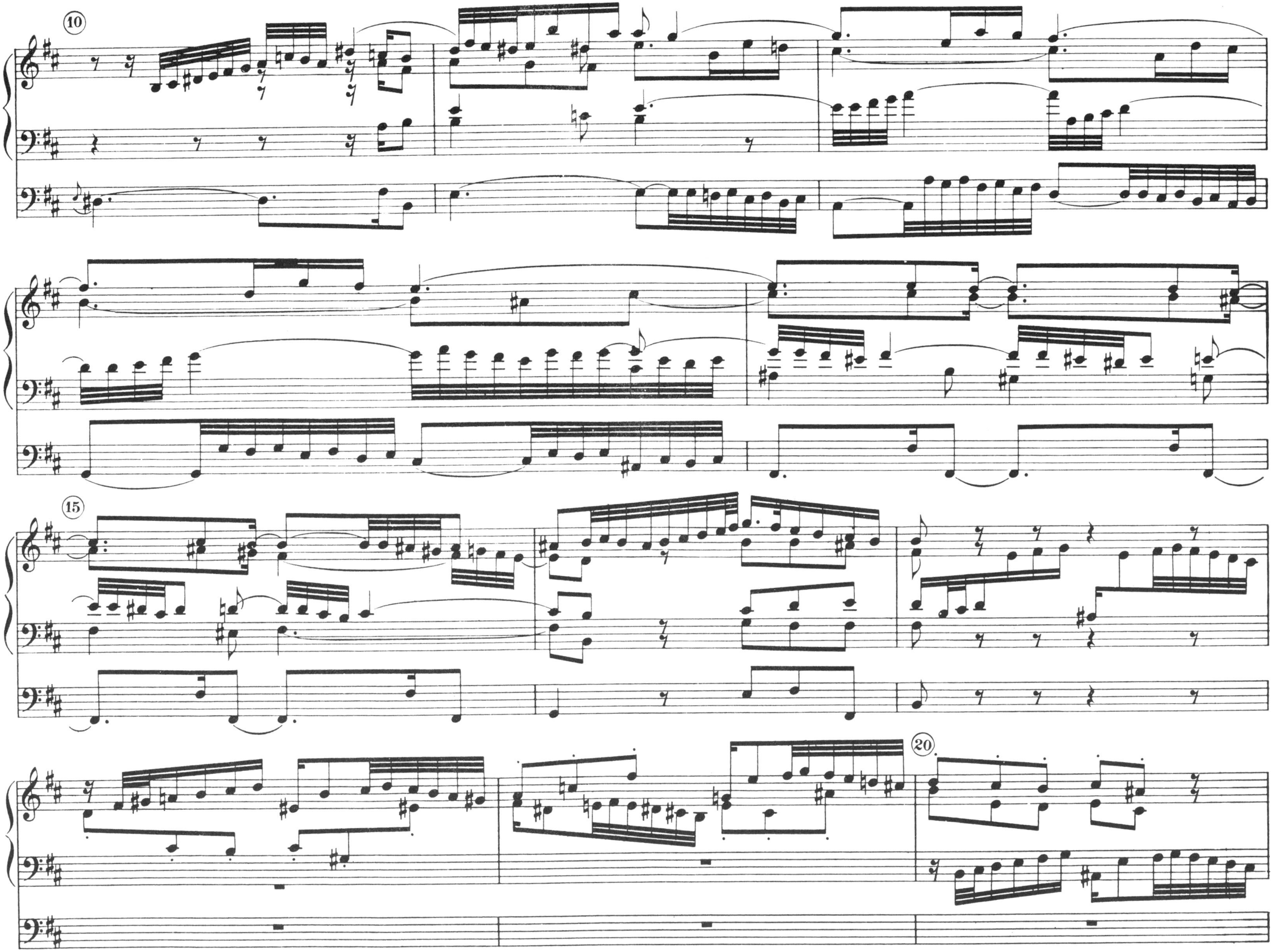
10
15
20

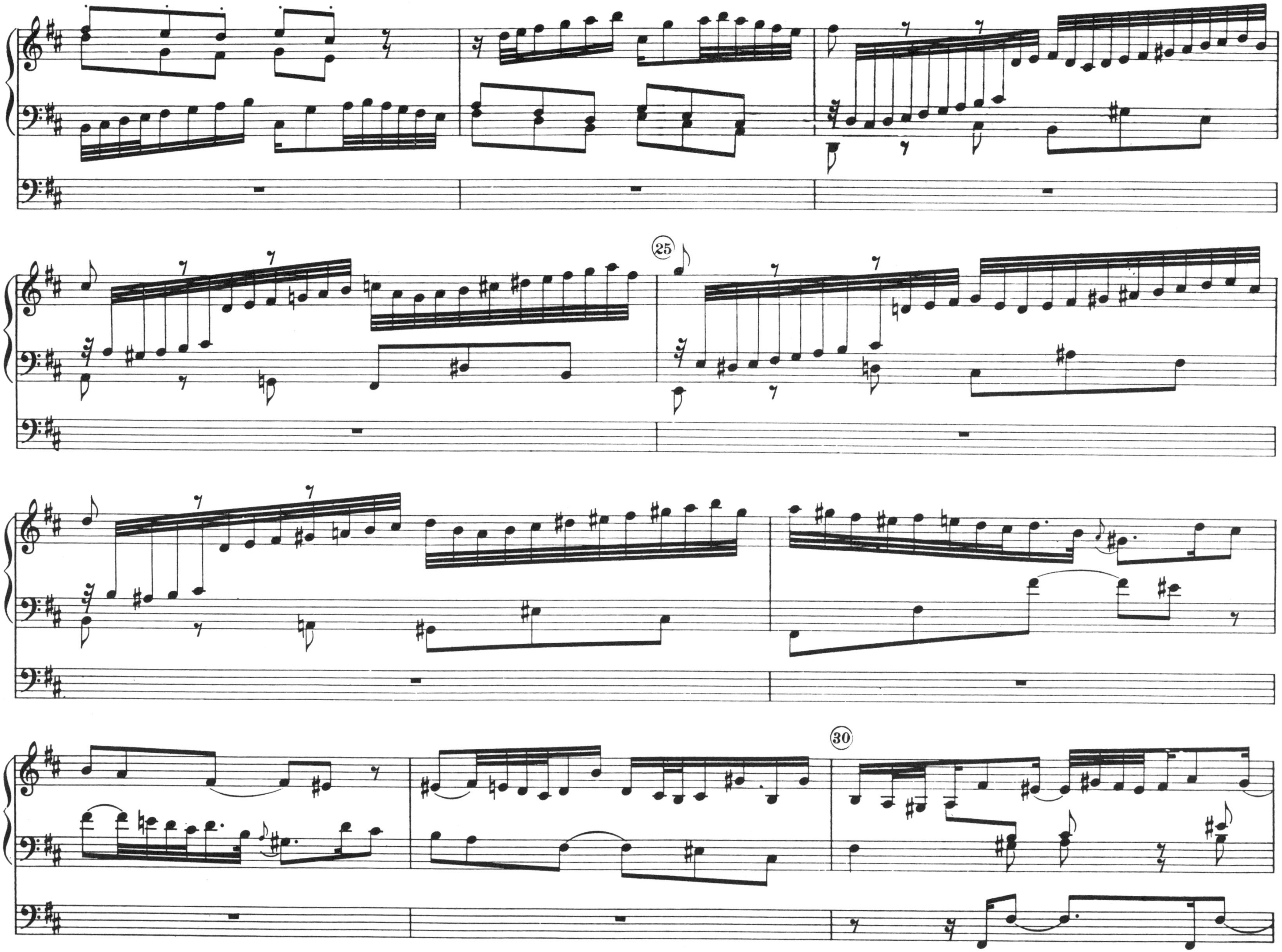
25
30

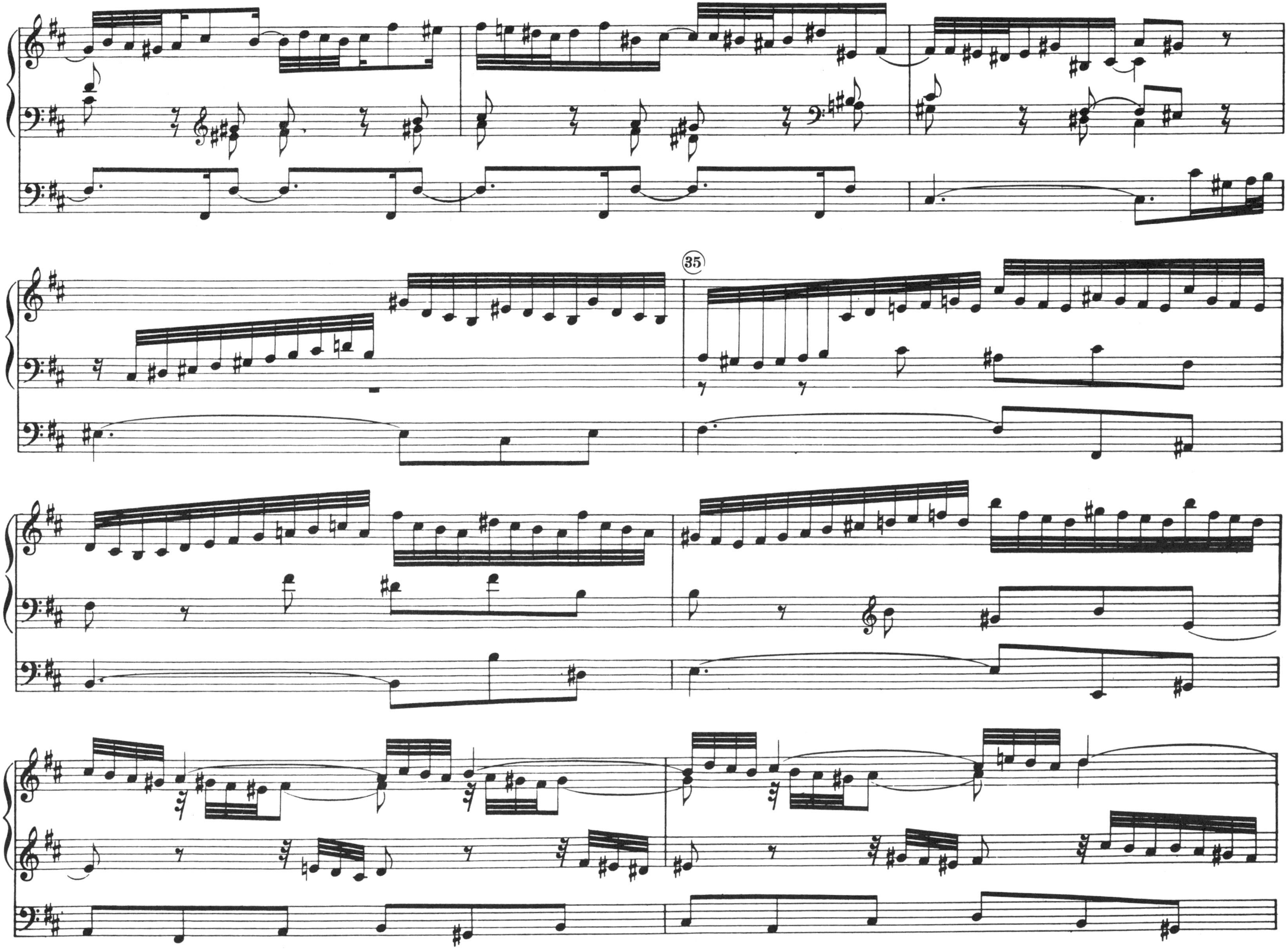
35

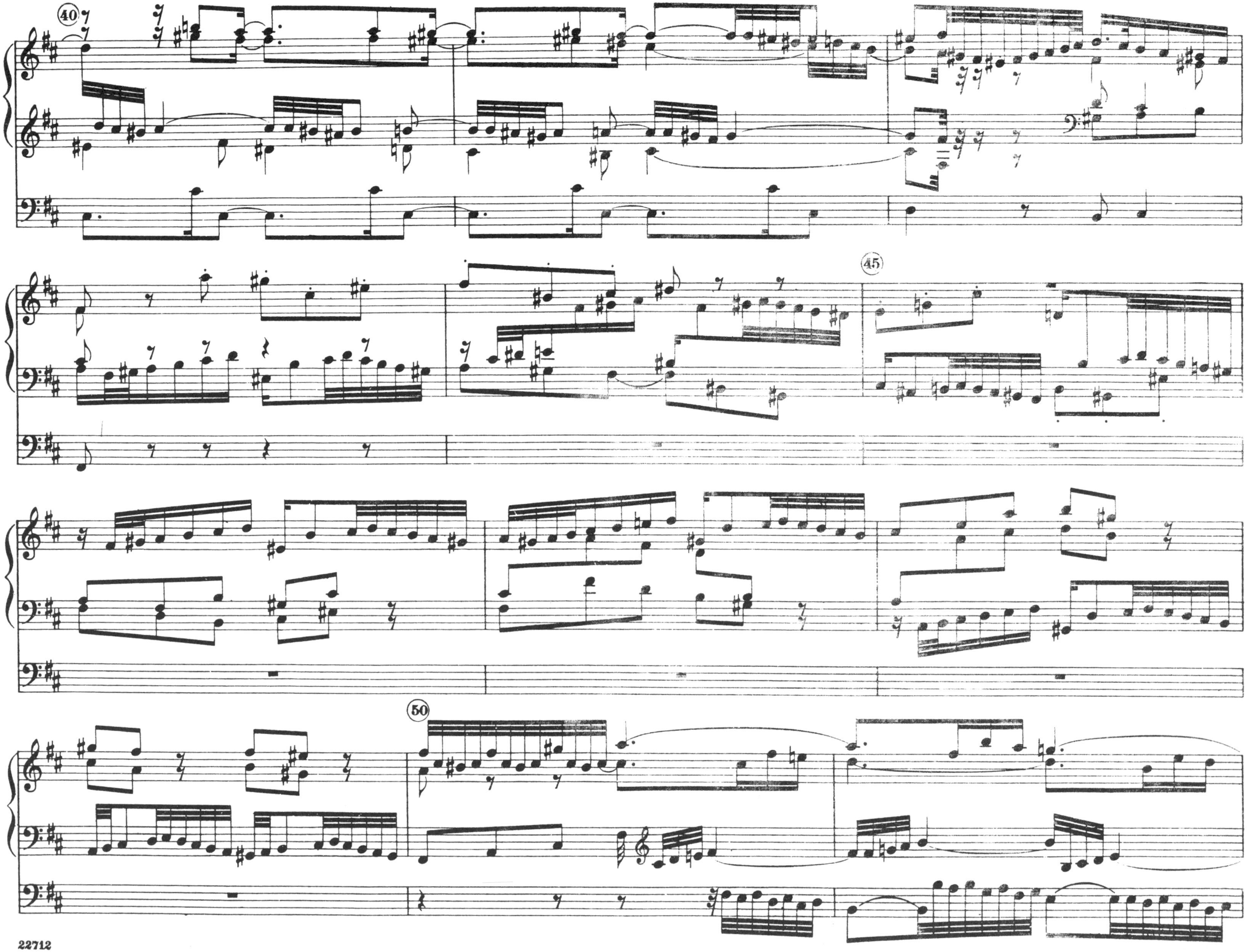
40
45
50

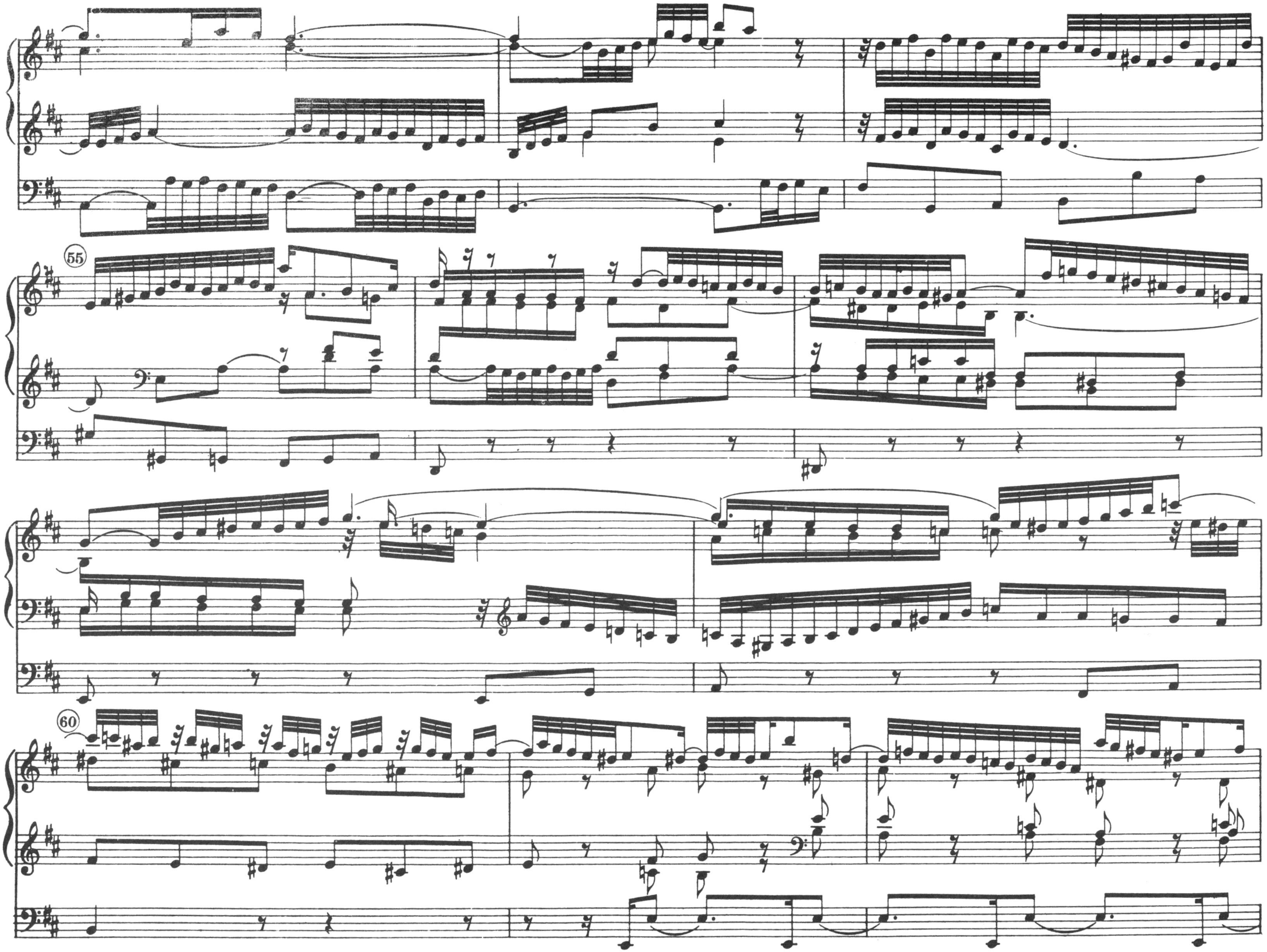
55
60

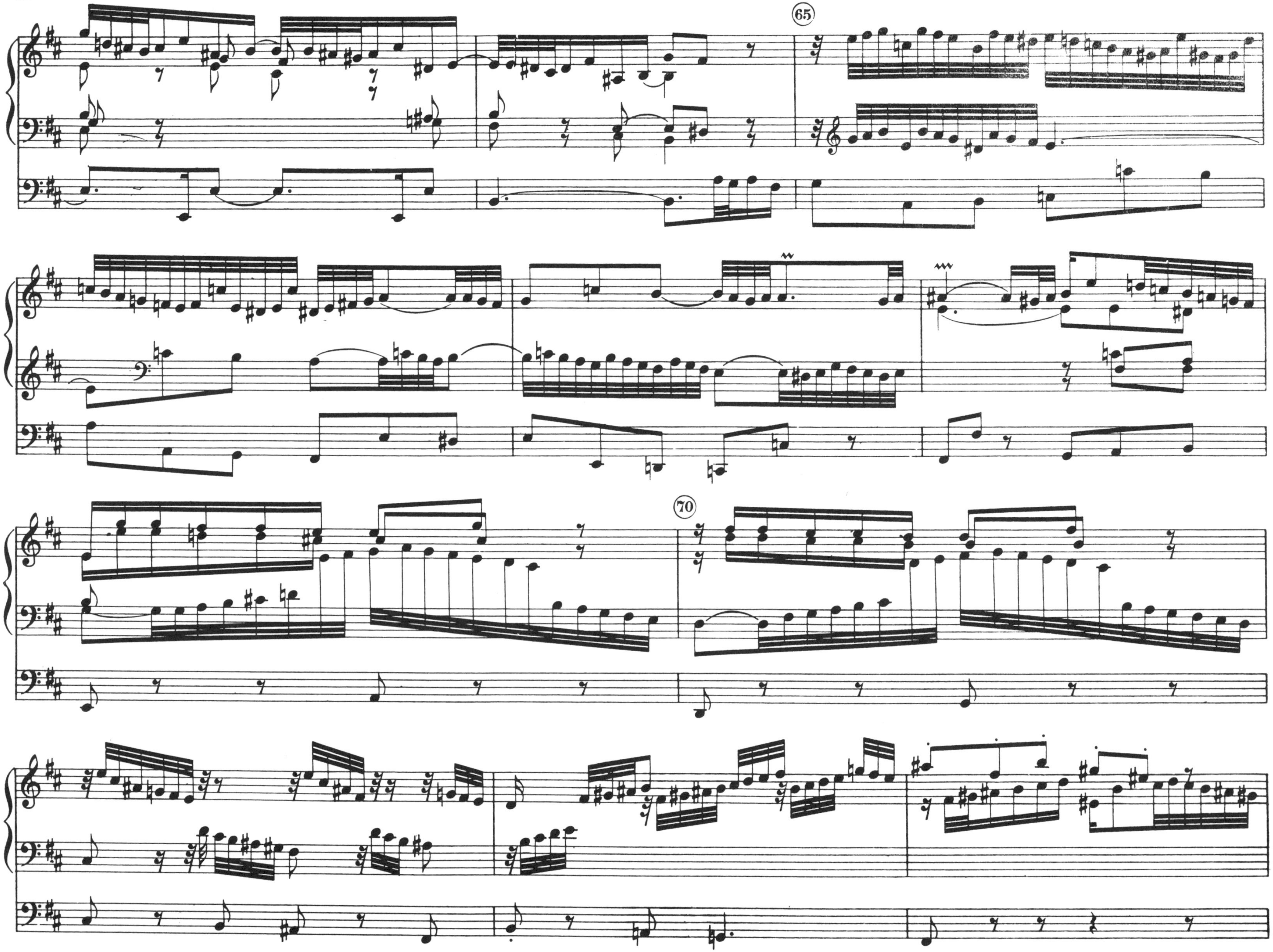
65
70

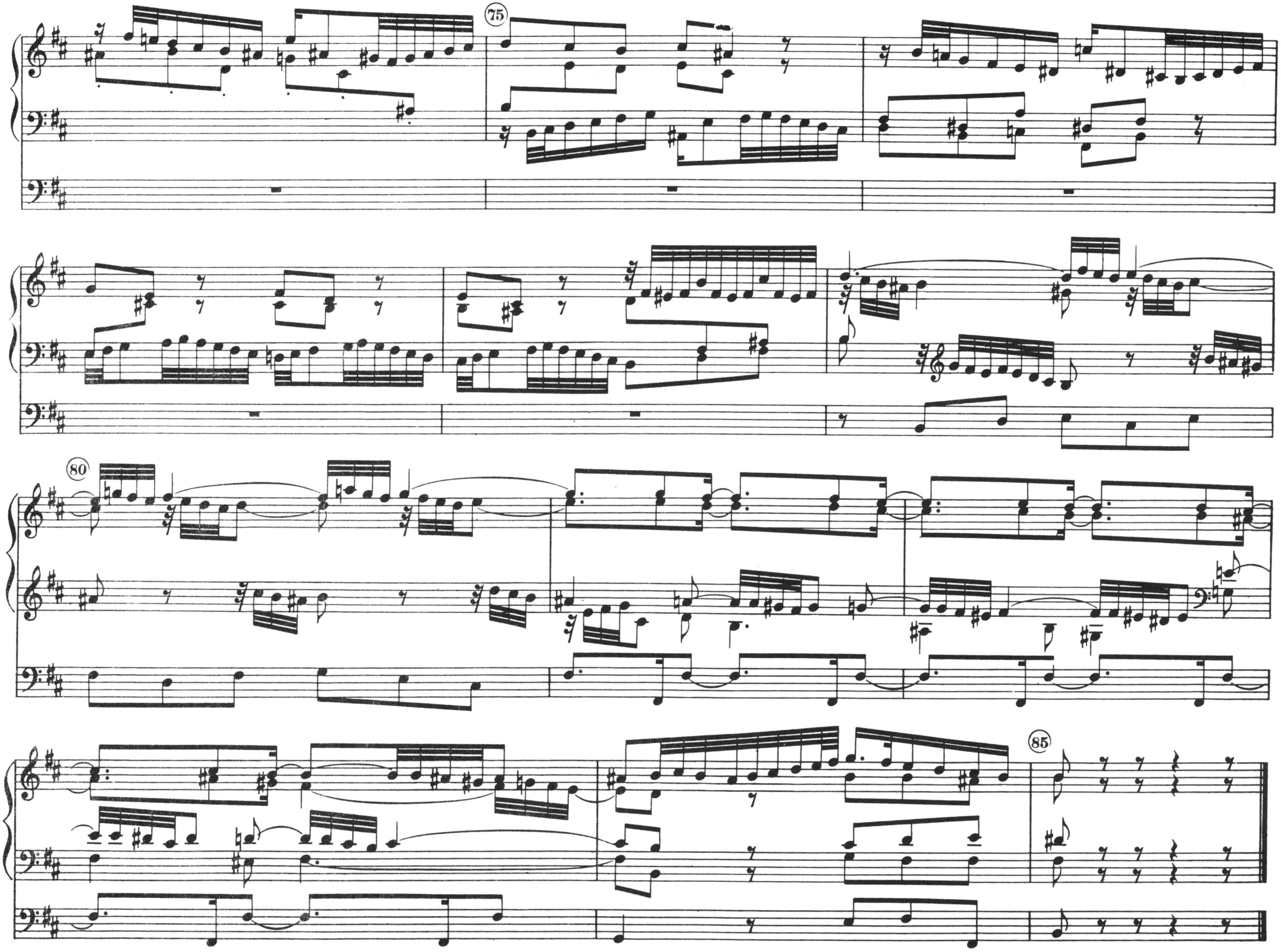
75
80
85

Fuge

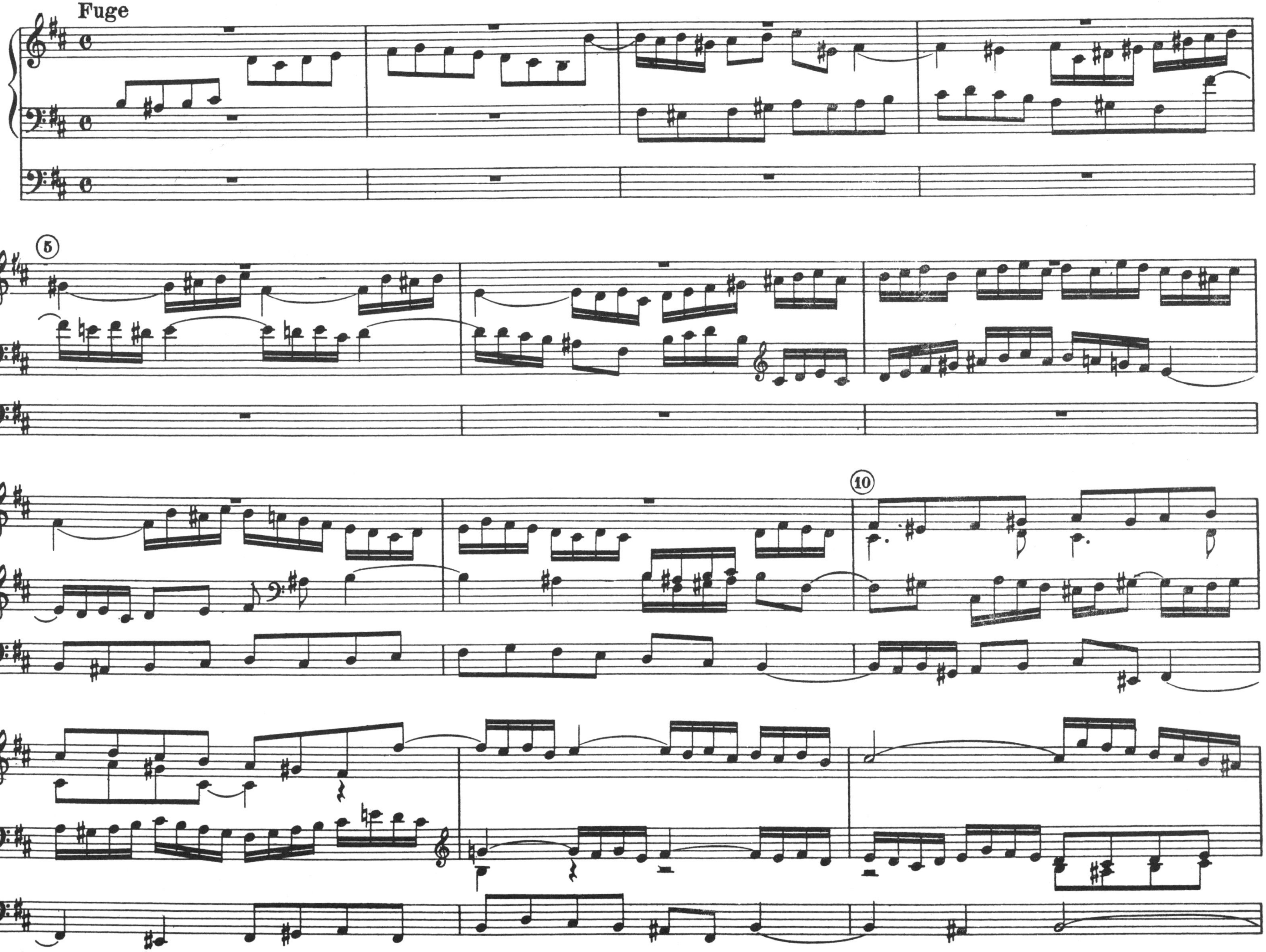

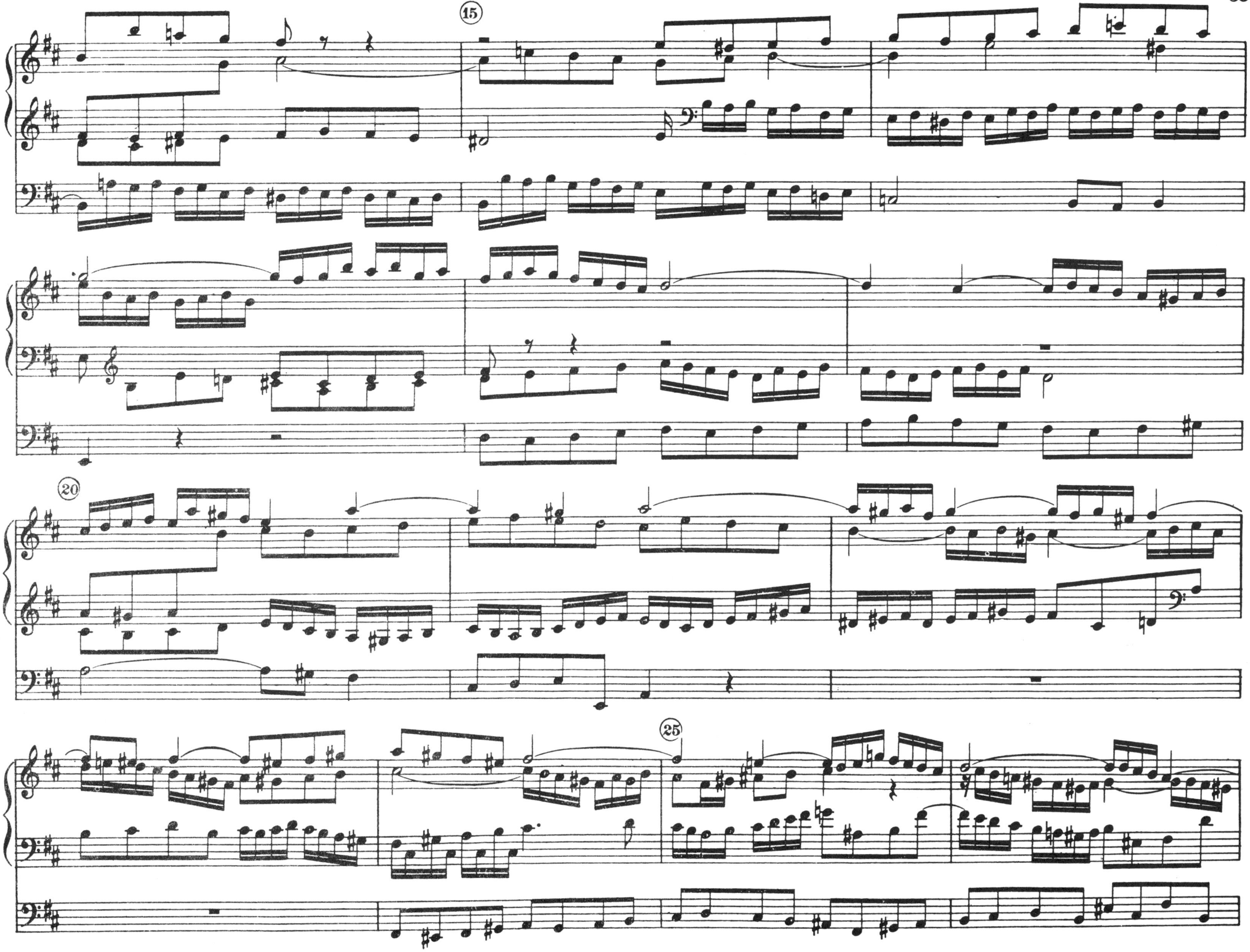
15
20
25

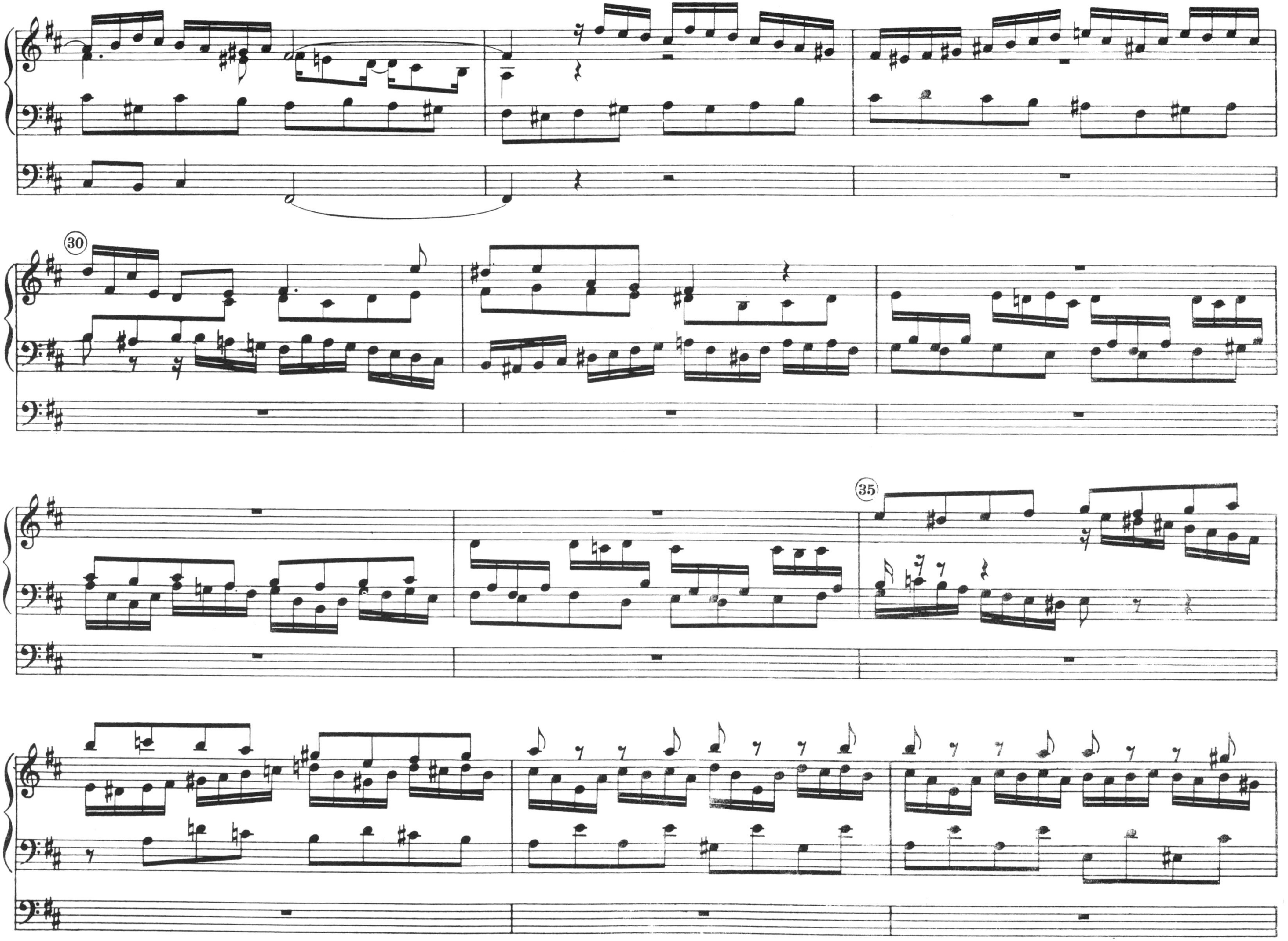
30
35

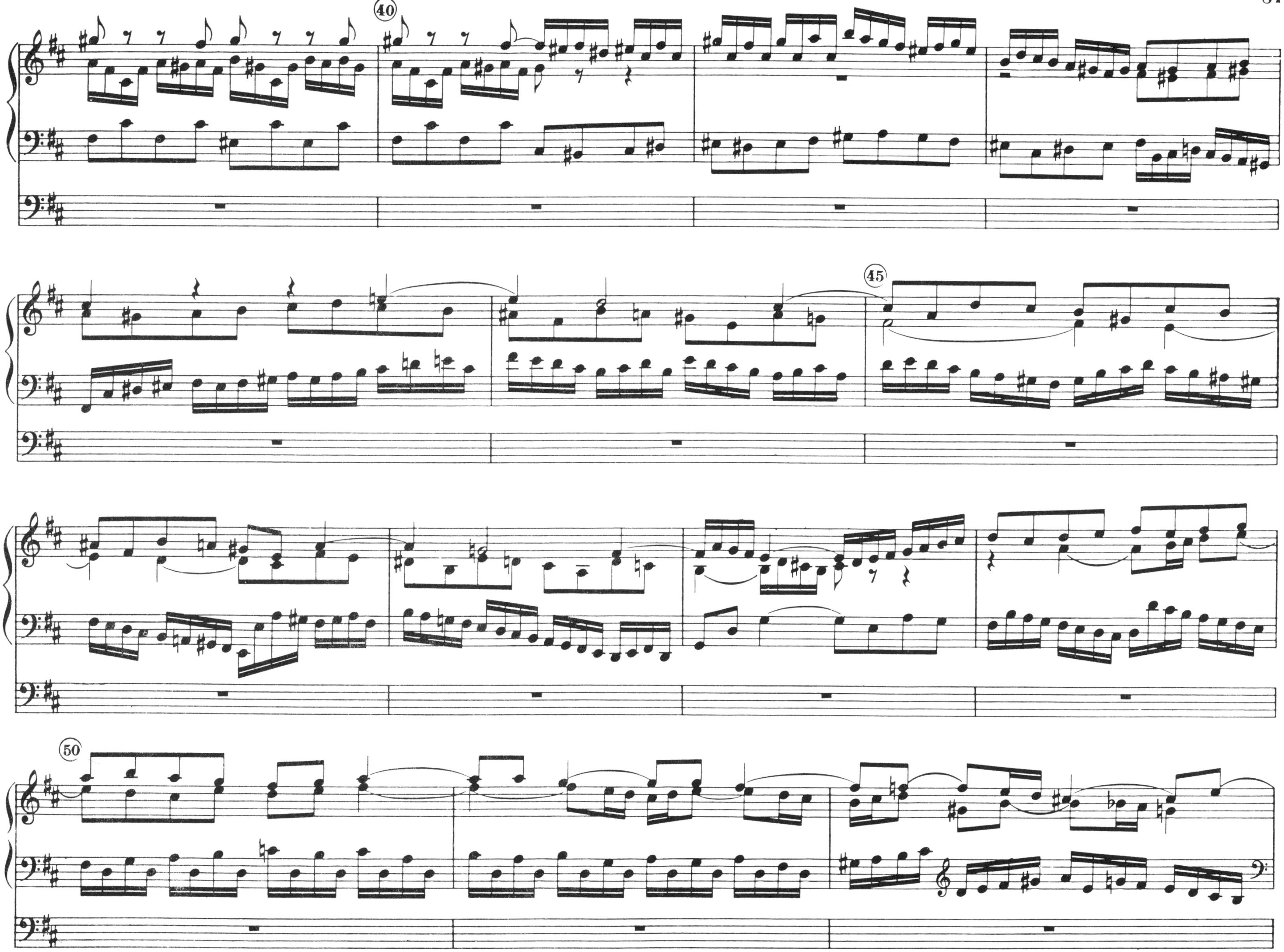
40
45
50

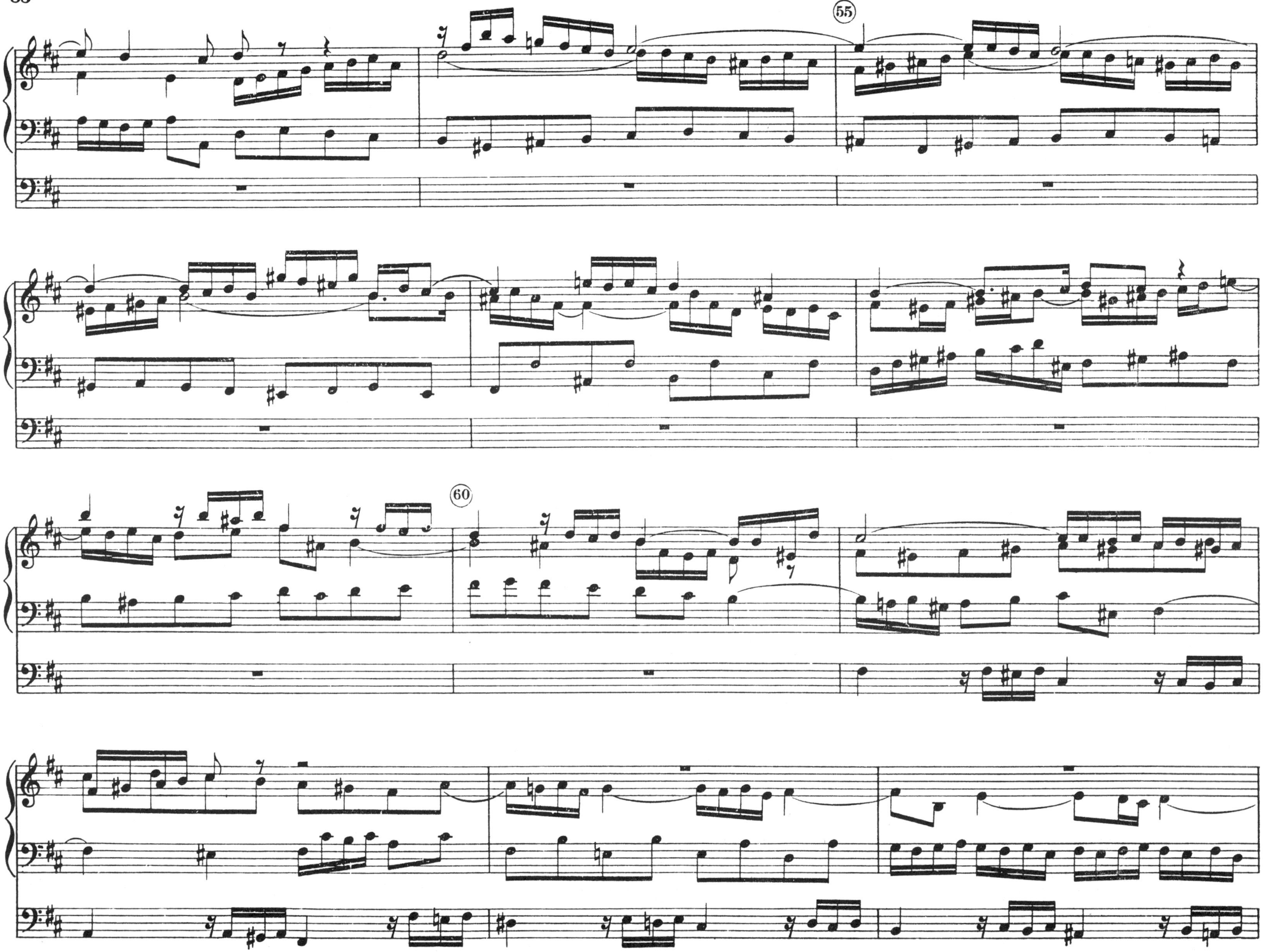
55
60

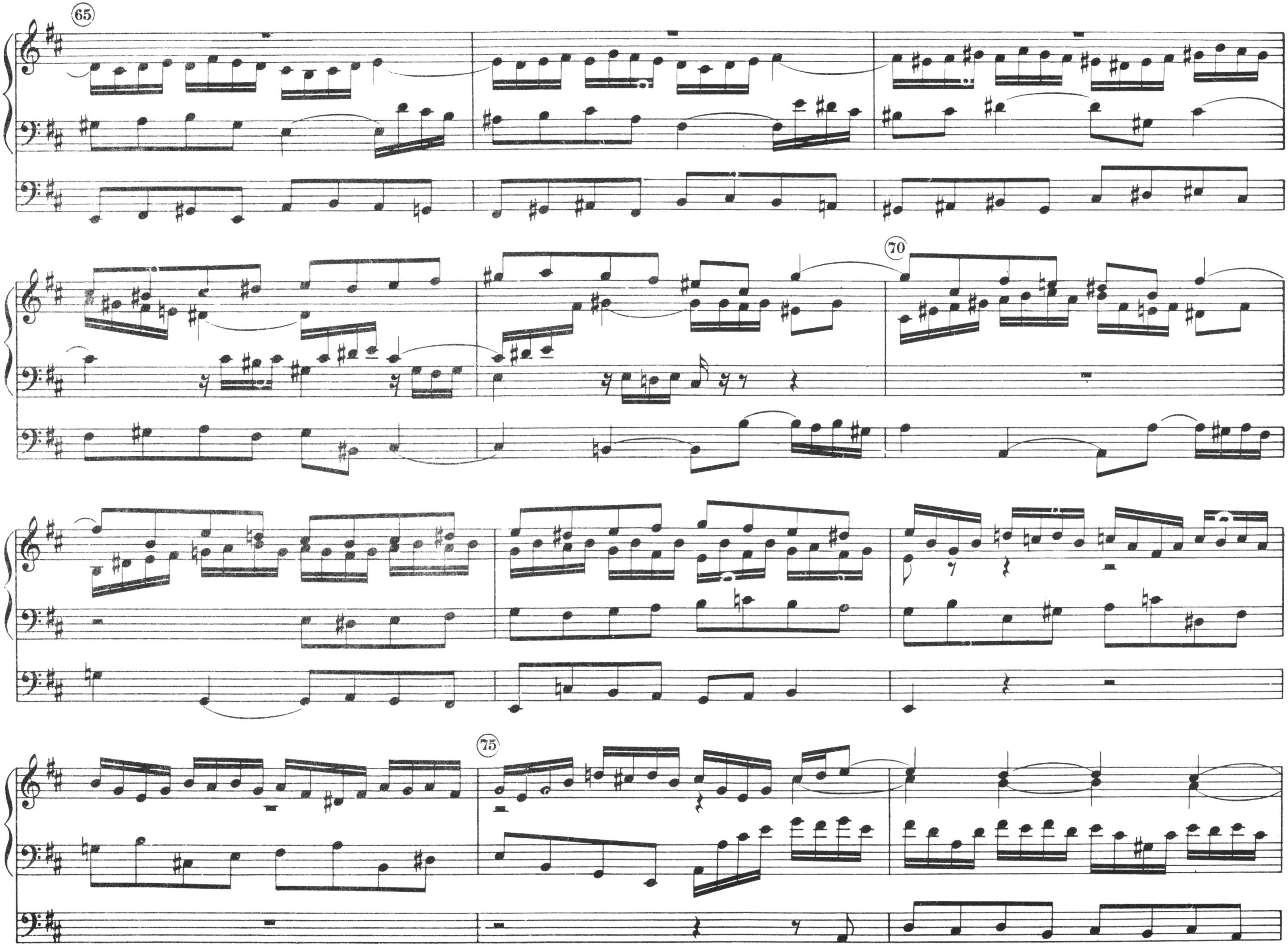
65
70
75

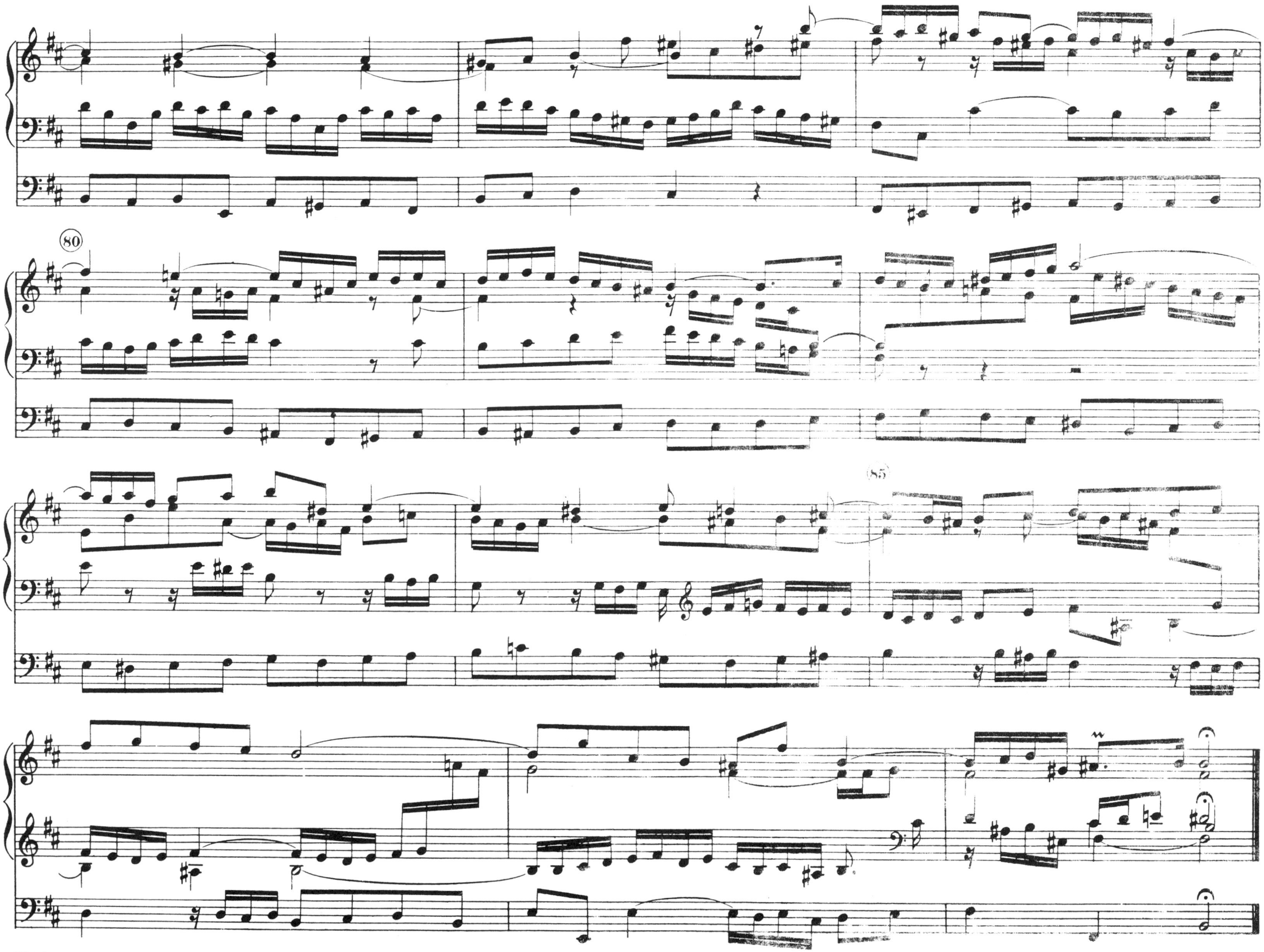

80
85

VIII
Passacaglia et Thema fugatum in C-Moll

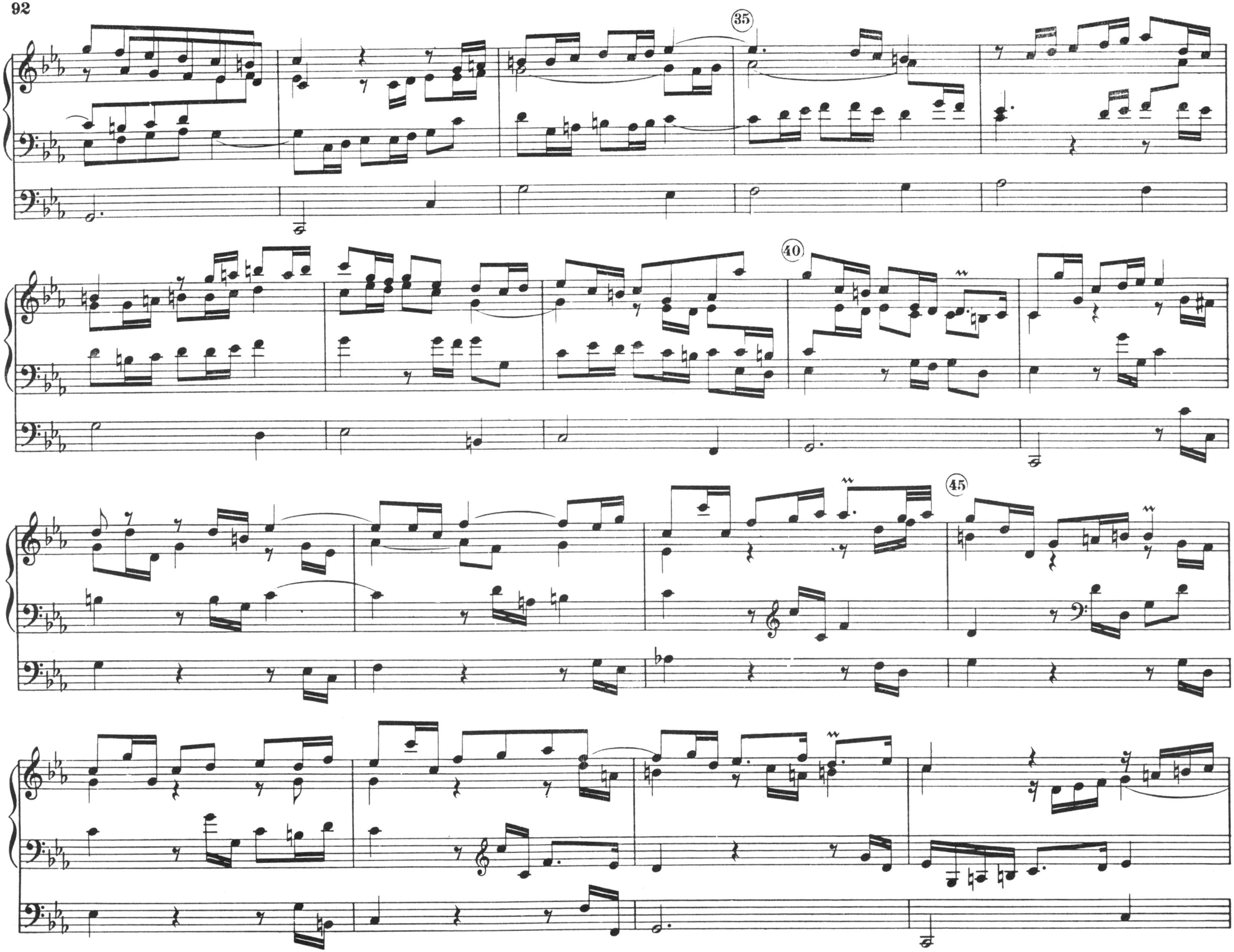
35
40
45

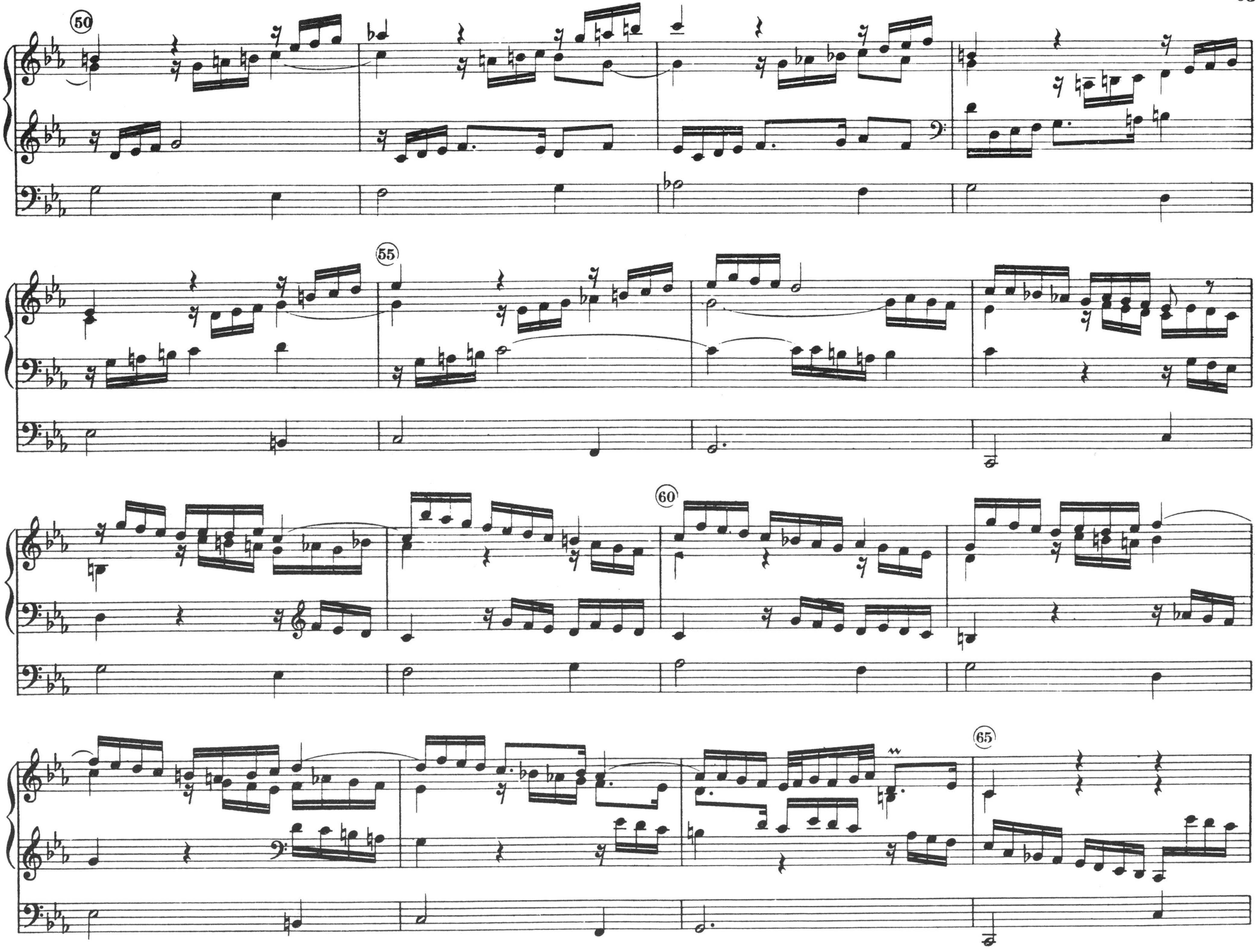
50
55
60
65

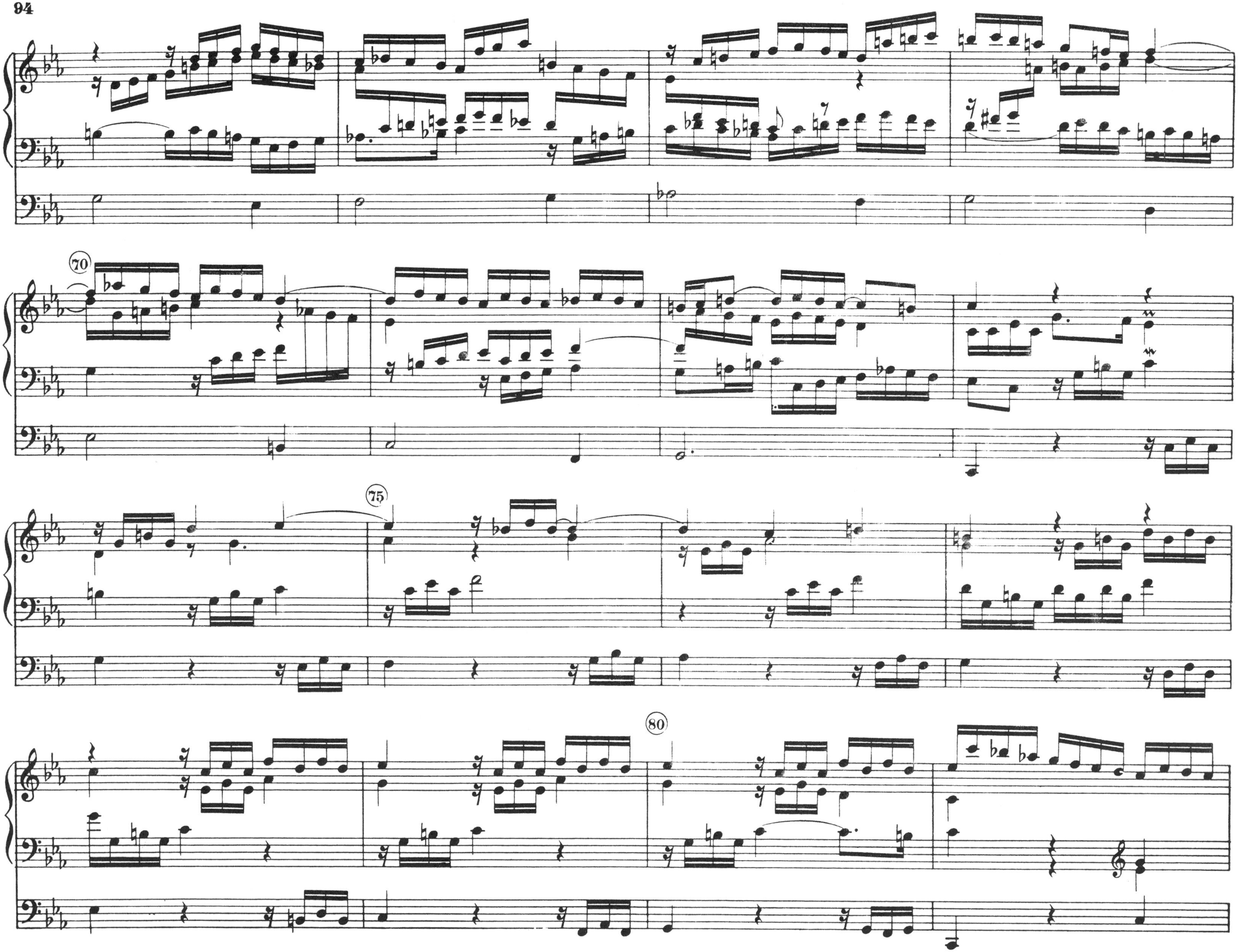
70
75
80

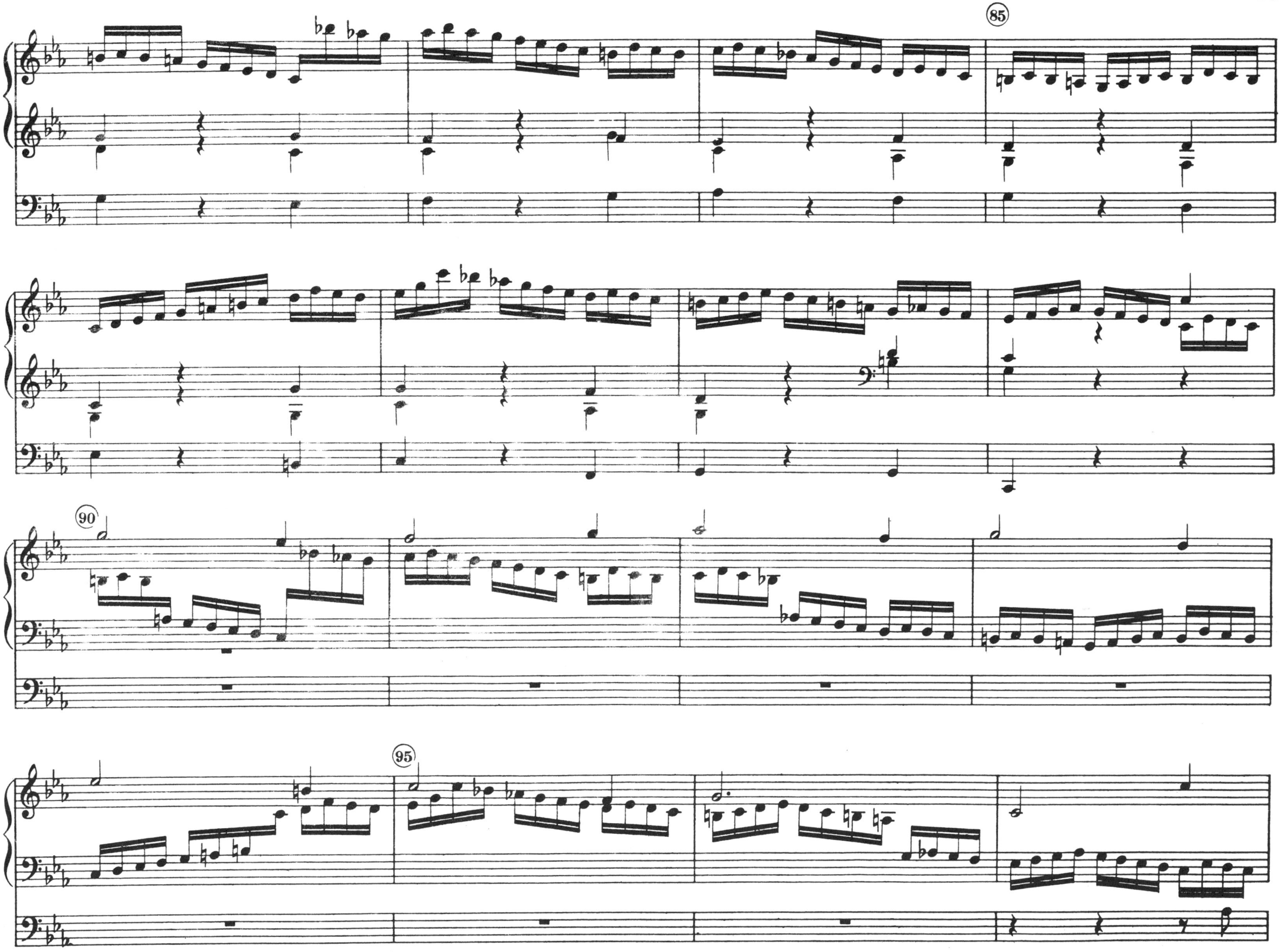
85
90
95

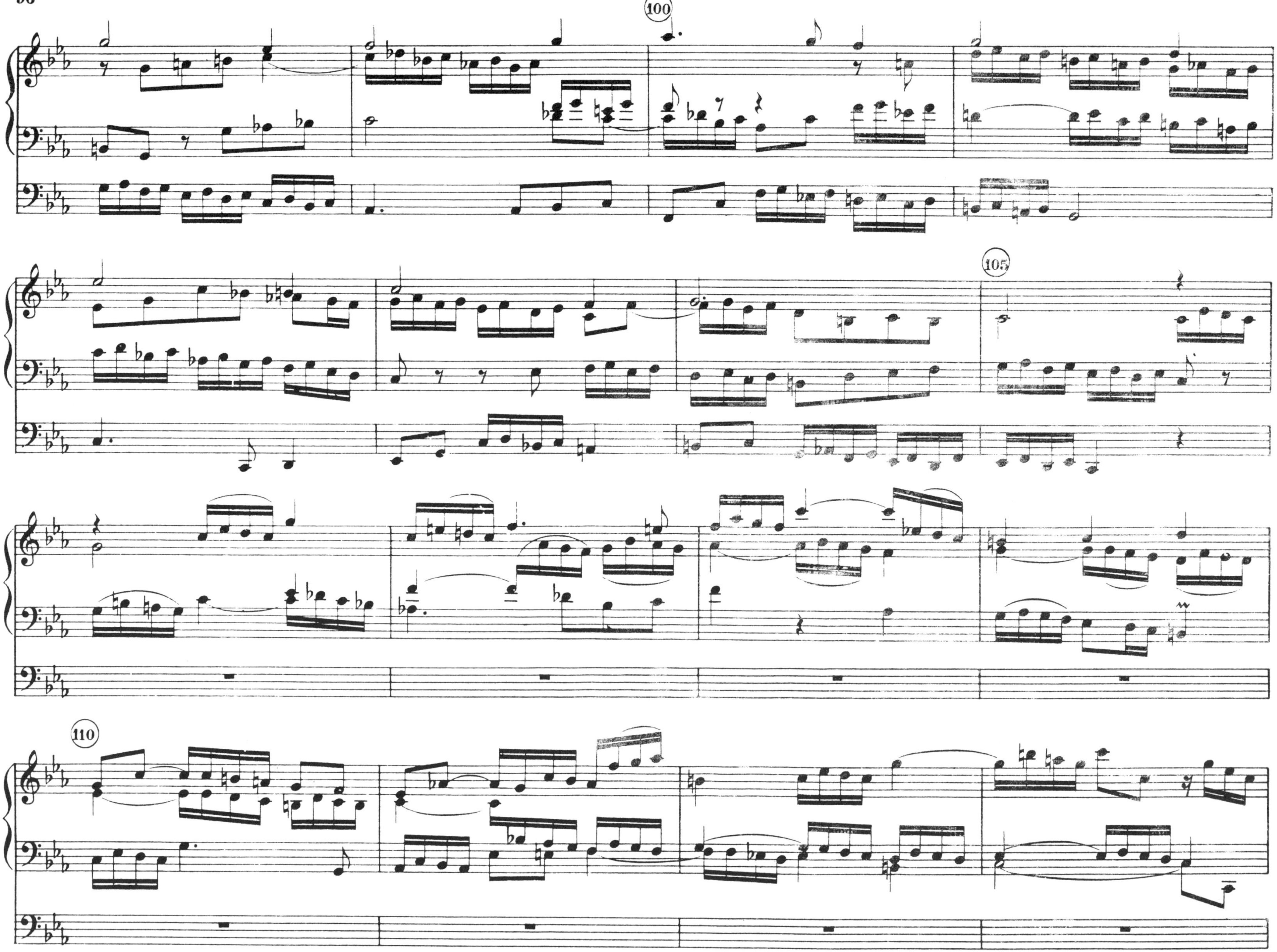
100
105
110

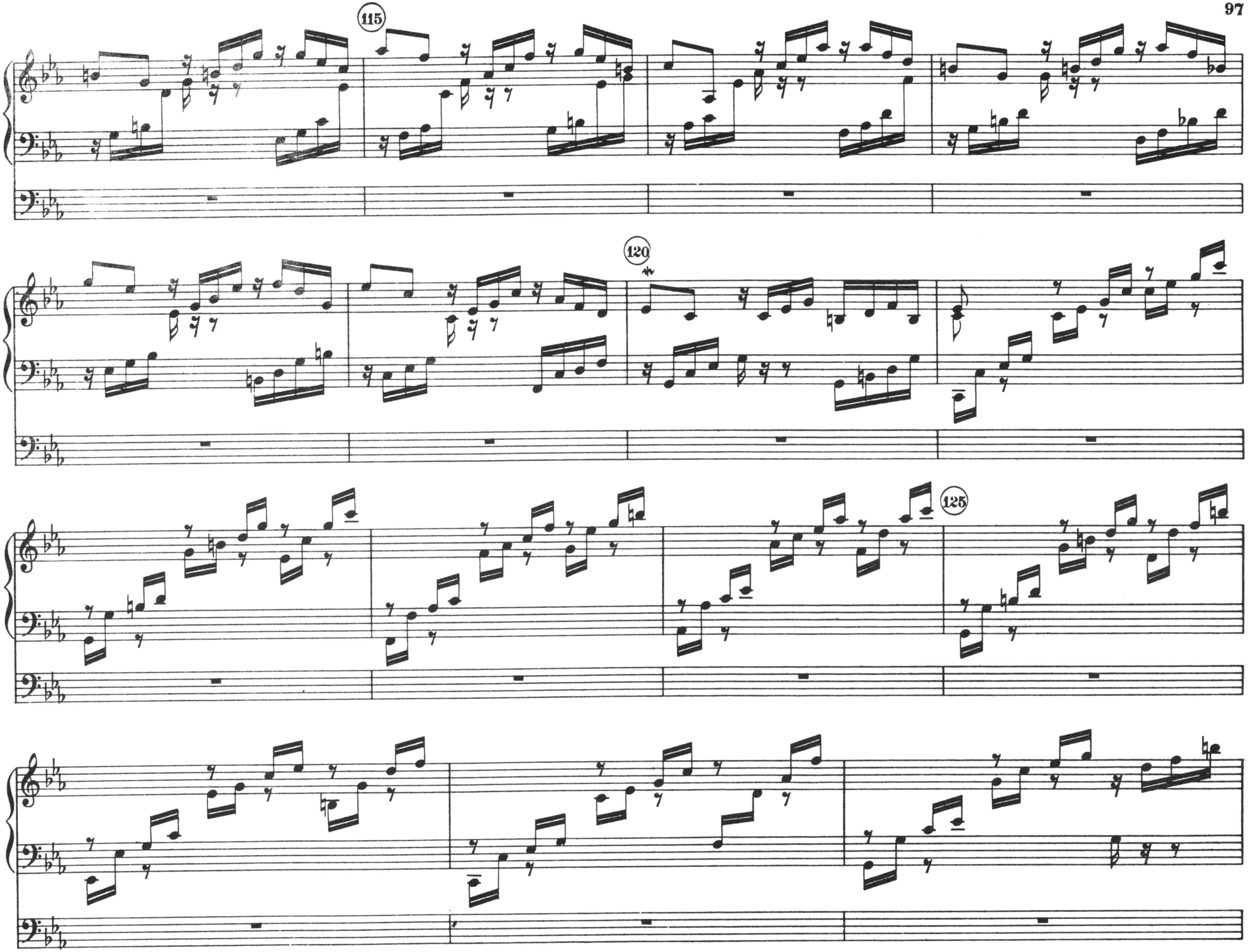
115
120
125

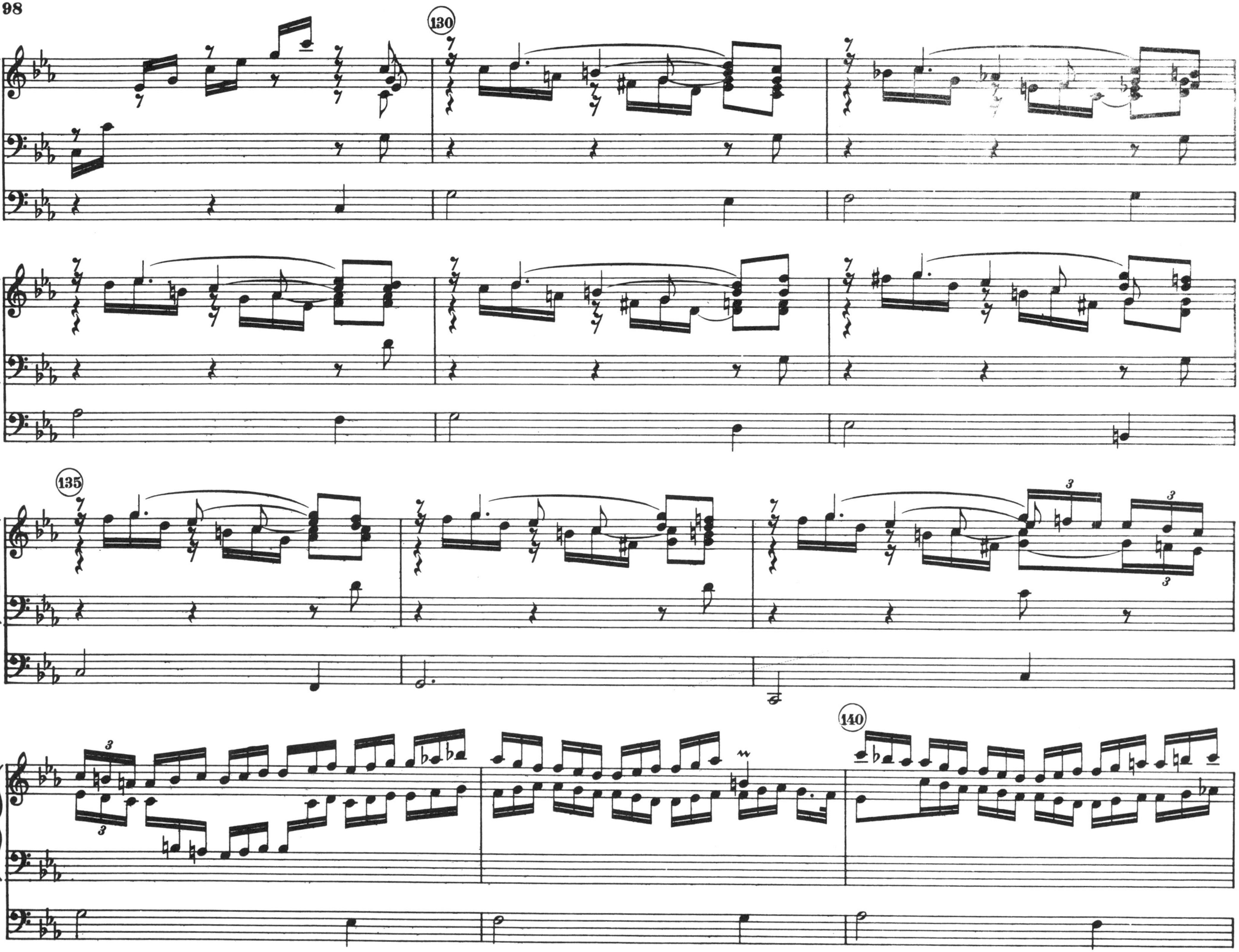
130
135
140
3
3
3
3

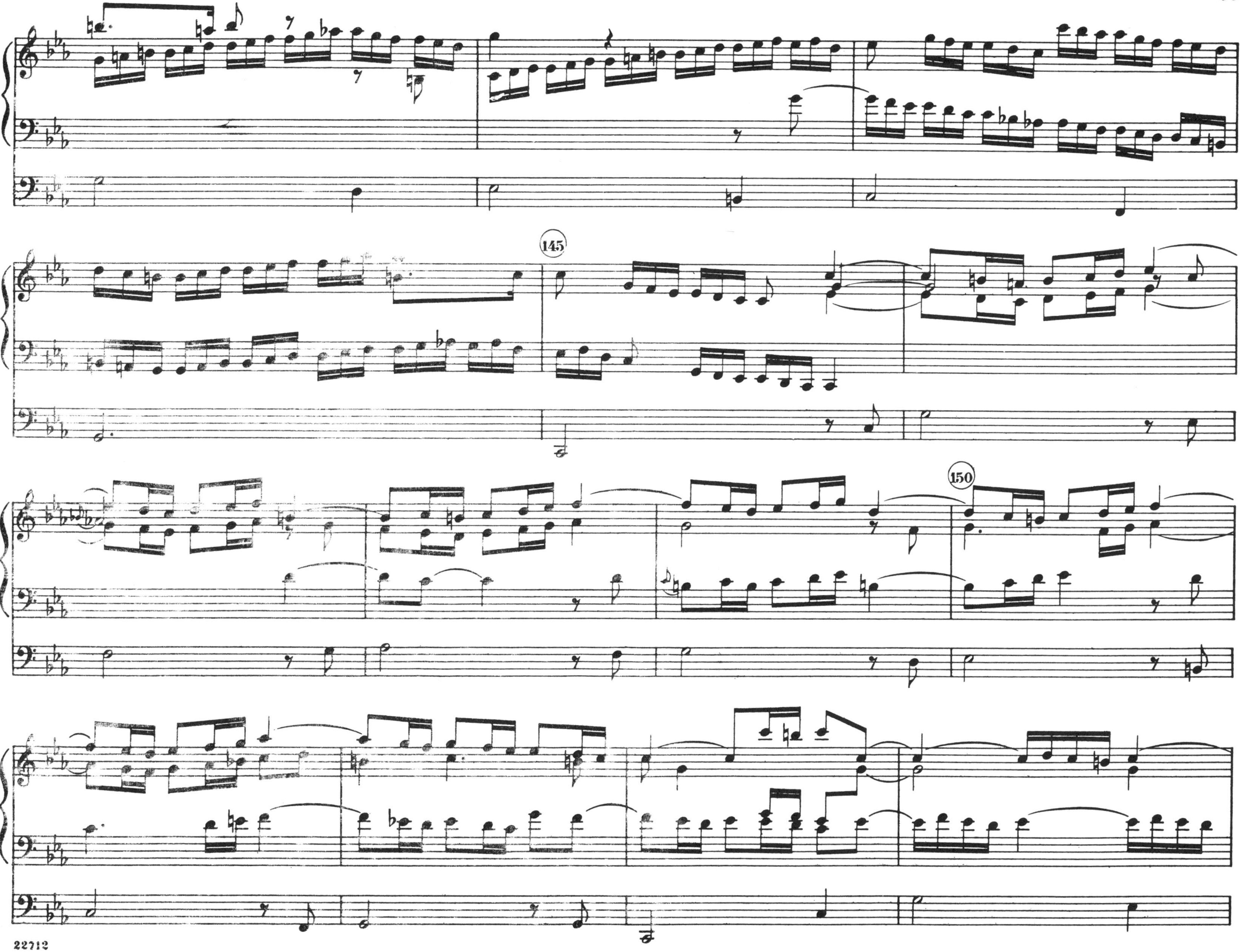
145
150

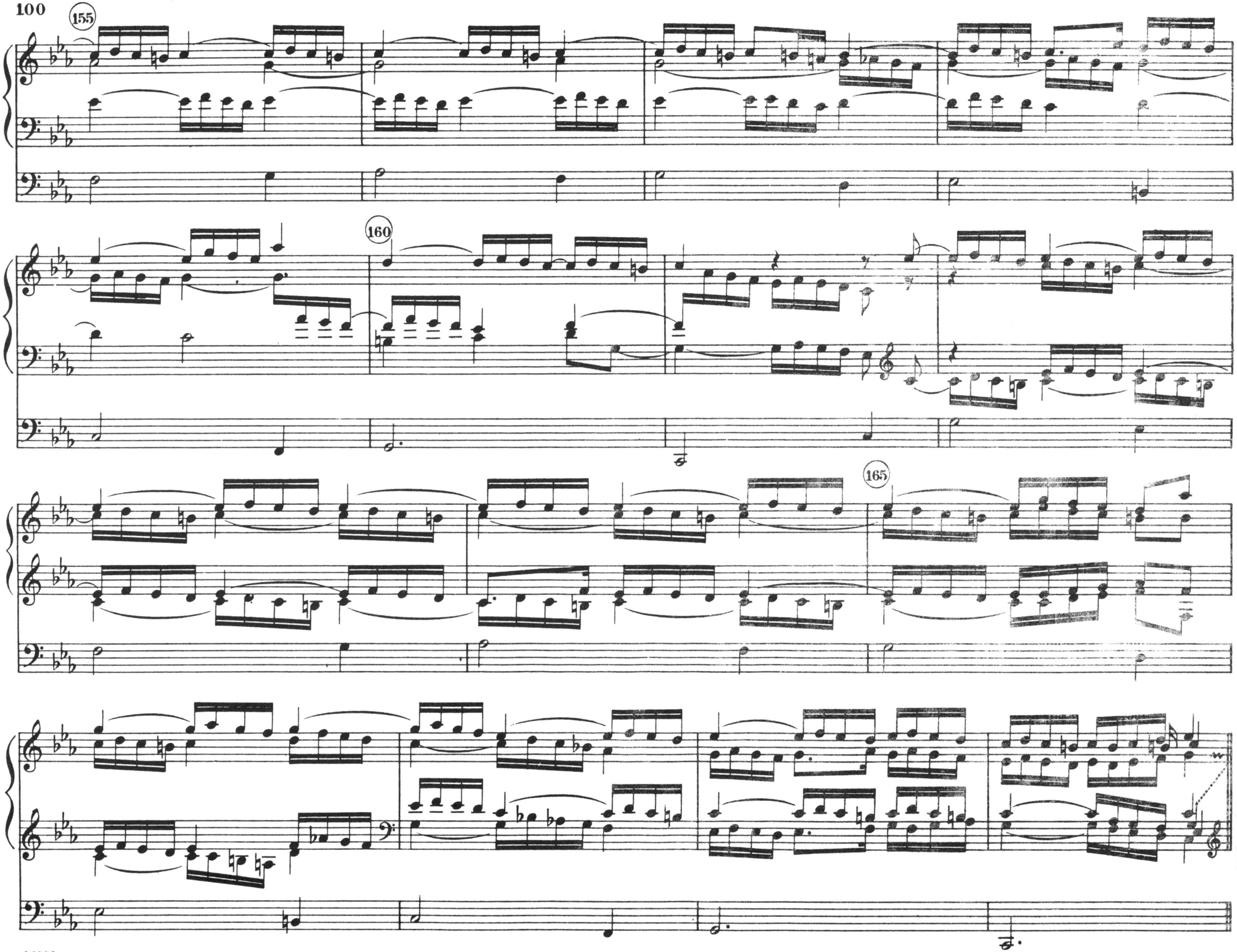
155
160
165

Thema fugatum

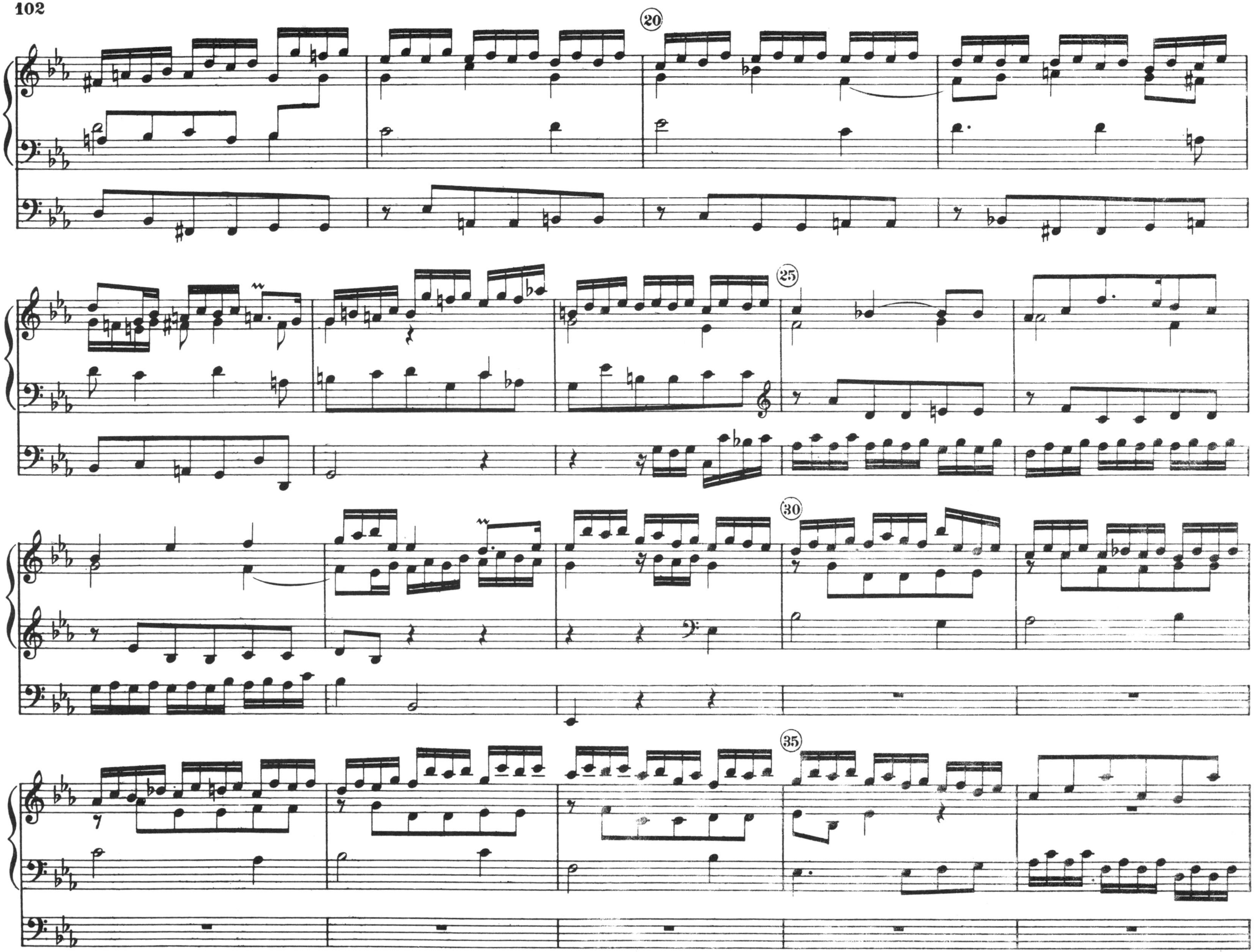
20
25
30
35

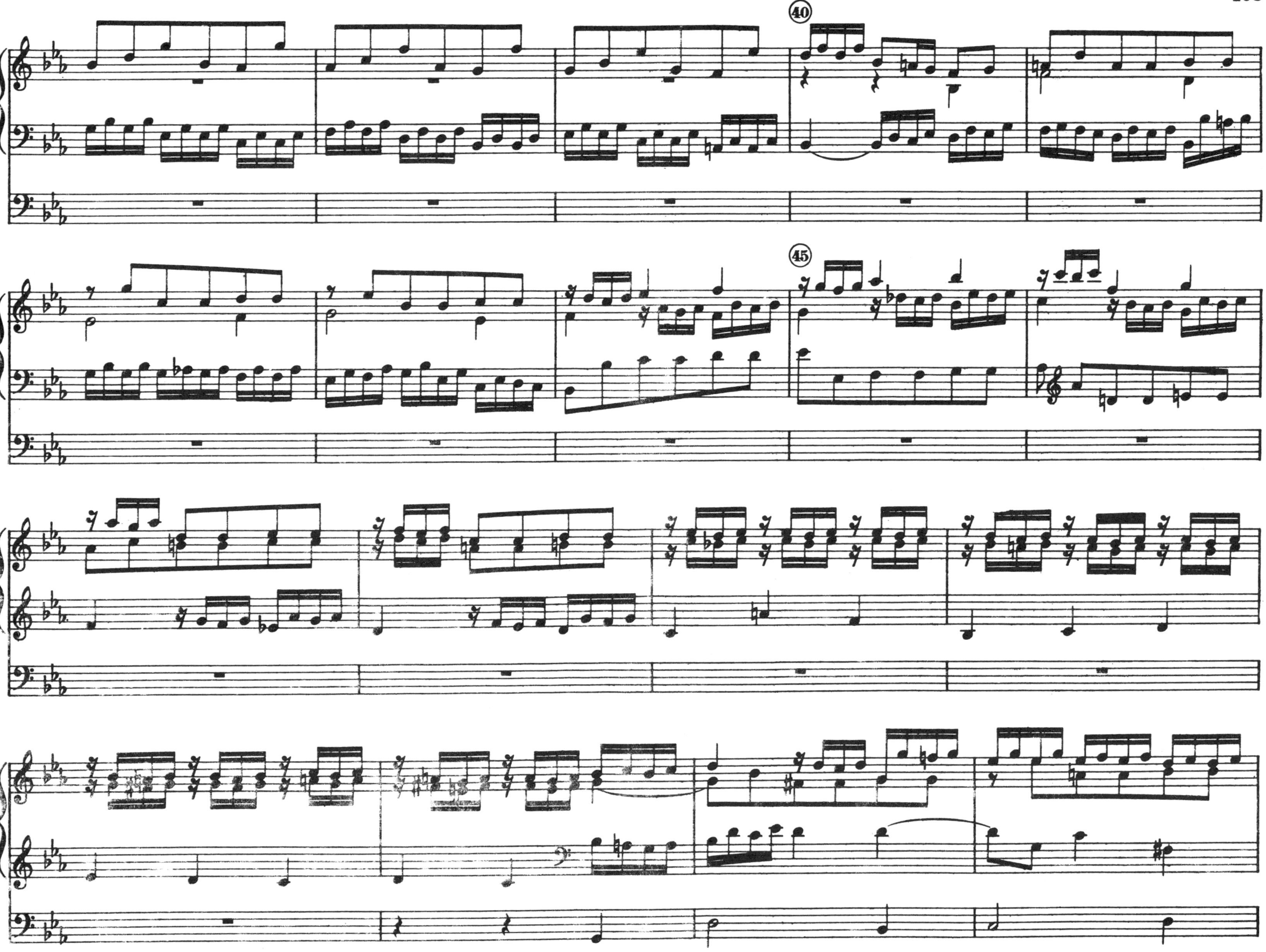
40
45

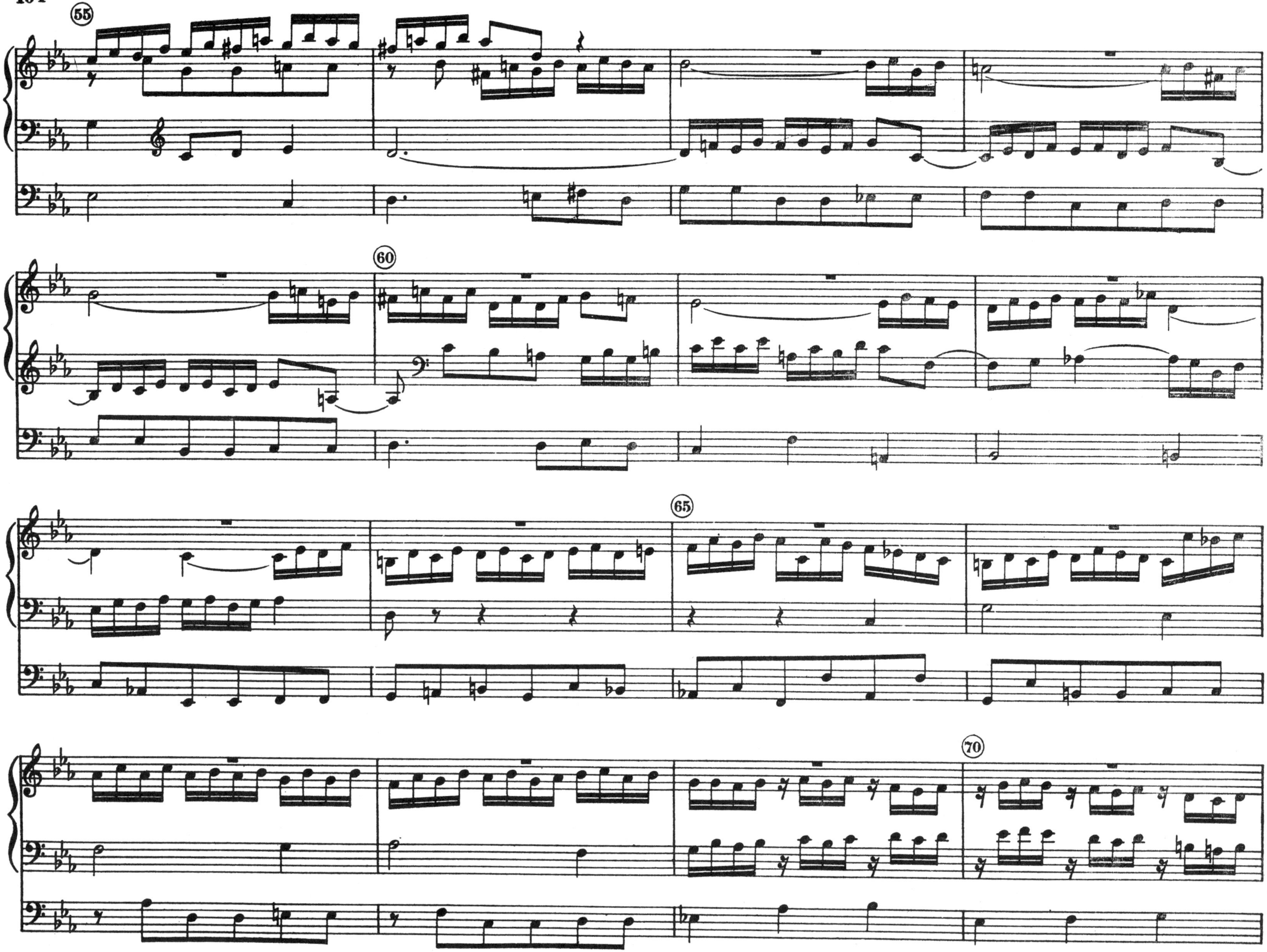
55
60
65
70

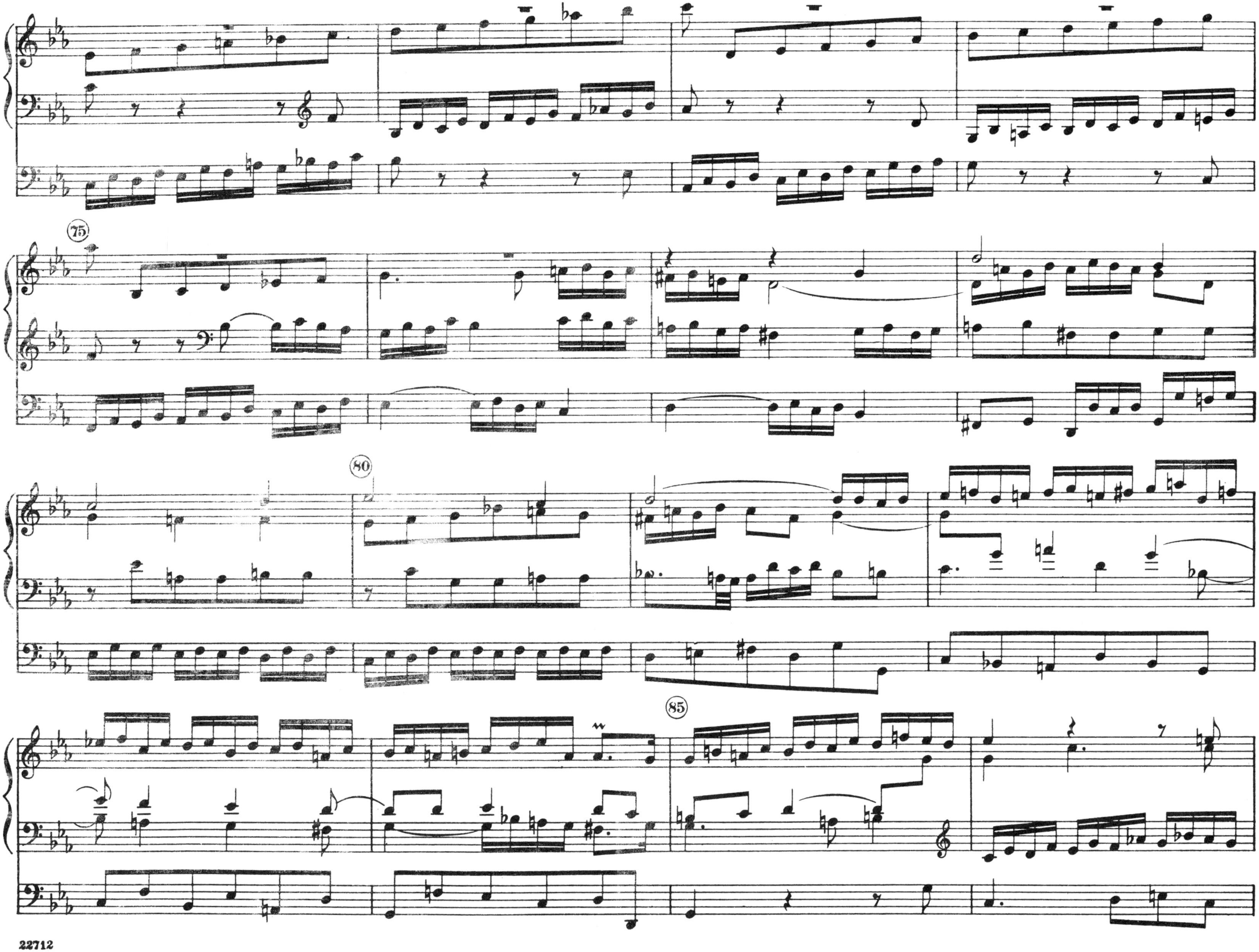
75
80
85

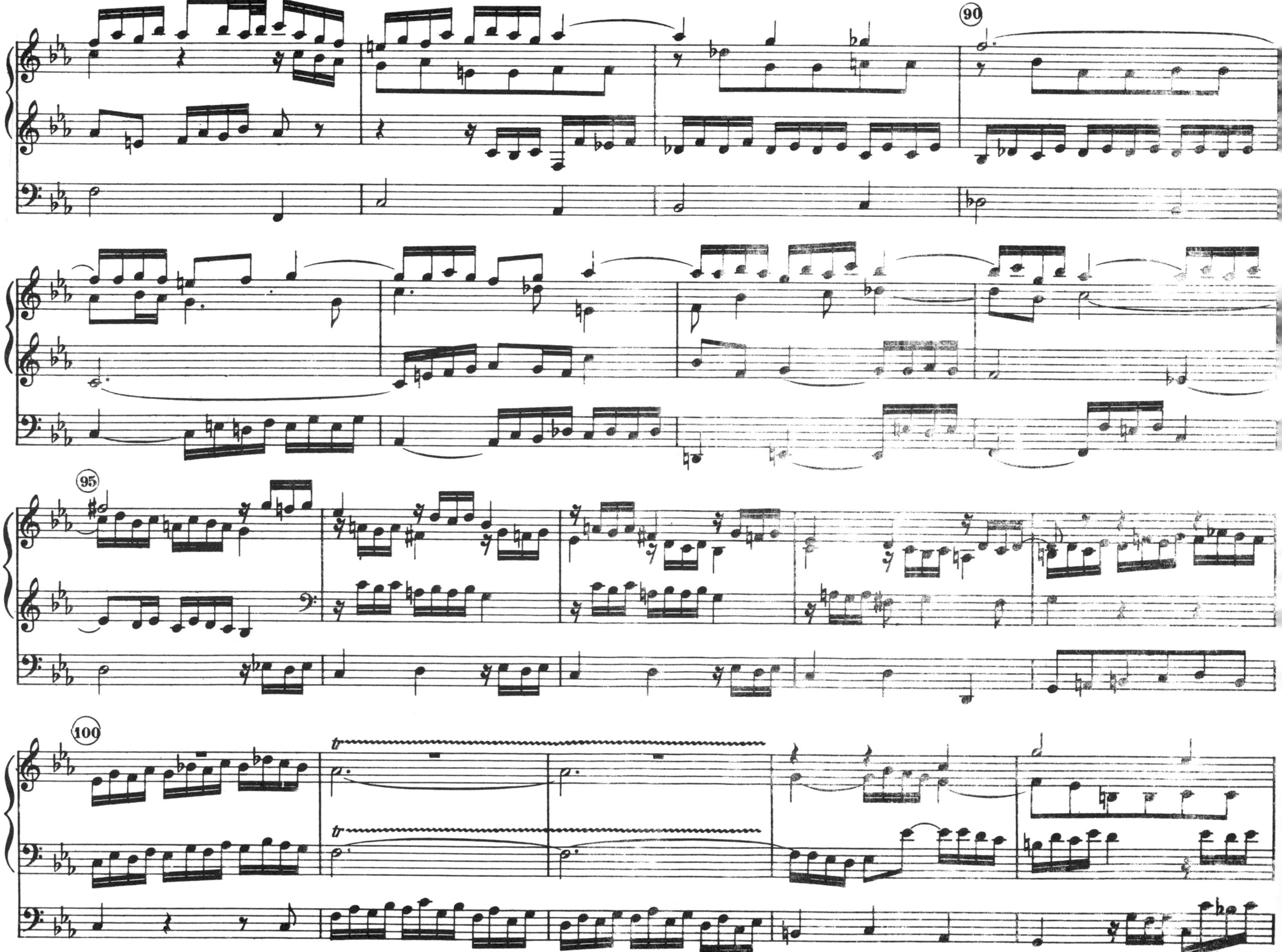
90
95
100
tr
tr

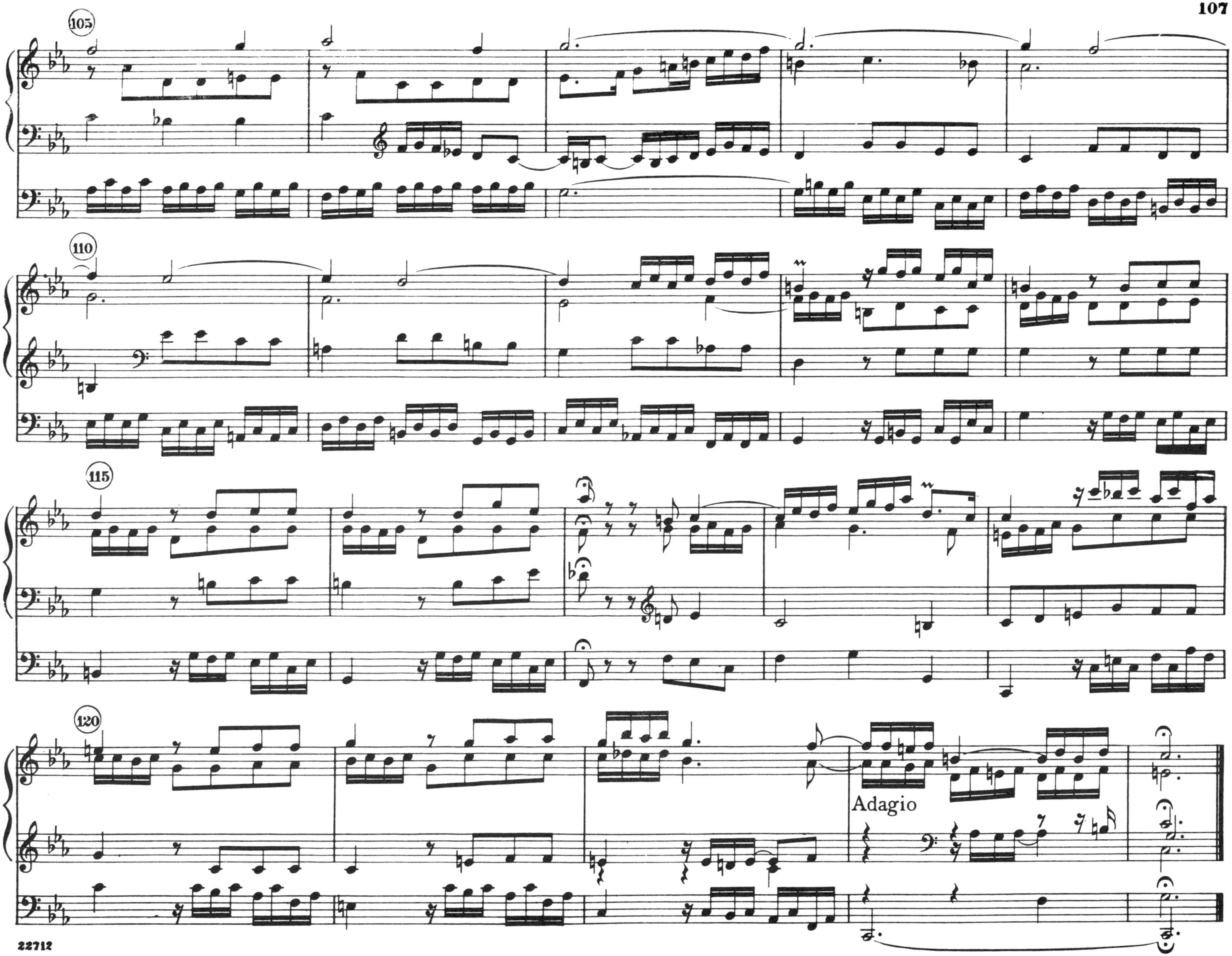
105
110
115
120
Adagio